Best wishes

'THE WAITER'

A NOVEL BY DALE LYONS

Dale

Published by New Generation Publishing in 2024

Copyright © Dale Lyons 2024

First Edition

The author asserts the moral right under the Copyright, Designs and Patents Act 1988 to be identified as the author of this work.

All Rights reserved. No part of this publication may be reproduced, stored in a retrieval system or transmitted, in any form or by any means without the prior consent of the author, nor be otherwise circulated in any form of binding or cover other than that which it is published and without a similar condition being imposed on the subsequent purchaser.

ISBN: 978-1-83563-485-1

www.newgeneration-publishing.com

New Generation Publishing

Dedicated to Joseph Robinson Lyons who led by example.

ACKNOWLEDGEMENTS.

The inspiration for The Waiter was suggested by my partner Janet without which I would have laboured to find a suitable subject. In addition, her erudite counselling, suggestions, editing, proof reading and tireless good humour has been of incalculable help. My daughters Kyla and Iona provided an insight into the protagonist's characterisation and experiences which provided substance and realism to the narrative. Marathon man Paul for his error spotting expertise. New Generation publishing experts David and Gemma have brought their usual professionalism and marketing expertise to the printing and distribution. Many friends and colleagues have knowingly and unknowingly provided ideas, observations and food for thought. I'm indebted to Google and MS. Edge for enabling easy access to facts, figures, information and places.

BACKGROUND INFORMATION FOR THE READER

The source for The Waiter concerns life and times through two world wars and the 20th century of my father, Joseph Robinson Lyons. 'The Waiter' is based on actual events and experiences although many of the embellishment are the writer's, including **The Voice**. Don's marathon quest from John O'Groats did take place although some of the on-route issues were the authors. The Waiter I hope will demonstrate that human endeavour and bloody mindedness can turn tragedy, depression and helplessness into hope and fulfilment. dale@5rhg.co.uk

CHAPTER 1

CRISIS

The night was pitch-black with driving icy rain off the North Sea. War had been declared on Hitler's Germany after they had invaded Poland and Britain was under a blackout, a recent government edict. Don Sullivan had just finished a late assignment, covering the annual Rotary Ladies Night at the Cliffe Hotel and was anxious to get back to a warm house, a Bells whisky, his wife Mary and his young son Malcolm. Only a month earlier he taken possession of a new motorbike, a Rudge Ulster and was justly proud of its 350-cc performance and its angry lion growl. At 11 pm the coast road was empty of traffic with a few pedestrians hurrying out of the rainy, cutting wind gusting from the North Sea. His main beam lit up the empty road ahead as he leaned into a bend, passing the Crown Hotel on the seafront with only 2 miles to Monkseaton and home for a well-earned rest and day off. A flash of light caught his eye as a black shape hurtled off a minor side road. It was too late to swerve out of its line and braking wasn't an option. To avoid a collision, the car turned away but all in vain as Don and his beautiful machine smashed into the passenger side of the car in a 30 mph explosion of metal, glass and motor-cycle engine.

    The car hit the bike side-on and took Don and his machine, skidding out of control, onto the pavement and came to rest just above the drop to the Tynemouth beach. Don's fragile body was catapulted onto the car bonnet and somersaulted finally onto the road in a tangled heap of flesh and bone. He was barely conscious but knew something was seriously wrong as he lay, now some yards away from the impact. His leather cycle coat had been ripped apart from the crash and he could just see his right leg torn away at an angle. The car's driver was clearly distraught as he looked down at Don mangled leg, his face now a white sheet. 'I didn't see you, you know – the, the light was so poor and, and – are you all right?' Silly question. 'What can I do to help?' Don was clearly in shock – the pain hadn't kicked in but he knew he had to keep a clear head. 'Oh my God I can see your leg bone it's sticking out and there blood everywhere.' The driver was now in a complete panic and frozen with indecision.

    Don had to stay conscious as he drifted towards a blackout, 'take my tie off and put a tourniquet around my leg above the knee – quick as you can.' Don gritted his teeth as a wave of nausea swept over him. 'There's a phone box just across the road – call 999 for an ambulance. We're just outside the Crown Hotel on the Coast Road – but make it quick I'm losing it.' Don attempted to stay awake through waves of semi-consciousness for what seemed an eternity until he heard the ambulance bell and in the split second before his slide into oblivion, Don's thought was of Mary and his young son Malcolm.

Two ambulance men look down at Don's mangled body and the motorcycle wreckage. 'What a mess – OK let's get him into the wagon pronto, the RVI's (Royal Victoria Hospital) the best although he probably won't survive by the time we get there – he's lost a lot of blood.' Don's breathing was shallow and his face now a pallid white as he was eased onto the stretcher and slid noiselessly into the brightly lit vehicle for the 8-mile journey up the Coast Road to Newcastle.

*

'It lucky for him he's type 'O' blood, bog standard, otherwise he would be in even more trouble.' The trauma surgeon exclaimed to the anaesthetist who gently placed the oxygen mask over Don's mouth. 'I'll give him 10 cc of morphine after we get him patched up although I don't give him much hope. The loss of blood and shock hasn't helped, and his injuries are the worst I've seen in a while but if he can stay with us for the next 24 hours he could have a 25/% chance – but no bets.'

News report in the Newcastle Argos on September 1st, 1939

MOTORCYCLIST FIGHTING FOR LIFE AFTER CRASH AT COAST.

A Triumph Herald and motorcycle crash leaves rider's life hanging by a thread.

Late last night a car and motorcyclist crashed at the coast near the junction of Bellview Road and Manor Middleway and left the rider in a critical condition. The male age 37 was treated at the scene by an ambulance crew and rushed to the Royal Victoria Infirmary where surgeons were fighting to save his life.

The police have arrested the car driver and charged him with dangerous driving while over the alcohol limit and are appealing for witnesses to the incident which occurred at 10.30 p.m. August 31st. The Rudge Ulster was considered by Police to be a write-off and was taken away for inspection as part of the investigation into the cause of the accident. Informal reports suggested the car driver was speeding at the time of the accident. (accident phone number attached)

CHAPTER 2

GROWING UP

Having an elder brother, Don would be the butt of Sidney's nasty pranks when his parents were out of sight. He would tell Don it was fun to put his fingers in the clothes mangle and the sadistic Sidney would slowly turn the rubber rollers, squashing Don's little fingers in the process. His screams would usually alert his mother Gracie, and his brother would be speedily chastised for his juvenile entertainment. Gracie's pain avoidance therapy on Sidney was short lived and it wasn't long before he coaxed Don to have a good sniff of a 'perfume' bottle, 'it smells really nice' as he enticed the gullible youngster. Don ill-advisedly took a good sniff, only to shriek in pain as the 'perfume' was ammonia bicarbonate, commonly known as Smelling Salts. Sidney was thrashed this time and Gracie hoped he might grow out of his bouts of bullying, but she wasn't confident.

Don would spend his weekends either helping his mother Gracie with the chores or at the local beach, fishing the rock pools or scraping winkles off the rocks with his pals to take home, boil and eat them with a bent pin. Sometimes friends and school mates became enemies and enemies' friends. It wouldn't take much to start a confrontation such as a game of marbles. On one occasion, Don had 'lagged' the first marble along the gutter closely followed by another rolled by Brian, a neighbour's son which diverted off a pebble and into the adjacent storm drain – lost for ever.

'Hey Don, you pushed me arm just when I was gannin to lag so you should giv me a one of yours.'

'I was nowhere near you, it's your mistake so you're not getting any of mine.' At which point Brian tried to grab Don's marble bag and received a punch in the face for his trouble. He was older and bigger than Don so he decided to teach this 'youngster' a lesson and ease his frustration at the same time. Little did Brian know that Don's uncle Clifford had been a champion boxer in the Merchant Navy and had on his regular visits to the Sullivan household taught Don a few elementary defensive moves. As they struggled to their feet Brian swung a fist that had it connected would have ended the fight then and there, but Don easily swayed out of the way, and powered a fist into Brian's solar plexus who staggered back in total surprise and eyes wide. Brian was not finished and rushed forward to crush Don. Big mistake - Don ducked under the flaying arms, stepped neatly aside and hooked his right leg around Brian's pulling him off-balance. As he crashed to the ground Don connected a left fist to Brian's ear and knocked out what fight Brian had left. Don's bemused 'friend' sitting on the ground wondering what had gone wrong with his superior assets.

'Had enough?' Don enquired, a smiling victor, 'let's help you up and you can have one of my marbles, I've plenty.'

'Where did you larn te fight like that Don. Maybe you could giv me lessons?' Said Brian, friends again.' Don secret training wouldn't be shared but would thank his Uncle Clifford next time he came to tea.

CHAPTER 3

At ten years of age Don decided to emulate his brother Sidney who was a regular smoker, usually Woodbines as they were the cheapest and anything that 'big brother' did was 'status' and would be copied whenever possible. Don's friends had already experimented with 'fags' and allowed Don a puff or two which wasn't enough to say he had 'smoked'. One afternoon Sidney left his cigarette packet on the kitchen table with seven in the packet of 10. Don thought he would be unlikely to miss one and helped himself to join his pals for a proper smoke. After a great deal of coughing and spluttering and to the great amusement of his friends who were 'experienced' smokers, Don was able to inhale properly although he didn't really see what all the fuss was about and decided that a sore throat and a lot of coughing were not worth the effort or the money at 8p for a packet of 10.

Saturday mornings were reserved for film club at the Gaumont picture house where Don and his friends would sing along to the on-screen introduction.

'We'll come along on Saturday morning greeting everybody with a smile, we'll come along on Saturday morning, knowing it's well worth while. As members of the GB club we all intend to be, good citizens when we grow up and champions of the free. We'll come along on Saturday morning on Saturday morning greeting everybody with a smile, smile, smile, greeting everybody with a smile!'

A sure-fire way to build a patriotic Britain. There followed an hour of cartoons, short comedy sketches of Abbot & Costello or Laurel & Hardy and end with Buck Rogers escaping terminal extinction only to emerge safe and sound the next week.

*

Eddie was a butcher's son, big and full of testosterone for his age and on a boy's camp demonstrated a lasting lesson in self-gratification. 'Gather round', Eddie said smiling, 'I'll show you something you'll enjoy' pulling down his pants and proceeded to stroke his penis to a lengthening erection. Accompanied by sighs of pleasure and frantic rubbing a foamy froth soon bubbled from his stiff member as his heavy breathing relaxed. 'It's easy, just think of a girl's tits and fanny when you rub – you'll soon get to enjoy it,' as a sedated Eddie grinned at his amazed audience – and they did!

Always short of money, Don applied to a local chemist advertising for a shop assistant. Before his interview Gracie checked he was neatly attired with a clean shirt, jacket and polished shoes when he presented himself to Mr Jackson, the chemist. After a short interview in which Don's literacy was confirmed, he was duly hired as a chemist's assistant. This involved running errands with prescriptions around the local community on Saturdays and some evenings, earning more than his grocery deliveries. Being quick witted, curious, and helpful the chemist taught him the Greek names of the various potions and tablets on the glass jars and Don became well versed in the etymology. He was even allowed to mix simple potions under supervision.

Before Jacksons he had delivered groceries for Nesbit's the grocer and occasionally received tips which he spent on trips to the local pork butchers, where for 1 penny they would provide a thick slice of bread and beef dripping, Don's favourite snack that kept him going until supper time. Another visit to ward off starvation was to Askey's the grocer who sold biscuits by weight and a quick call of; *'any broken biscuits please, Mister/ Misses?'* would sometimes yield a few pieces of digestives or 'nice' biscuits.

When the chemist was out of the way Don was soon mixing sodium bicarbonate and powdered acid (cream of tartare) and sugar which made a very acceptable sherbet dip substitute especially when dipped with liquorice root and made him very popular with his schoolmates. A riskier venture was making mild explosives with peroxide (inorganic) when mixed with barium, sodium, and potassium, the combustible ingredients. Don's first attempts fizzled out harmlessly as he dropped the lighted match onto the mixture but with the additional ingredients he smuggled from the chemist he added more potassium and packed the contents into an empty tin and fashioned a fuse from a an old firework. He decided to invite his buddies to the event on a piece of wasteland well away from prying eyes.

'OK lads, stand back it could be a bit dangerous.' Don warned, keeping his fingers crossed in the hope that his home-made 'bomb' would work better. Wow! Did it ever! Five seconds after he lit the fuse there an ear splitting craaack and the obliterated tin rose twenty feet in the air like a miniature rocket, scattering Don and his mates. The perforated tin was inspected, admired, and kept as a souvenir, assuring Don's status as a bomb maker.

*

Don's unhappy, punishment-based school days were now over so what was in prospect for his employment? He certainly wasn't going to follow any of his friends into the Tyne shipyards or down coal mines and couldn't think of anything worse even though his elder brother Sidney worked at the local Heddon pit in the office. Although he had enjoyed his time at the chemists he would have had to spend many years studying to qualify and wanted to be trained and start earning at the same time, so Don scoured the local papers and eventually saw an advertisement under '*Food Service Positions*'.

'TRAINEE WAITER. Good prospects, training, uniforms, accommodation and meals provided. Apply to the Rubicon Club for an application form (phone number inserted with reference number).'

With his mam Gracie's help, he composed a letter with the application form and a few days later a letter embossed with the Rubicon Club's logo invited him for an interview. Don brushed up his only jacket and smart trousers, obtained a glowing reference from Mr Jackson and impressed the two interviewers with his smart turnout and quick answers and was duly appointed at a starting weekly wage of fifteen-shillings as a Junior Waiter, all found. Don was on his way!

CHAPTER 4

Don bid farewell to his Mam and siblings; elder brother Sidney and younger sister Sadie, clutching a worn but polished case containing his meagre belongings of a spare shirt, pair of socks, underwear, pyjamas and toiletries, his stomach tied up in panic-mode knots. His mother had presented him with a bag of his favourite sweets for the journey – liquorice all sorts – and a big hug. 'Now be on your best behaviour and be a credit to the Sullivans. And make sure you write and let us know how you're doing Don, otherwise I'll be worrying. Promise me to write just as soon as you're settled.' Gracie said tearfully but proud of her young son.

'Yes Mam I promise to write and thanks for the sweets.' Don said as turned sadly away, leaving home for the first time and to be sleeping in a strange bed in an even stranger place was an unnerving experience but he was resolved to be a credit to the family. He had no idea what to expect even though he had been given an outline of his duties at the interview.

The Rubicon Club was a bastion of high privilege and exclusivity for the major movers and shakers of the Northumbrian industrial powerhouse. Mine owners, shipyard owners, industrialists and bankers were the clientele who demanded and received the best quality service. Conveniently situated opposite Newcastle's Central Station, the Rubicon Club had a Victorian brooding quality, rising some five floors on Rubicon Street with an imposing pillared frontage that sported a gleaming brass plaque – polished daily. This grand façade seemed to say, 'if you're not impressed with this, just wait until you get inside.'

Crossing the road from the Station he looked up at the grey sandstone block building, swallowed hard and rang the inset polished brass bell. A tall liveried uniformed, top hatted figure looked down at Don. 'Can I help you, young man?'

'Yes, please Sir, I'm here to see Mr. Sinclair the Head Butler.' Don replied in as firm a voice as he could muster.

'Ah yes, Mr. Sinclair – go around the building to the Tradesmen entrance – they'll take care of you there.' He gestured the direction in an imperious tone and closed the door before Don could say 'thank you'.

An elderly man in a brown tunic embellished with a Rubicon Club logo sat in a tiny cabin with a sign – *'All Deliveries Report Here'* – and looked up as Don repeated his request, 'Wait here,' was the gruff response as he dialled a number. 'Mr Sinclair will be down to see you soon; you can take a seat over there,' indicating a threadbare sofa.

Shortly afterwards an imposing, middle aged man sporting a pristine uniform and a silver badge; EAMON SINCLAIR – HEAD BUTLER, who filled out the polished buttoned uniform. Don stood up to attention. 'Ah Donald Sullivan is it now?' Eamon asked, more of a statement, in a pleasant Irish brogue and a mischievous grin. 'So, you've come to help us?' Sizing up Don's turnout and demeanour appraisingly.

'Yes sir, I hope so sir.'

'Good now it is, and so do I, so do I. So come with me and we'll get you sorted Donald.' As he strode off at a pace.

'My name is Eamon Sinclair but you can call me Mr Sinclair. So, the first thing we'll do is give you a little tour of the building, get you fitted out with your uniform and show you to your accommodation. On the way you'll meet some of the staff, so you will. You'll be alright at the Rubicon Club, oh yes. Come with me now.' Eamon Sinclair was an imposing 6', had a full rosy face, piecing green eyes and a full head of russet hair. He walked with a rolling gate perhaps the result of some time spent in the Merchant Marine.

'You'll be wearing your uniform all the time you're on duty in the public areas and when off duty you're restricted to the back of the house.' Warned Eamon. 'So don't be caught off limits, is that clear?'

'Yes Sir I won't, certainly.' Don agreed, secretly thinking how fortunate he was to have been selected and now to have his first new suit and it hadn't cost him a penny. He was now provided with a brand-new uniform (2 sets) and shiny black shoes (2 pairs). Don was surprised to find that the knife edged trousers and braces would fit him neatly as did the shiny buttoned waistcoat, a jacket with short tails trimmed with green cord, white shirts (2) and a dark green silk tie with a woven Rubicon Club crest at its centre! 'So far I've made the right choice,' Don thought. He could hardly believe these acquisitions were his. Eamon put Don's possessions in a hessian bag and ushered him out of the housekeeper's office but not before he was introduced to the Club's Head Housekeeper, Mary Macdonald who was a shapely, doe eyed young lady with a winning smile. Don was smitten!

The Rubicon Club had been founded in the early Victorian era on the back of Britain's growing World influence, resulting from the industrial revolution. A group of mine owners, shipbuilders, bankers and industrialist decided they needed a private place to discuss collaborative ventures and the potential for growth worldwide. Its present location had been selected in clear view of the rail station and a new building of rugged stone, plate glass windows fronted by majestic marble columns testified to its occupants' power and influence over the wider community.

Inside, no expense had been spared. A palatial dining room, an oak panelled conference room, a marble floored reception area, several meeting and dining rooms for private tete-a-tetes and ensuite bedrooms (a novel development). Eamon opened a door into a pristine billiard room boasting a memento filled glass cabinet surrounded by pictures of moustachioed past members. The final room contained a magnificent bar with an array of spirits and an impressive range of whiskies with walls featuring paintings and sculptures of national and international artists. It was truly the last word in Edwardian luxury.

Don stood open mouthed in wonderment, eyes wide in disbelief until Eamon nudged him. 'Here's something that will surprise you, Donald.' Eamon took out a large bunch of keys, two of which were used to unlock a storeroom just off the main dining room. 'This is what we called 'Fort Knox.' He said, almost like a prayer as he crossed himself. Inside was a veritable Alladin's Cave of glittering, highly polished silverware that would grace a royal palace. Pile, upon pile of assorted silver-plated dining room ware, all embossed with the RUBICON CLUB coat of arms. As his eyes became accustomed to the brightness of the silver, he gazed in awe at enormous soup tureens; shelves of assorted cutlery; 'what are those Mr Sinclair?' 'Lobster crackers!' Eamon answered smiling. A carving stand just for Palma ham; dozens of toast racks; stacks of wine coolers; a plethora of serving salvers - small, medium and large; a polished wood table inset with a double gas ring under which were two highly polished copper-bottomed sauté pans. 'This is our 'piece of resistance' Donald,' Eamon said proudly, 'It's for making our signature dessert, 'crepe suzette', pancakes flamed and served at the table to impress the client, very swish eh?'

'What? You set fire to the pancakes, but don't they burn? They wouldn't taste very good then would they Mr Sinclair?

'No, they don't burn Laddie, no,' he replied laughing, 'they taste delicious and you'll see how it's done in due course. This dessert is French as are most of our dishes – it's called 'cuisine francaise' which means French kitchen and it's a very special style of cooking and very new to Britain but you'll learn about it during your training.'

'When does my training start and how long will it take?' Don was anxious to show willing.

'Well young man, it's already started with your tour of the building and 'Fort Knox'. But tomorrow you'll be provided with some learning materials because we expect you to make notes as you learn. Each day you'll write up a diary of what you've done, oh yes it will. And it will be regularly monitored.'

'Will I have a teacher too and have an exam or anything? Don asked slightly concerned at being tested.

'Your 'teachers' will be the various heads of department like the head waiter or maître d'hôtel as we call him or the head barman and wine waiter. Let me show you your accommodation and then I suppose you could do with something to eat? We do have a staff dining area and about this time they will be serving lunch.' Don's stomach had been rumbling for some time as his meagre breakfast had been hours away.

Eamon led the way up two more flights and into a small dormitory with four beds, neatly made up, next to which were four small cabinets and wardrobes. In the centre was a table covered with gingham cloth and four chairs on linoleum with a paisley motif and a patterned carpet. A small settee along one wall and a side table on which stood a dark brown Bakelite radio. Some local prints of the seaside, river and fells on each wall made up the room's decorations.

'Well Donald this is your home-from-home and your bed is that one in the corner – pillow cases and sheets are changed every week. Your three colleagues work in various departments, and you'll meet them in due course. So how to you like it?'

'It's very comfortable Mr Sinclair and I'm sure I'll fit in. Did you say there was a staff canteen Mr Sinclair?' Don asked but didn't want to seem disrespectful.

'Yes we do and you're right Donald – I could do with a bit of nourishment myself, so I could, so let's see what's on offer.' Lunch was shepherd's pie, cabbage, stewed plums and custard and for Don, a real feast!

Through this eye-popping wonderland, Don was escorted by the Head Butler, his head swivelling left and right as he peppered Eamon with questions, leaving no stone unturned as Don soaked up this unreal world that would be his home for many years, he hoped. 'Will I get to serve some famous people?' Asked Don, feeling a little more confident.

'All in good time after your training Donald, so observe and remember because it's the fine detail we strive for at the Club.'

*

Don's first day's training was with the maître d'hôtel, Pierre Toulemon, a dapper little Frenchman who was the 'chef' of the Pullman restaurant.

'Ah, I was told by M. Sinclair you must be Donald ze new apprentice so welcome to my fiefdom, if you will. Now 'ow it works, you 'elp me and I 'elp you, then we get on oui?' He explained as Don struggled to understand the strange accent. No expense had been spared in kitting the restaurant out in lavish European style with renaissance pictures, art déco sculptures and a chandelier centrepiece comprising hundreds of crystal shards which took Don's breath away. He had never seen anything as beautiful.

'Ah oui I can see you are impressed mon ami but we 'av work to do n'est pas? First you will learn to set ze table for all meals – petit dejeuner zat is le breakfast, then dejeuner – lunch and finally diner – dinner of course. 'Eers where we keep ze table clothes and all ze cutlery, le 'dumb waiter' we call it. See, everything in place in zee felt covered draws.' Pierre waved his arms expansively to cover the restaurant as he deftly unfurled a tablecloth and spread it to settle in one smooth movement.

'See, the edge of ze cloth 'as to be underneath. We lay out the cutlery for ze déjeuner. I tell you in French because le menu is in French which you 'av to learn. You will enjoy zis and we are an 'appy team and an 'appy team keeps the clients 'appy also – oui?'

'Oh yes, M. Toulemon, I agree, certainly.'

Later that morning they ran short of napkins so Don was instructed to go to the linen cupboard on the next floor where a linen maid would sort him out. He entered a storeroom in error and was brought up short by what he witnessed in progress. A well-dressed middle-aged man was engaged in an activity with a young member of staff. His trousers and underpants were round his ankles leaning on a table and the man was thrusting himself energetically into the young man's rump, slapping his buttocks in the process. The young man was grunting as he was pushed forward and the man's face was flushed as he increased the tempo. Fortunately, they were facing away from Don and oblivious to his presence, so he quietly closed the door and went next door to the linen pantry, and collected two dozen, double damask napkins from the laundry maid and quickly returned to the restaurant.

Don, at this point was unaware that what he had witnessed was not an isolated practise at the Rubicon Club. Although the management had their suspicions, they were reluctant to create a situation with their clients because if these practises were investigated and exposed it would have serious consequences for the club and its membership. Don decided to keep his discovery to himself, as least for the time being until he knew a lot more of what was going on. 'What other surprises am I about to experience,' Don wondered.

CHAPTER 5

'What took you so long to get those napkins Donald,' demanded Pierre, 'We 'ave the dejeuner to set up, you will 'ave to be quicker if you want to make a good impression.'

'I'm sorry M.Toulemon there was a queue for the laundry.'

'Now, 'ere is the table setting for the dejeuner.' Pierre indicated with a sweep of his arm.

The maitre d'hotel laid out an array of knives (2), forks (2), spoons (2), water glass (1), wine glass (1) and then proceeded to fold a starched napkins into an amazing bird shape.

'Donald, make a note of the setting and copy it for the other three setting on the table. I will check when you've finished but don't worry about ze napkin fold, I give you a demonstration when you've laid up ze places; it's quite an art and anozer skill for you.'

Don took a tray to the sideboard after making a note of the arrangement, loaded the requisite amount of cutlery and made a reasonable copy of Pierre's placement.

'Ah bon Donald, let's see – you 'ave to put the knife and fork for the first course on the outside but is not bad for a first attempt. Now 'ere is 'ow you fold the napkin so pay attention.'

By the time they had laid up the 40 settings for the dining room Don was mentally and physically exhausted by the effort. 'I thought being a waiter was going to be an easy job.' he thought, 'there's a lot to learn but I'll make sure they won't fault me for trying.'

'I sink you did well once you got going Donald, so once the lunch starts at midday just follow me around and keep your eyes and ears open. When you see a client waving at you, see what he wants and fetch me straightaway. For your first day it's unlikely to 'appen but be on your toes. You can pour the water when ze glasses are a quarter full, I show you first – always serve from ze right-hand side.'

Pierre showed Don the lunch menu, much of it in French and briefly described each dish and garnish but most went by in a blur. Four other waiters were on duty, two experienced and two commis (second) waiters, one about 3 years older than Don and his roommate. When service started Don was positioned near the sideboard with a napkin over his right arm and told to stand upright and pay attention to the action. As the service speeded up Don was told to remove the soiled plates to the kitchen and wash-up which kept him busy most of the time. Pierre demonstrated his skills serving silver service style for the main courses and for a dover sole he rolled a trolley to the table and expertly removed the bone, placing the fish fillets neatly onto the plate along-side lemon quarters which he squeezed onto the fish after a nod from the client. Don was so impressed he almost applauded. Almost all the places had been taken within the hour and as Don stood at his sideboard station scanning the room his gaze locked onto a rather overweight client he recognised. 'Yes, that was the man he had seen in the storeroom earlier in that compromising situation.' Don realised, momentarily losing concentration.

''ow are you enjoying the service Donald 'eet is good eh?' Pierre nudged Don.

'Err … a lot thank you M. Toulemon, I'm enjoying it and hope I'm making a good impression?'

Don's response would hopefully get him a good report to Eamon his Mentor, as he was on trial for 3 months and if satisfactory would be given a permanent position and a salary raise to £6 a month, half of which would be sent to his mother Gracie to help with the family housekeeping.

After the service, Don paid a visit to the staff canteen for a well-deserved rest and then returned to the restaurant at 5.30 p.m. to lay-up for the dinner service. Pierre had told Don he would help serving the first course, with soup served from a terrine at the table. The other first course dishes had been completed in the larder; hors d'oeuvres and shrimp cocktail.

Although Don had been demonstrated the soup service, he was naturally nervous especially as his customer was the club member he had seen abusing the young man. As Don carefully ladled the soup into the bowl a passing waiter jogged his elbow – accidentally or deliberately, the result was the same. A small amount of lobster bisque was deposited on the sleeve of the customer who reacted as though the whole terrine had been deposited in his lap.

'You stupid boy, why don't you be more careful that's my best lounge jacket. Pierre, Pierre hasn't this boy had better training?' The man cried out, loud enough to be heard by nearby customers.'

Don stammered his apologies but was quickly taken away by Pierre who took his napkin to wipe away the offending drip of soup.

'Many apologies Lord Backgammon, just an accident and I'll have your jacket cleaned and returned to you by tomorrow. The young man has just started with us and I'm sure he is very sorry. I'll make sure he is suitably chastened.' Pierre said in his best obsequious tone. 'I'll bring Donald over to you to apologise in person.'

Don was summonsed to Lord Backgammon and stammered his apology using lots of 'Sirs' and 'sorries' in the process. The Lord was duly mollified and took a closer look at Don who was a handsome young man and liked what he saw.

'Humph, I suppose he has to learn but he should be more careful in future if he intends to remain here.' He said smiling meaningfully at Don for the first time.

'Well done, Donald, you've made a good impression with Lord Backgammon and that's all to the good. These people are very influential and you don't want to get on their wrong side.'

Don was lost in thought about his accident with Lord Backgammon and as he turned into the corridor that led to the staff quarters, not paying attention and barged into a young lady carrying a tray of toiletries, sending the entire contents flying.

'You should look where you're going young man,' Mary the head housekeeper said angrily. 'I just hope nothing is broken or damaged or you'll have to pay for it.' She warned as she picked up the scattered bottles and packages.

'I'm terribly sorry Miss, I wasn't paying attention, let me help you.' Don stammered an apology as he picked up some of the items. 'I'm new here and still finding my way around.' Don said by way of an excuse. 'My name is Donald, and you are Miss Macdonald aren't you, the Head Housekeeper?'

'That's right I am and pleased nothing has been damaged.' She said, less angry with Don's apology and help. 'You're in M. Toulemon's department aren't you?'

'That's right, he is very good and I'm learning lots but it's quite tough at times with all the menus in French, but I suppose I'll get used to it, eventually.'

'With hard work and the right attitude, I'm sure you will, Donald.' She replied in a more friendly way. 'I must be on my way; I've been delayed long enough.' Giving Donald the glimpse of a smile as she quickly made her way down the corridor.

'What a way to meet such a beautiful young woman. She called me 'young man' but she can't be much older than me, two or three years?' Don thought, 'I'll try to see her again but what excuse could I use?'

CHAPTER 6

When Don returned to his room, he was introduced to Brian another apprentice of six months standing who had also been serving in the dining room. He lived in North Shields and said his father was the owner of Mary Bell, a trawler and his mother looked after the finances and fish sales.

'There was nee way I was gannin te follow me daah on the trawlers.' Brian said with some conviction. 'I did gan oot with Daah twice, aye was sick for days and it frightened the life oot'a me when we woz caught in a farce 8 storm, I thought I was gannin te die, the waves were the height of hoozes and I was soaked through. I divn't nah how they dee it day after day, aye, the North Sea is so unpredictable, but daah seems tee enjoy it. Ah prayed for me return to solid land, so a landlubber ah will remain.'

Brian was a good head taller than Dan with ginger hair, a square cut chin, brown eyes and a Geordie accent you could cut with a knife. He was slim and carried himself confidently, probably the result of Pierre's training.

'I see you've made a hit with Lord Backgammon, but you better watch your back Don, it's said he quite likes young men and there are other clients with similar preferences. There's a rumour that one or two male staff have got involved to boost their wages.'

Don wasn't quite sure he understood but acquiesced. 'Thanks for the tip Brian, maybe we can keep each other informed for our own protection?'

'Yeah, why not, so tell me a bit about yourself Don – you look as though you can handle yourself.'

Don kept his martial skills to himself and briefly mentioned his family in Shields making Brian laugh about his antics as a chemist's assistant. Don's two other roommates, Charlie and Darren were visiting their families near the Roman Wall, in Hexham and Corbridge.

'They're both good fun,' confided Brian although Charlie's a bit of a loose cannon and plays stupid tricks. I'm not sure how long he'll last because Pierre doesn't rate him and gets disciplined regularly for sloppy service. Darren is the deep one and does a lot of reading but is reliable. You'll get on with both just don't take Charlie seriously. If we can arrange our day's off I'll show you where my Dad works at the fish quay, it's really interesting even if you don't like fish.' Brian said quite enthused with a new friend.

'Well thanks Brian for the offer, it sounds fine. Maybe when I've settled down but I need to check on my family, especially as my Dad's away a lot as an Army medic on the front line. He's a specialist with fractures and rehabilitation and there's plenty of that where he's stationed, near a place called the Somme.

*

During the evening service Don had been on lookout for the young man who was being abused in the storeroom but wasn't in either the restaurant or bar. Don's priority was to develop his restaurant skills and become indispensable to Pierre. That way a promotion to a commis waiter was his next step and improved earnings. Don had it all mapped out.

But only a week later events at the Rubicon Club took a turn for the worst when all hell broke loose with the arrival of the Newcastle Constabulary in the form of four uniformed officers and a plain clothed detective. Several staff were called into the manager's office and incarcerated for three hours. After which two members were escorted from the office and into police vehicles. It wasn't long before the grapevine revealed that a body of a young man had been discovered by a dog walker near the river just above the waterline. Identification on the body had revealed that he had been a chef in the Club's kitchen. Although the police were tight-lipped at this a stage regarding the time and cause of death there was little doubt that the death was not accidental. It was also rumoured that the young man was sexually active with other men.

'Suspicious death of young Club chef.' (Headlined the front page of the Newcastle Journal the next day.) *'Last night Police were alerted by a member of the public to a body on the riverbank opposite Waterloo Quay. The young man's details not been released nor the cause of death until family members have been informed. Personnel of a famous Newcastle club are being interviewed for information on the circumstances of his death. At this time the police are keeping an open mind until an autopsy has been conducted.'*

It was the only topic of conversation throughout the Club, and everyone had their own version of what had happened. The consensus was it was not accidental, leaving only one alternative - murder. Don wondered whether the victim was the one he had seen in the storeroom but wouldn't know until his photo appeared in the newspaper. Don would have to bide his time.

Both his absent room-mates Charlie and Darren had returned, Charlie was in the restaurant and Darren who was a 2nd commis in the kitchen and a prime source of speculation about the death of Desmond Lawson a chef tournant and a recognised homosexual. It was rumoured he had been blackmailing one of the club's clients and had paid the ultimate price.

Darren's secret informant was Rubicon's chef de cuisine who had been privy to the manager's involvement with the police. Prior to any disclosures in the press, two staff members taken into custody by the police had under questioning revealed some of the secretive practices and payments by the Rubicon's clients, but no names and little evidence of a reliable nature had surfaced. This had allowed the police to develop a picture of the unlawful sexual behaviour undertaken at the club, but they would need eyewitnesses for any real progress to be made.

CHAPTER 7

'This is a rat's nest Super, we're dealing with a situation which, under the law involves prison sentences but the only evidence we have is hearsay by two totally unreliable witnesses who say some clients of the club and pillars of society are engaged in homosexual activity. Some are senior members of the Government and captains of industry with everything to lose. Their lawyers would make mincemeat of our witnesses if it ever came to court. On the other hand, we have a dead young man who, whatever his sexual orientations didn't deserve to be tortured and die in this way.

We have to get some justice for him and his family but unless we unearth some reliable evidence or witnesses, we're snookered.' Mark Breland, the senior detective in charge voiced his frustration at their impasse.

I feel the same but our best approach for a breakthrough is two-pronged. Mark's supervisor advised. 'Firstly, check again with that dog walker who found the body and secondly, we'll quiz the two Club youngsters again and widen questioning of the senior staff. They could have heard things from among the clients – but discretely, we don't want to have Division or even Scotland Yard come down on us for any harassment of public figures – right?'

'Absolutely Super, I'll get on it and let you know if we get any leads; one of my sergeants is friends with the maître d'hôtel, as he likes to be called. What he doesn't know about the Club's clients is not worth knowing.'

'Fine, we'll meet up asap when you've something to report but we want speedy progress as I'm being leaned on from on high.'

Two days later the police issued an appeal to the public for information in the Telegraph and issued a photograph of the victim, adding that their investigation had now moved to a murder enquiry after the autopsy had revealed serious injuries consistent with a violent assault. Desmond Lawson aged 24 from Denton was confirmed as the deceased and his family had made a tearful public appeal for information. '*If you have any information about this evil crime on our dearly loved son who had his whole life and prospects of a successful career ahead of him, please contact the Police.*' Desmond's photo showed a smiling fair haired, smartly attired young man in his chef's uniform.

'Well, that's confirmed what we knew already.' Brian said resolutely handing the paper to Don after the restaurant service. Don took one look at the victim's photo and visibly blanched as he realised that the face in the photo was the young man he had seen in the storeroom. He was now a key witness of both the victim and of someone who had a motive for the murder, but what was he to do? Keep quiet or reveal what he saw to the police? It was an unenviable choice but Don decided he wasn't going to let it jeopardise a career that he had set his heart on. On the other hand, how could he allow a possible murderer to remain at large?

CHAPTER 8

Two weeks after the murder of Desmond the police interviewed Don, along with all the Club's service staff and still no arrests had been made which, according to the Rubicon Grapevine Management wasn't surprising.

'So, Donald how well did you know Desmond? Was he a pal of yours?' Asked Mark Breland in a manner that suggested he would rather be down the at the Kings Head supping a pint of Best Scotch. Instead, he was obliged to conduct these pointless interviews because the chief had insisted they leave no stone unturned.

'I'm new here Sir and I work in the restaurant so I only knew he was one of the chefs in the kitchen.' Don said hoping they couldn't see he was sweating.

'So have you heard any gossip from the other staff as he was known to be a 'brown nose?'

'A 'brown nose?' Queried Don, unfamiliar with the term which didn't elicit a reply. 'Except they said Desmond liked going out with older men and didn't have a girlfriend.' Don said evenly hoping it would be enough to get his release.

'OK son but if you hear any more, you'll let us know, won't you?' Giving a piecing stare that made Don tremble.

'Yes, certainly I will Sir – thank you. Can I go now? I'm on duty for the dinner and M. Toulemon is a stickler for timekeeping.'

'OK son, run along but don't forget what I told you. Any information you hear WE want to hear it first?'

Don made it with seconds to spare with Pierre checking his watch as he looked up.

'OK Donald we 'ave a special party tonight from the Rotary Club and I want you to serve the 1st course of bisque d'homard you know what that is?'

'Yes M Toulemon, it's lobster soup but will I be serving it at the table?'

'No zat is too tricky for your skills now, we'll serve it from the trolley and you will take it to the table and make sure you serve it - from which side? Yes, the left and don't spill it.' Pierre emphasised stroking his little moustache with a casual twist, a la Poirot.

Tyne Central Rotary Club had a membership of the movers and shakers of the business sector. The dinner was an important occasion for cementing relationships and arranging business deals although members would be shocked if it was suggested that this was their primary purpose. Its true role, constitutionally, was fostering companionship and raising significant sums for selected charities and these endeavours, in addition oiled the business wheels.

It was just Don's bad luck to be serving a group which included the last person he wanted to see – Lord Backgammon. Realising all too soon that he would have to serve the bisque to the Lord. Again, nerves took over as he slopped the soup over the soup dish's rim.

'Ah merde alors Donald,' squeaked Pierre, 'bring ze dish back and take a clean one, now try again and slow down.' Don swallowed hard and tried to calm himself as he ladled a little less soup into the bowl returning to place the dish in front of the Lord looked up and exclaimed in voice that carried down the table.

'Ah, this is the young man who ruined my best jacket last time he served soup, but I see he's improved somewhat this time. Come to my room tomorrow and I'll give you a reward for your obvious improvement in serving skills. Now don't forget, I'll have a word with the M Toulemon about it.'

What was Don to do? How could he distance himself from his invitation from the Lord because if he didn't attend his job could be forfeit. The alternative was keeping the appointment and hoping he could come up with a plan to spike the Lord's intentions. Maybe Pierre could advise him because surely, he must know about the Lord's predilections with young men?

'After your little mishap Donald I thought you performed very well on ze dinner service so I'm going to 'ave you pour ze wine tomorrow but first the little instructions. Show ze bottle to the client then pour a little into the glass, about 'alf an inch and they will taste and if it's good 'zay will nod, and you will pour 'alf a glass, no more – understand?'

'Yes Sir, I understand.' Don replied but thought 'what's not to understand, I'm English and ee's French and 'ee can't even speak proper eenglish,' doing a passable Franglais behind Pierre's back made Dom smile.

'Good, now keep a close watch and when ze glass is a third full offer to refill, but not until. For ze good selling if they 'ave finished the bottle then ask if zay would like anozer. If they want a bottle of something different, excuse yourself and find the wine waiter, we call him the Sommelier.'

After lunch the next day Don's 'promotion' to wine server was considered a success as he sold two more bottles of wine after consulting the Sommelier on popular reds and whites.

'Well done Donald we'll make ze waiter out of you yet.' Pierre congratulated him with a pat on the back. 'Don't forget you 'ave to see the

Lord this afternoon but do not agree to anything he suggest or to see 'im again if 'ee asks. Tell 'im you 'ave to talk to me first unerstand?' Pierre looked closely with an earnest expression that was more a warning than a question.' Don was relieved that Pierre had his personal interests at heart and approached the meeting in a more settled frame of mind.

*

Don tapped on the Lord's apartment door hoping it wouldn't be answered but there was no such luck as an imperative command bayed him enter. 'Come in, come in young man don't be shy. I'm not an ogre you know. Have a seat there.' Pointing to an easy chair a little too close for Don's liking but he had no choice. 'Would you like a drink I've some lemonade or would you like something stronger? A beer perhaps?'

'Er, a lemonade please Sir I'm not old enough to drink alcohol.'

'Quite right, quite right I was only teasing. 'His half smile which didn't reach his eyes, suggested he wasn't. 'I've been watching you and thought you conducted yourself admirably on both occasions so I thought it was right you should have some reward for your efforts. You know I like to encourage new members of the Rubicon staff.' The Lord continued as he handed Don his lemonade contacting with a damp hand in the process. 'Now this is for you Don as a little reward, and if you play your cards right it won't be the last,' handing Don a ten-shilling note and endeavoured to hold Don's hand as he did. Don was too quick and stepped back smiling.

That's very kind of you Sir and I appreciate your generosity, but we're not allowed to accept money from the Rubicon's clients. It was one of the first thing we were told. There's something called a tronk where client tips are placed and shared out among the staff each month, that's the rule Sir.' Looking directly at the Lord as he finished his lemonade.

'Well, that's very commendable of you Donald and I will of course abide by the Club's rules. Now while you're here why don't you tell me a bit about yourself and your family. I like to get to know all the staff because we're really one big happy family here so see me as friend, as well as a client.' Laying a hand on Don's knee.

Don moved away and quickly gave a potted version of his background trying to disregard the Lord's increasing interested and hurriedly stood and excused himself as he had to be on duty for the evening service.

'Well, that was a very entertaining get together, learning about your family circumstances. I must be hard for your mother bringing up a family in these difficult times, so you must let me know if I can be of any help Donald. You will, won't you?'

'Yes Sir, thank you Sir. And good day Sir.' Don managed a smile as he edged out and closed the door, breathing a heavy sigh of relieve as he returned to his room to dress for his restaurant duty. Whatever happened in future he would stay clear of the Lord at all costs and vowed there was no way he would return to the apartment for another tete-a-tete.

*

Don arrived earlier for service to report his meeting to Pierre who listened closely to his account.

'You did the right thing Donald, refusing his gift as eet would have made you beholden to 'im. I 'ave a plan if 'ee tries any funny business in future and tomorrow I will tell you what I 'ave in mind. But, tonight, we are not very busy so I want you to 'elp with the silver service. You know 'ow we've been serving the main course and vegetables with the spoon and fork?'

'Yes, M Toulemon, do you think I'm ready because I kept dropping the vegetables when we practised.'

'OK let's 'ave a little practise now before the service with the bread role. I think you'll be fine just make sure you get the vegetable tureen or the platter close to the plate that way if you drop anything it drops *ON-THE-PLATE,* right?'

'Yes Sir, that's a good tip so I'll get close.' As Don deftly transferred the roll onto the plate. After the service Pierre drew Don to one side and away from any eavesdroppers.

'I 'ave an idea to sort your problem with Lord Backgammon.' Pierre whispered looking around. 'I weel tell 'im your father is in the police and keeps a close eye on you and your training and was interested that the Lord had invited you to his private apartment. 'Zis maybe enough for him to lose interest in you, but we see.'

After Pierre's intervention it was noticeable that the Lord's interest in Don had withered. Matters were taken out of Don's hands two days later regarding the murder when a press announcement revealed that £1,000 had been donated by Rubicon clients for any information that would lead to the arrest of Desmond's killer. The lead detective's phone was red hot for the next few days with informers hoping to receive some of the bounty. Several suspects were rounded up from the police records of local 'nasty' criminals who had previous convictions for GBH (grievous bodily harm). Photos of rogue's gallery were shown to informers who had seen someone around the time of Desmond's assault. Two of those questioned had heard that a 'hit' had been ordered on Desmond by an unidentified bigwig, with a substantial sum as an inducement but were reluctant to admit they knew of anyone directly involved despite being leaned on as to the consequences of compromising a murder enquiry.

When this information filtered through to the Club management and inevitably the staff, Don thought this might be the time to disclose his information about the Lord but how to do this? Any information about what he has seen could easily be traced to the Club and Don himself. Maybe it was better to do nothing, but he was reluctant to let it rest. Desmond's life had been cut short for no other reason than he had been deluded to blackmail someone who would stop at nothing to protect their identity. Don was determined to right this wrong and perhaps ensure that the Lord's criminal act was avenged. He had no one to advise him as they could also be dragged into the mess so gave himself two days to reconsider and hopefully make the right decision for Desmond and justice. Don knew he could be in mortal danger if his involvement was disclosed before anyone was apprehended.

CHAPTER 9

Don's training was moving on a pace both in the restaurant and at the local tech. where he had been enrolled in a City & Guilds 706 Intermediate Waiting & Bar programme. He was now adept at silver service and with the help of the Sommelier his knowledge of wines covered the Premier Crus of the Medoc and the Loire white wines. His favourites were the sparkling wines of Champagne encompassing areas of Epernay and Reims which included the famous Moet & Chandon brand. It was all heady stuff for someone who had previously only sampled the sparkling 'wines' if Tizer or Dandelion & Burdock. Don had broken free from the North East's traditional employment expectations into an industry that rewarded hard work and where promotion through the 'ranks' was based on merit.

Don was still a young man and like most of his colleagues, full of testosterone and masculinity in building status and hierarchy. Fights, though short-lived were a feature of the staff accommodation and pranks even more likely to be inflicted on the weak or less aggressive such as 'apple pie beds' and 'water willies' initiating bedwetting on the unfortunate victim. Most gave as good as they got with an element of tit for tat. The club management was usually tolerant of these low-key activities and turned a 'blind eye' for most transgressions.

Initiation to these activities could be excused as part of the female starved world to which these young men were subject. However, when these high jinks got out of hand then the hammer would come down. One such occasion was dreamed up by Don's roommate Charlie when he was offered some left-over porridge by a colleague in the kitchen. The prank was to 'bomb' late-night revellers who regularly passed under the Rubicon Club's parapets. With a pint of porridge and spoon, Charlie, had pressurised Darren and Brian to collaborate in the escapade, but Don was having none of it as he could see it would end in disaster from on high.

Don excused himself, 'Unlike you lot I'm still under probation so I'm not risking my career on something which is likely to end in dismissal. Think about that before you start.' Don said resignedly. 'Once your japes involve the public you're involving the reputation of the Club, and that's a risk you shouldn't be taking.'

'Ah c'mon Don it's just a bit of fun, no one is going to get hurt, at worst they might get some new hair tonic so let's go.' Charlie laughed at his joke as he and his co-conspirators left and made their way to the crenelated flat roof of the Club. Darren was posted as a look-out with Brian in-charge of the porridge bowl with Charlie ready to spoon some porridge on the unfortunates below. As 11 o'clock chimed from St. Bartholomew's church, a raucous group of young males with their escorts meandered in an alcoholic haze under the 'bomb' site and as the wet and sticky globules found their mark on coats, hair and dresses the group scattered. Our three miscreants pulled back from the parapet doubled up in mirthless laughter as the victims craned necks upwards screaming abuse at the source, fists shaking. Attempts to remove the glutinous mess was half-hearted in the gloom and the ragged group muttered their collective frustration and anger as they wandered to the rail station and home, vowing retribution.

'Was that good eh? Better than I thought so let's wait a while for another group, we've got enough porridge left.' Charlie said still laughing, hugging the others in delight. Unfortunately for Charlie and his comrades the next group that suffered the same fate were much older and in their midst was a client of the Rubicon Club. In paroxysms of laughter at their double success they were unaware of the events unfolding below. Lord Sheffield, the Club client in question had been spared the assault, but not his wife, who was doubly distressed as her brand-new haute couture dress, specially purchased for the charity ball had been ruined by the gluey adhesiveness of the chef's top quality Scott's Porridge Oats.

Our three musketeers stole quickly back to their lair buoyed up by their better-than-expected success and gleefully explained to Don. 'You should have seen the mess and confusion it was priceless and no-one's the wiser.' Charlie crowed, luxuriating in his heightened status, knowing word would quickly transmit to his peer group. Don was not amused in the slightest and realised that involving the public so close to home could involve him in the collateral damage but at this stage he could only hope that Charlie's prank would not back-fire. Unfortunately, they would all be disappointed.

Lord Sheffield summoned the night porter to rouse the manager, who respectfully replied that he was in bed and should not be disturbed.

'What? I don't care whether he's in bed with the housekeeper or the butler get him down here at once or his job is on the line and move as quick as your little legs will carry you.' Lord Sheffield's whiskers quivered as he barked this ultimatum to the porter who scuttled off, sweat breaking out on his rubicund cheeks.

'Oh dear! Oh dear! Oh dear! I'm the meat in the sandwich here. I don't know how it will end and it should be my day off.' Fred the porter muttered to himself as he knocked with increasing force on the apartment door until a grumpy 'who's there? What d'you want?' replied the manager huffily, barely awake.

'Sir, its Frederick the night porter. Lord Sheffield wants to see you immediately and he's very angry.'

'Lord Sheffield? Are you sure? Have you been drinking Fred? If this some kind of joke – I'll have your job!'

'No Sir, honest Sir, he's at reception and about to blow a fuse so come down now, it's very serious.' Fred added even though he had no idea what the problem was. After a few expletives, the manager said he would be down directly.

'Right Sir, I'll tell him you'll be down but be quick Sir he doesn't like to be kept waiting.' Fred said agitatedly.

'What the hell can he want at this time of night, it must be serious, or he's had a skinful and wants a bed for the night.' Cyril Longbottom, the Club Manager deliberated as he hastily pulled on a dressing gown.

'I want action and I want it now Longbottom or heads will roll!' The Lord shouted his face puce from frustration of an evening ruined, not to mention his wife's dress.

Completely oblivious as to what the Lord was on about Cyril attempted to calm the situation until he had some idea as to how to proceed. 'Of course, My Lord, certainly I'll do what I can. Er...can you tell me what the problem is we're talking about and the kind of action you want taken? '

'Ah yes! Obviously, you are not aware of the facts of the matter. One or more of your malcontents showered us with a sticky mess, narrowly missing me but showered my wife ruining her dress AND-I-WANT ACTION! The culprits must be members of your staff, so I want them apprehended and dealt with in short-order or I'll know the reason!' Longbottom was puce with anger, as spittle sprayed the manager's night wear.

'That is terrible, and I'll deal with the matter urgently My Lord. In the meantime, does your wife want something to change into or cover up the damage? Cyril said, swallowing hard to stop himself laughing out loud at the lumps of porridge dripping onto the floor. 'I can get you a taxi immediately sir and will report back to you personally tomorrow when I have investigated this very serious breach of our rules and staff guidelines. I can only apologise for the inconvenience to you, your wife and your party for the distress and damage. Naturally I will have the dress cleaned and repaired or replaced as a priority.' Cyril laid on his apologies and his solution with a veritable trowel in the hope that the Lord would cool down sufficiently to get him into a taxi and out of the Club so he could resume his slumbers.

'Right, yes, good, something to cover up the mess, a housecoat perhaps and a taxi home. I'll expect to hear from you first thing tomorrow with what action you propose to take.' The Lord's frustration filled balloon had been successfully pricked by Cyril's diplomacy and expert grovelling.

CHAPTER 10

Cyril called a meeting of his senior staff early the next morning to investigate the shenanigans of the previous evening; the maitre d', head chef and butler who were given the facts and subsequent fallout involving Lord Sheffield. It was clear that those responsible were service personnel bearing in mind that 'porridge and kitchen' were closely linked to the fracas. The breakfast chef was the first to be quizzed and both the maitre d' and butler were asked to question the likely suspects particularly those with a record of misdemeanours.

'Lord Sheffield was spitting tacks last night and gave me a thorough dressing down so I want this sorted today and the culprits brought to book. I have to report back to the Lord this morning so get to it and report back to me by 11. We can then decide what to do with the culprits because I suspect there was more than one.'

'Eamon, quiz the younger on-site staff as to their whereabouts last night' the manager advised, 'as this should narrow down the perpetrators.' The head butler shook his head in disbelief at what had happened but had a fair idea where to start his investigation.

'Zer are some of my boys 'ooh could be involved so I will talk to 'zem before ze service.' Pierre offered. On investigation by the head chef, the breakfast cook initially denied any knowledge of what had happened to the left-over porridge but was warned that unless he told the truth, his job would be forfeit. 'I don't think you realise how serious this is. We are talking about an offence to one of the most senior members of this club and the police could be involved. If you come clean, I'll do what I can to save your job, but I can't promise.' The possible involvement of the police frightened the cook into a spluttering confession naming the Charlie as perpetrator in chief.

'But I didn't know what he was going to do with it. I thought it was something involving the other lads in a practical joke.' He stammered; shaking with concern as to his likely punishment.'

'I should have guessed it might be Charlie, that little toerag, we'd be better off without him.' The chef thought, recalling Charlie's lack-lustre period in his kitchen where he could never be trusted to do any job without close supervision.' The Chef rang Eamon the Butler first and identified Charlie as the main culprit who in turn contacted the manager. I'll interview him first Mr Longbottom and find out who else is involved, then we can meet in your office and decide on what action to take.' Eamon suggested.

'Thank you Eamon I'm very grateful to you and the chef for your swift action; I'll see you in my office later.'

Summoned from his room to Eamon's office, Charlie realised that he was in serious trouble from the outset. He was told the game was up and he better tell the whole story as an assault on a Club member had been committed. Charlie's face gradually changed to an ashen shade of grey with his bowels in an uproar as the consequences of his folly dawned.

'It wasn't my idea really it was the others, I only got involved to help and I didn't know it would involve outsiders, honest. I thought it was just a bit of harmless fun.' Charlie's futile attempt to exonerate himself from the action fell on deaf ears.

'Don't test my patience Charlie, we've talked to the others, and they've fingered you as the instigator and leader of the assault so cut the bullshit because you are now in very serious trouble. I want a full account of what happened, **now and no lies!**' Eamon shouted the demand, seething with frustration that he had been involved in this crass escapade primarily because he was also responsible to the club for these young men's behaviour.

The two culprits, Darren and Brian lay the blame four-square on Charlie's shoulders, stating they had been forced to participate. They had 'definitely not' been directly involved in the porridge cascade on the Lord or anyone else. In the process of the Butler's interviews, Don was asked why he had not reported Charlie's proposed 'bombing' plan? Don agreed he had tried to dissuade Charlie at the outset but he was not a snitch. As the junior member of the group he had little influence and didn't know what they had planned.

'Don't forget Donald, your allegiance is to the Club first and foremost and not to a personal code of honour to colleagues. Knowing them, they'd be unlikely to give you same 'omerta' if they were pushed. Anyway, you're not off the hook, it'll be up to the manager as to what action he considers appropriate.' Eamon knew Don wasn't involved but might still suffer from the fallout.

*

All the heads were agreed that swift and severe action had to be taken on the miscreants when they resumed in the Manager's office. Charlie had too many black marks on his CV, so his dismissal was to some extent a formality. Any further action by the police if they were involved would largely depend on the Lord's reaction after he had the report. Of the other offenders, Darren and Brian would be docked a month's wages and were given a final warning to toe the line. It would be up to the manager to butter up the Lord by reporting that the main perpetrator would be dismissed, and his helpers severely punished with a final warning as to their future conduct. He didn't want to lose two skilful and hardworking members of staff in Darren and Brian if he could help it. Don was fortunate to be given a reprimand and told to act more responsibly in future.

The Manager's report to the Lord, said the matter had been investigated thoroughly and action taken on those involved and he hope a line could be drawn under the matter. The Lord's wife's dress was returned good as new having been cleaned and repaired and a large bouquet of red roses accompanied it's return with a bottle of Krug as a sweetener.

'Well Cyril I hope those tear-aways have learned their lesson and understand that innocently conceived pranks can go too far. I know, I've had my fair share of punishment for japes that got out of hand so we shouldn't be too harsh, should we?' The Lord confided after reading the report. 'Maybe sacking that young man is rather harsh as no one was injured so perhaps you might reconsider? We don't want to ruin his career for some unruly behaviour, do we?' The Lord suggested, in a sea change to his previous night's demeanour, when it seemed he wanted the culprits hung, drawn and quartered!

'That is very generous of you My Lord and I will review his punishment and give him a last warning and hope that having the Sword of Damocles as a threat will guarantee his best behaviour from now on.' The Manager heaved a silent breath of relief at the outcome and would relish giving Charlie and the other two a sound verbal kicking for putting him through 12 hours of torment. He was satisfied that the other departmental heads would also pile on the agony. Lessons had to be learned if discipline at the Club was to be maintained and he was determined that the consequences of this prank would circulate.

CHAPTER 11

The murder of Desmond still haunted Don's waking hours but he was still no clearer about what to do about his dilemma. Wait until matters were taken out of his hands; was an option, but for how long? Shouldn't he do the right thing and help the police to find the culprit? Wasn't it his public duty if he wanted to get justice for Desmond and his family?' One of those who had responded to the offer of a reward had provided a description of a man near where Desmond had been found culminating in the arrest of a known villain.

Don heard through the grapevine that the murder investigation had stalled through lack of reliable eyewitnesses even though a local villain had been arrested and accused of an attack on Desmond. He just had to figure out a way of disclosing his eyewitness account to the police without jeopardising his career and decided to seek his mentor's advice.

'I've a problem Mr Sinclair and I'm not sure what to do.'

'If it's to do with the porridge incident don't worry, The Lord decided to drop the matter and no one's going to be sacked.'

'No, it's not that Mr Sinclair, it's to do with Desmond's murder.' Don whispered and looked around.

'Alright Donald, my office is probably the best place to talk,' Eamon ushered Don in and sat him down. 'Now take your time and just tell me what you know, then we'll decide what to do – if anything.'

Don revealed what he had seen, and until Desmond's murder had decided to do nothing and tell no-one, until now.

'You see Mr Sinclair, I didn't really know Desmond, but he had his life and career and now it's gone, and his family haven't a breadwinner or a son anymore. Whoever was responsible for his murder should be caught and punished, that's right isn't it Mr Sinclair?' After his agitated disclosure Don was out of breath.

Eamon knew it had taken Don some personal soul searching to unburden himself. 'You're right Don the guilty should be punished and you were right to tell me but we are not the law and we do have the police. We should also consider what could happen if we tell the police as you are the only eyewitness directly linked to Desmond's murder. If the police take it further, defence lawyers will say you could have been mistaken as to what you saw. They might even take a dim view that you didn't come forward with the information when they interviewed you. And if they did take what you saw as hard evidence, the person involved is a heavy weight of the first order, and very influential. He's a pillar of the community with bags of influence where it matters with top legal support. His life and position would be forfeit if convicted or even charged and perhaps that's why Desmond is now lying in a grave because he threatened this man's position. I'll have a quiet word with Mark Breland because we have close family ties and see what he thinks. Leave it with me until I've seen Mark as he's in charge of the case.' Eamon smiled as he placed a fatherly arm on Don shoulder as he left. Don felt a great weight had been lifted but worried about what would happen next.

*

In all the excitement he had forgotten he was the de facto maître d'hôtel that lunchtime as a reward for passing his interim City & Guilds waiting exam, so he better check the dining room layout and allocate sections to his three-waiting staff. He just hoped no-one would order the crepe suzette because the last time he was rather generous with the Napoleon brandy and Pierre had to snuff out the flames with a well-placed cloth. The customers thought it was all part of the show and applauded loudly – what a let off! Surprisingly, his faux pas was a five-pound tip - the largest of his tenure. A week later Eamon called Don into his office and said he had talked to Mark at length, and with Don's written evidence in support, was about to bring Desmond's murderer to justice, but at what cost to Don and his career at Rubicon?

CHAPTER 12

National newspapers had picked up on the disclosures by the police concerning the murder of Desmond Lawson and the involvement of a high-profile member of the Rubicon establishment. Admissions by Turner-Smythe who was the ADC of Lord Backgammon, claimed that that the instructions and money supplied to Desmond's attacker, Bart Spencer had originated from Backgammon's private secretary. Turner-Smythe eventually admitted his involvement when his fingerprints were found on the money in Spencer's possession and these revelations involved the grooming of young men in homosexual activity, lured by substantial payments and gifts.

Don's evidence proved to be a crucial part of the eyewitness evidence that eventually brought Lord Backgammon, as well as other VIPs into the High Court, accused of *'committing acts of gross indecency'* a criminal activity. It was only due to their highly paid lawyers and societal positions that saved them from prison sentences, but their careers and public standing was ruined.

Don was the centre of attention for his involvement in the very public trials which didn't sit well with the Rubicon Club management – even though Don had declined interviews and kept a low profile throughout. The Club prided itself on its privacy for members and as Don had been a key witness his days at the club could be numbered even though he was a valued cog in the restaurant team and now deputy to the maître d'hôtel. Nevertheless, press reports regarding the Rubicon Club revelations continued so the manager called a management meeting to stifle anymore speculation.

'There's a view that Don is the source for these news items which is untrue. We all know that he is a loyal employee, but, he is seen as a reminder of this unsavoury period at the Club.' The Board had hoped the press would have found more tastier news for their columns.'

'Why should zis young man's career be compromise when iz conscience and disclosure elped to catch Desmond's killers?' Demanded Pierre.

'Point taken but the fact remains that as long as Don remains, we're under the press microscope. This atmosphere is affecting membership applications.

'What if we give Don some paid leave of absence until things settle down because punishing Don is the very person we ought to be supporting. We can always use the agency to fill the gap?' Eamon the Head Butler added a viable alternative and Pierre nodded in agreement.

'Yes. That is worth considering Eamon. What's your view Chef? After all this whole situation revolved around one of your staff. Er, that is, I mean - I hasten to add that neither you or your department were in any way culpable.' Cyril's quick apology was to deflect any possible volatile response from the Chef who was on the verge of challenging the perceived rebuke.

'I'm with Pierre and Eamon on this. Donald is a model employee and has always had the Club's interest at heart, so having him forced out leaves a very big question in the minds of the rest of the staff, which is; however valuable I am, my job could be at risk for no fault of my own,' Chef asserted.

'Alright, alright, I take the point Chef that we're agreed to find a way around this issue without penalising Don. So, give him a leave of absence and if there's no more disclosures, we're good?' The manager then hoped to convince the board that because his department were united, Donald should stay. Any other action would be counterproductive.

Don was given the manager's decision by Eamon. 'Until things cool down Donald it has been decided to give you two weeks paid holiday and a bonus to cover sustenance costs while you're away. This is no reflection on your work but the management are concerned that your on-site presence is still a press magnet so please decline any interviews my boy?' He regretted being the conduit as Don was entirely blameless.

'Yes, Mr Sinclair I understand. I'd never do anything that would hurt the Club. They've – you've done so much for me. But if my going away for a while will help then that's fine.' Don replied knowing he was being made the scapegoat but at least he wasn't being financially penalised. At that time Don was unaware that a portion of the reward money, £200 of the £1,000 for the arrest and conviction of Desmond's killers had been allocated to him. An enormous sum and equivalent to a year's salary!

CHAPTER 13

As the tram rattled over the Tyne's High-Level bridge towards Low Fell and down to into Shields, passing Saltwell Park, Don recalled fond memories of playing on the longest Banana Slide in the World when was just a toddler, taken into Low Fell by Granny Tearse. The 15-minute tram-ride was a short walk to his home at 33 Dakar Street. His earlier letter to his mam explaining the reason for his two-week break from the Rubicon had initiated a celebratory 'welcome home Donald' party with bunting over the door and windows. It was the first time Don had been home for many months, so he would use this 'home' time to reconnect with his pals and consider his next career move because he felt his time at the Rubicon Club could be over, despite the reprieve.

'My, my, look at you Donald all grown and turned-out smart as a pin. I hardly recognised you as the waif who left here over three years ago.' His Mam gushed, 'We're all very proud of what you've done, so come here.' Gracie cried, her voice betraying the emotion she felt, her eyes shining as she gave Don a maternal hug for good measure.

'It's good to be back Mam, it really is and I've got some good news as well.' Don said choking up at his welcome.

His elder brother Sidney, who had grown apace to over six feet tall, and Sadie, his little sister, chattering away and skipping with excitement, were next to welcome their famous sibling. Clifford, his uncle and ex-boxer was a rare visitor who had taught Don self-defence and boxing moves.

Although rationing was still in force, Gracie had saved up the points by using her forceful personality to persuade the pork butcher to keep some prime cuts 'under the counter' and two pounds of pease pudding for good measure. Accompanying the beef brisket were roast potatoes, tomatoes and turnips from the allotment and a rare tin of pears, made for a mouth-watering feast for the ever-hungry family.

'We read all about the shenanigans at your Club and were quite shocked, but it was a lovely photo of you in the Gazette. You were the talk of the street, with lots of neighbours wanting the details. We couldn't really tell them much though.' Gracie gave Don a questioning look to elaborate but Don shook his head, lips pursed.

'Thanks everyone for such a welcome home.' Don's eyes misted over at having such a supportive family.

Little remained of the meal except two portions of pease pudding which would be used later as a filling in the stottie cake either at tea or supper. The party had taken on a somnambulant state of sated satisfaction when Don handed out a few presents. A block of cheddar cheese, a roll of black-pudding and a fruit cake that the chef had insisted he take for helping to get justice for Desmond. In addition, a colourful plaid scarf for his mam, a striped, blue tie for his brother Sidney, a pair of socks for Clifford and a book about The Famous Five by Enid Blyton for Sadie. Everyone said he shouldn't have but very pleased, especially Gracie with his boost to the pantry supplies.

'I told your friend Jimmy you were coming and said you would be around to see him once you'd settled in. He was here with some of your other friends so they'll looking forward to hearing all your news.' Sidney said as he got up to leave for the night shift at Horden colliery where he was now a deputy.

'Thanks for that lovely meal Mam, can I have a word?' As Gracie turned and smiled, her sun-browned arms covered in suds. 'I received a reward for helping the police and I want you to have some of it. I don't have any real expenses and it will make things easier for you, but don't tell anyone else, that is unless you want to.' Don separated £150 which he had placed in an envelope for his mother.

Gracie stifled a shriek when he told her the amount. 'Donald, that is a huge amount are you sure? Won't you need it for your career?' She asked, recovering from the shock that would make life much easier for some time. Don was adamant he had enough for anything he needed.

Don was left with his thoughts as Gracie busied herself with the washing-up from their meal with Sadie engrossed in her prized new book. If he was determined to leave the Club, his first job would be the situations vacant in a trade paper. The Caterer was the weekly that he had occasionally leafed through in the Rubicon staff room. WH Smiths in Shields town centre would have a copy and he could meet his friends at their usually haunt on the Links for a kick-a-bout as Newcastle were playing away that weekend.

Don greeted his five pals as he kicked the ball back, 'Hi Jimmy, it's good to see you again, how's the hand?' Don asked his pal as he was shown the gnarled hand minus two fingers and two others with only a knuckle each, after the rail accident.

'Hi Don, it's not too bad, as I can just about hold onto somethings. The surgeon is getting a sort of artificial hand that can strap on. I've already been for a measurement and I'm going back to the clinic next week for a fitting.'

'That's good news Jimmy and how's everyone else? All got jobs? Girl friends?' Don asked turning to his other friends as they shook their heads – jobs were few and far between on Tyneside.

Getting any job with soldiers and sailors returning from the war was hard with only part time work at the docks or doing labouring available which was poorly paid. Coal mining had been rejected out of hand by his pals because of the long hours underground in dangerous, cramped and in an unhealthy environment where 'miners' lung' was an ever-present risk from the coal dust. Accidents had invalided out a few of their fathers and friends from the local pit and this only served to underline their aversion to a life underground.

'You two can be Sunderland and we'll be United,' Jimmy said taking Don's jacket as part of the goal post. 'The first to score 5 goals wins the game.' He added taking the football and tossing the coin calling out 'heads' to see who would have first kick-off.

After 10 minutes with the game at 2 – 2 a Park Inspector approached them.

'Hey, can't you read the notice.' He shouted. 'It's in the King's English and says 'NO BALL GAMES' so cut out the football.

'We're not bothering anyone and there's plenty of space to play.' Jimmy replied angrily.

'I don't make the rules. This park is for everyone to enjoy, and you could hurt someone if they were hit by the football. So be off with you or I'll have to report you and you could be fined.' He added with a final coup de grace.

'What a killjoy. I'll bet he loves ruining people's enjoyment for no reason.' Don said in a stage whisper.

'I heard that and don't be cheeky or I'll report you anyway for abusive language.'

'C'mon let's find somewhere else to play, what about on the beach; there no law there about playing games.' Jimmy said moving away with the football.

'I've a better idea, the Marsden Café is open and it looks like rain so let's have a some tea or pop.' Don suggested and added. 'My treat as I've been given two weeks leave with pay, OK?'

All agreed and quickly decamped to the warm fug of the Café for drinks and cakes as they applauded Don's generosity.

*

Don caught the local trolley bus from the corner of Beach Road opposite the Wheatsheaf pub to the town centre near the Market and picked up a copy of the Caterer at Smiths. Back on the trolley towards Dakar Street he leafed through the magazine and spotted what looked like a promising position.

EXPERIENCED WAITER REQUIRED FOR 4 STAR HOTEL

4 Arrows Hotel. Cumbria. Phone or write for application.

Good starting salary plus bonuses. Live-in option. Uniform provided. Confirmation of Training. Qualification & Reference required. Traveling expenses paid. Phone Newcastle 326 or write for application form to the Personnel Officer (address given).

Once at home, Don put pen to paper and wrote off for the application form in his best handwriting giving his address as the Rubicon Club. There was no rush as he would have to give some notice of leaving anyway and even if he were offered that job, which was a long shot, an interview would be good experience for future applications.

'What's for supper Mam?' Sadie called out, ever hungry as she returned from playing with her friends in the lane.

'Wait and see.' Replied Gracie smiling at her cherubic daughter. 'And go and wash your hands, they're filthy. Supper will be ready by six so give your brothers a call, I think Sidney's in the garden, but I don't know where Don is.

Finally, they were all assembled round the polished table covered by a linen cloth with a decorated multi-coloured crocheted centre piece and Sidney, as head of the household said grace, adding 'and protect Dad from harm, where-ever he is, Amen'. Their meal of baked ham, roast potatoes and cabbage followed by a steamed syrup sponge was a rare treat, thanks to Don's financial windfall.

'Ooh this so tasty.' Sadie blurted out with a mouthful. 'But isn't there any gravy Mam?' Looking round the table.

'Hunger is the best sauce my lass and don't speak with your mouth full, I won't tell you again.'

The brothers smiled, giving knowing looks at each other on hearing this reply by their mam. Don helped Sidney with the washing up and told him he was thinking of buying a motor bike to see more of Northumberland on his days off. 'My BSA Bantam cost £35 second hand, but you could get an Ariel 250 second hand for about £40.' Sidney replied.

'Let's see some bikes at Baxter's showroom on the Parade tomorrow as I have a day off.' Sidney said, 'and if you're keen, I'll teach you how to ride if you like?'

'Oh yes, thanks Sid, that would be great to see the selection and what I could afford.' Don hadn't told Sidney about his windfall. 'Could we go on your bike?'

'OK Don, if it's not raining. I've a spare crash helmet and put on a big coat it's a bit draughty.'

Gracie wasn't too pleased Don was thinking of a motorbike but couldn't object too much as her eldest son was already an experienced motorcyclist and would take care of his younger brother. 'Make sure he holds-on tight Sidney and don't go too fast, I know what you're like.' Gracie warned her eldest, her anxiety showing with what she considered dangerous transport.

CHAPTER 14

'Hey Sid, they've an amazing selection haven't they.' Don marvelled over the glittering array of BSA, Ariels, Triumphs, Nortons and even a BMW. The cheaper end of the range featured a Francis-Barnet but a Harley Davidson was not for sale, not that Don could afford it anyway. Prices for 2nd hand machines ranged from £35 to £00's and a BSA 250 caught his eye at £45, with a red petrol tank, sprung forks back and front and six months warrantee for any non-accident faults. Salesman Vince could see the pair looking at the BSA were in buying mode.

'The BSA has just come in and is in very good condition and has only 2,000 miles on the speedo.' Vince explained, 'If you put down a deposit today, I could add a helmet, good riding gloves and a leather jacket. What do you think?'

'We're just looking for a first bike for my brother and haven't made our minds up yet, but something in the £35 - £45 range. If we decide to buy would you give a discount on the price?' Sidney asked, always looking for a bargain.

'Certainly, we can do you a deal so have a good look around; they've all been serviced and are guaranteed for 6 months. We can also provide the insurance cover to get you going. I'm Vince Pembroke, at your service and here's my card.'

A comprehensive search of the showroom's bikes, Don's notes revealed that only two bikes ticked all the boxes in terms of price, quality and mileage. The BSA 250 and an Ariel 200 both at £45. 'What do you think Sid, which would be your choice bearing in mind what I want it for?'

'Both are in good shape for the price and are very reliable makes but for me the BSA edges it on reliability, MPG (Miles Per Gallon) and it's got fewer miles on the clock. But it's your bike after all.' Sidney added. 'I'll ask Vince if I can have a test ride on your choice.'

Sales had been a bit slow at Baxter's for a while, so Vince bent over backwards to close the sale at £40, adding the extras he'd promised earlier, and the deal was done. Sidney took the bike out for a 10-minute spin along the coast road to Marsden and gave it the all-clear.

'I can't really believe it's mine.' Don proudly polished the bright work for the third time, back at Dakar Street. 'Will you be able to give me some lessons at the weekend.' Don pleaded, hoping Sidney would agree to get him started.

'Don't rush things Don you've plenty of time. It's important you know how the machine works and understand its limits. That way you get the best performance out of it safely.' Sidney had the same enthusiasm when he bought the Bantam but had to make sure Don didn't short circuit any steps. Motorbikes could be dangerous in the wrong hands and most motorbike accidents occurred within the first few months, especially with young riders full of testosterone. Don wouldn't be let loose on the bike until Sidney was convinced he was ready otherwise he would have Gracie to answer to, and that didn't bear thinking about!

After a few lessons, Don was ready for the open roads with Sid as a chaperon. 'OK Don, you've passed all my safety checks and you're riding well enough to have a spin on your own and make sure that 'L' plate is secured so enjoy yourself; just watch out for the others.' Sidney smiled a warning, satisfied that he had done a good job for his younger brother.

'Thanks Sid, for all your help, I couldn't have done it without you.' Don shook his brother's hand, kick-started his BSA and eased away down Dakar Street giving Sidney a wave as he turned the corner. Little did Don know that his first outing would not be the joyride he anticipated and wished he had taken a different route that morning.

CHAPTER 15

Don accelerated along the Shields grassy seafront towards Marsden and the Rock his newly acquired BSA 250 purred like a well-fed cat. His friends had gathered at their regular haunt the Wheatsheaf to welcome him and his new motorbike. His status as a mini-press star resulting from his involvement in the murder trial made him the leader of the pack. The gang were naturally envious of his chromium bright machine and Don had promised each a spin so they fussed, inspected and discussed the attributes of his proud possession after he braked to a halt, pulling the bike expertly onto its stand. He took his pal Jimmy to get the drinks of Best Scotch, Newcastle Brown and a Tizer for himself, as Sidney had warned, alcohol and bike riding didn't mix.

Each of his four friends in turn whooped and hollered from the pillion as Don roared along the seafront getting disapproving frowns and head shakes from locals enjoying the sun and light breeze off the sparkling North Sea breakers. Don had never been so happy or proud of his newfound status but was he just buying their adulation?

'We're so proud of you and that bike is one of the best around, so look after it.' Said Jimmy as he showed his disfigured hand to Don, almost accusingly. 'The surgeons have grafted skin from my bum onto the two of the fingers to get more feeling and manipulation back.' He added, turning his damaged hand for Don's fascinated inspection.

'You know when it happened, I thought you might lose your hand when I saw the mess, but now it's looking much better.' Don said with some relief because he had always blamed himself for that accident playing on the mine's railway.

Sated with their bike ride and beers, Don was given back-slaps by his pals as he remounted and with a boisterous engine rev. roared away along the seafront to the waves and shouts of his friends.

Three miles later as he was negotiating an 'S' bend a fox darted out of a hedge almost under his wheels. Instinctively Don braked. Skidded on the loose chippings. Slid out of control. Hurdled a narrow ditch. Through a bramble hedge. Over the wire fence and into a newly ploughed field, catapulting Don off his BSA like a circus acrobat, his breath knocked out like a pricked balloon. Don's spectacular tumble was witnessed by a nearby tractor driver who quickly dismounted and ran over to help.

'Boy! What a mess!' He exclaimed, leaning over the prostrated Don. 'Are you alright, young man?' He asked anxiously, fearing the worst.

'Whaaaa ….. t happened', Don mumbled, coming too, ' Oh, aye, I'm fine, I think, no serious damage. ' Don stood unsteadily to inspect the damage to his muddied machine.

His leather riding coat had helped to protect him from the barbed fence and more serious injury. The handlebars were bent and there were numerous scratches and scrapes along the bright-work and petrol tank but otherwise looked undamaged. Physically Don was uninjured, but his pride had been dented and was sick at heart having to face his Mam and Sidney.

'Let me help you with the bike so we can check the damage,' The tractor driver took control. 'The handlebars can be straightened but apart from that it looks alright. The soil's took most of the impact.' While the farmer manhandling the bike with the front wheel clasped between Don's legs to straighten the handlebars.

'I think you need to take a break. You don't look 100% so let's wheel the bike to the farmhouse and get you a drink.'

After sipping a hot, sweet cup of tea in front of a roaring fire in the cosy front room of the farmhouse, Don recovered to thank the farmer Fred Larkin for his Samaritan help. 'You're Don Sullivan from Shields aren't you?' I thought I recognised you from that picture in last week's Telegraph.' Don explained that a fox was the cause and not his speed. 'It's a pity you swerved, as one less fox would have been a bonus.'

After a desultory wipe down of the bike, Don kicked the pedal and the engine roared back to life seeming to demonstrate that a little ploughed field wasn't much of a problem for a BSA. His faculties back in command Don shook the farmer's hand and eased away, well below the speed limit. Back at Dakar Street, Sidney viewed the dishevelled bike with some concern thinking that speed was the cause as did his mother, until they heard the full story.

'I told you motor-bikes weren't safe Sidney, but you wouldn't listen, and Don could have been killed. Gracie cried, annoyed with herself and close to tears but mightily relieved that her son was unharmed.

CHAPTER 16

Don's brief break from the Rubicon had come to an end but he was still concerned with the thinly veiled ultimatum from the management to find alternative employment. He was resolved to go but only when he was ready. His conscience was clear as he had helped rid the Club of its criminal members and played a significant role in solving a murder. After reporting back to Eamon and given permission to park the BSA undercover adjacent to members parking, Don found a letter on his bed addressed to Donald Sullivan, Rubicon Club, Newcastle-on-Tyne with a 4 Arrows Hotel crest which he tore open and as he read, shouted 'Yes! Yes!'.

Dear Mr Sullivan,

Thank you for your completed application for the position of 'experienced waiter'. We would like you to attend an interview on a date to be arranged at your convenience. Please contact the Personnel Office on Carlisle 498 at your earliest.

Yours sincerely,

Elaine Dalrymple. Personnel Officer.

'Let's see, my day off is Thursday so I'll try to get the interview on Thursday afternoon.' Don was getting more excited as he read the letter again. 'It'll take me about two hours on the bike,' as he checked his road map.

'Yes, Thursday would be convenient so can we say 2 p.m.?' Ms Dalrymple, The Personnel Officer confirmed and gave Don the address and directions.

*

'Bonjour Donald, Bienvenu.' Pierre welcomed Don's return to action and told him he would be the maître d'hôtel as it was his night off. 'Ah well, in at the deep end again.' Don thought, 'It'll be good for my development though.' Don wanted more responsibility to add to his CV.

'Le dinner on Wednesday is not too busy but I 'ave allocated two of your friends, Darren and Brian. Also, the Sommelier is on duty and will 'elp out if required.' Don checked with Chef-de-cuisine Stuart to see if there were any changes in either the table d'hote or specials menu so he could brief his staff in good time.

'No changes on the standard menu but I've a couple of specials I'd like you to push. The fishmonger gave me a good price on some plaice so I've added 'Plie Bonne Femme', poached fillets in a white wine sauce with mushrooms.' Stuart explained as Don t the tasted the wine sauce and agreed it was 'very tasty'.

Half an hour before service Don did a tour of the room and briefed his friends on the additions to the menu. The Sommelier asked him to recommend a Chateau Latour '45 as it was a bin end at the reduced the price on the 6 bottles to £6.00 each– a bargain!

*

On his return the next day Pierre was delighted to be told that the 45 diners had had exemplary service and that most of the specials had been taken up. High praise also from the Sommelier as all the bottles of '45 Latour had sold. Don had also produced a flaming crepe suzette at the table without setting fire to anything but the pancakes. Lord Sheffield and his guests greeted the performance with a round of applause and a generous tip insisted upon by the Lord, with house rules on gratuities disregarded.

'Well done, Donald, I 'ear you and your team made a great success of the dinner and everyone was 'appy with the service. Leaving you to 'andle everything on your own was a good idea n'est pas?' Pierre's habit of lapsing into his mother tongue usually happened when he was nervous or in this case 'very 'appy.'

'Thank you M. Toulemon, I couldn't have done it without all the instruction and advice you've given me.' Don's praise for Pierre's training was heartfelt and not a ruse to boost his boss's self-image, although it didn't hurt Don's prospects.

'Well, that went well chaps, didn't it?' Don said to his fellow waiters who smiled in agreement. 'Many thanks for your efforts and to our customers for their generosity!' Tips were distributed in equal shares with a proportion to the kitchen staff. 'After all, the kitchen contributed to a successful evening.'

CHAPTER 17

Armed with his credentials; a waiting certificate, a curriculum vitae and a glowing reference from Pierre, Don set off for his interview at the 4 Arrows Hotel on his gleaming BSA and managed to negotiate the hilly and undulating A69 in just over 2 hours. The market town of Alston, highest in England was less than a mile from the hotel which was encircled by four acres of wooded pastureland. The Palladian styled hotel built in the early Edwardian period as a residence for the local Earl of Penrith had been sold off after the demise of the Earl and transformed into a 4* 40-bedroom hotel and restaurant.

Extensive modernisation over the past few years had added a spa, gym and a 15-metre swimming pool. Within the grounds was an all-weather tennis court, putting green and a 9-hole golf course and in season, alternate activities were archery, fishing and croquet. Within the hotel a plethora of activities included a games area with a billiard room, and an assortment of board games. In short, residents needed little else for an enjoyable and relaxing stay. 'What a place to develop my skills and move up the ladder,' Don thought and was sure his interview had been granted on the Rubicon's reputation as a superior private club and haute cuisine restaurant.

'Tell me about your responsibilities at the Rubicon,' the Personnel Officer asked before the maître d'hôtel quizzed him about his operational restaurant and wine experience. Don had done his homework on French cuisine, knowledge of wines and his deputy management role. Finally, the Hotel Manager questioned his reasons for wanting to leave the Rubicon,

'I've learned all I can at the Rubicon over 3 years and want to develop my career in a more commercial environment. The 4 Arrows is the step up to develop my skills in a more varied, busier environment.' Don explained confidently. The manager acknowledged Don's reasons for the move and confirmed that the Personnel Officer would be in touch with their decision in a few days. 'Thank you for my tour and an enjoyable interview sir.' As he departed with a smile, satisfied with his performance.

His return journey on the A69 was nothing like as smooth, due primarily to the escape of about 50 woolly jumpers from an adjacent field who blocked the road and delayed him for almost a half hour. Although fine weather had been forecast a band of cold air descended from the fells accompanied by driving rain that quickly soaked him through despite the thickness of his leather jacket. Eventually, three hours later he arrived at the Rubicon, shivering from cold and worn out but thankful he was not on duty that evening.

'You look like a drowned rat Don, better get those wet things off before you catch something nasty,' advised Darren his roommate whilst pouring him a tumbler of whisky, 'here get this down you, it might ward off the chills.'

'Thanks it's just what I need after that journey - bloody sheep!' Don gulped the whisky in quick time then out of his soaked gear and into a relaxing bath.

'So did you wow them with your high-level Rubicon experience and skills?' Darren asked pointedly as Don quickly squashed that question.

'I don't expect to get the job, it's a class operation and I think they want someone with a lot more experience especially with the salary of £7 a week they're offering.' Don didn't want to divulge his confidence in being offered the job, 'I won't be counting my chickens,' he replied, non-committally.

*

Pierre and Eamon buttonholed Don the next morning after breakfast service, anxious to find out how he had faired, hoping he hadn't impressed the 4 Arrows management.

'You never know what they think or what they're really looking for so I don't think I'll get the job because the interview was a tour and a grilling by the maître d'hôtel and the General Manager.'

'Well, from what you've said we could be losing you, doesn't it?' Eamon said sadly. 'You'll be a great loss to the Rubicon especially as you've become something of a celebrity and model member of staff. So, think carefully before you decide if you're offered the job.' Eamon warned, placing a fatherly hand on Don's shoulder. 'Grass is not always greener my boy.'

'Oh oui! I agree wiz Eamon mon ami 'eet looks like Donald makes ze good impression, but we don't want to lose 'im do we? Now that 'e can manage the restaurant. Maybe we give him more money to stay?' Pierre said, glancing at Eamon for support.

The question in Don's mind was that if he was offered the job was it a step too far? The 4 Arrows was a class operation and to be realistic would demand a more rigorous test of his ability which was still developing. He loved the Rubicon despite his problems and had still much to learn about the business.

*

The two weeks later he decided to make a detour to the housekeeper's office and pay a visit to Miss McDonald. Tapping lightly on the door the Head Housekeeper called a 'come in'. In his best manner and smiling – he had been told his smile was an asset – Don entered and stood before this vision of loveliness. Mary McDonald was to Don, a stunner with dimpled cheeks, wide green eyes and an apple pink complexion in an oval face with full curved lips with just a hint of colour. Don swallowed hard and was at a loss for words.

'Yes Donald? Can I help you.' She asked, sensing Don's nervousness.

'Eh, sorry to trouble you Miss McDonald I know you're very busy but now I'm M. Toulemon's deputy maître d' in charge of restaurant supplies I wondered if I gave you a weekly total of our linen requirements, would that be of help?' Ending his offer with a question.

Well Donald, and you can call me Mary as you're Pierre's deputy, we've managed to supply the restaurant well so far, unless of course you have a problem with the linen supply?' She paused waiting for Don's reaction.

'Oh no, no, Miss er… that is Mary, everything is fine, yes, we get all our supplies and the quality is spot on. I just thought this was one way of getting to know you a bit better.' Don was struggling to make any headway, just improvising to extend his stay and see if it could lead to a closer relationship.' Don wasn't really making any sense which he could tell from the quizzical expression and knitted eyebrows of Mary.

'Well Don, what I think and correct me if I'm wrong, but the reason that you came to see me with this rigmarole excuse about the linen situation that you just wanted to have a chat. And that is because,' she paused, making eye contact, 'that you quite like me.' Mary in turn did quite like this rather brash, young man who carried himself well and was quite handsome in a rugged sort of way. She had made some enquiries with Pierre and her housemaids after their first meeting, all of whom thought Don was a 'looker' with a very positive demeanour. After Don's press exposure she also realised that he was no pushover and had acquitted himself well with the police and the management.

Don blushed to his roots and didn't know where to put himself. She had hit the nail on the head and it was up to him either to defuse the impasse or apologise and backout. Don did neither and took the veritable bull by the horns.

'Yes, your right Mary I couldn't think of anything better as a reason for seeing you because I do like you and have done since my first day here. I'm sorry if I've offended you and I won't pester you again, but at least you know how I feel.' Don said burning his bridges in one fell swoop, but he had to know whether Mary had any feelings for him.

'Well Don, you haven't pestered me at all and I'm pleased you've been so honest as to your real reasons for your visit.' Mary eyed Don in a new light but wasn't giving him any hope for a relationship too soon. He was going to have to work for it. 'I'm sure we can work together but now I have work that is a priority so can we continue our 'chat' at teatime in the canteen. I'll be there at 3.30 today if that's convenient?' Mary thought she would get a better take on Don and his prospects but – slowly, slowly, it was early days.

'Oh yes Mary, thank you I'll be there at 3.30.' Don couldn't believe his luck that at the first attempt he had, albeit in an ungainly fashion been able to initiate a formal meeting with what he dreamed could be his first real girlfriend. Outside of Mary's office he skipped his way joyfully down the corridor and back to the restaurant, on top of the world, almost barging into a chambermaid who viewed his antics with raised eyebrows.

But for how long? If he took this job and it was a tempting prospect, he would lose Mary before he had the chance for their relationship to blossom. She could just become a distant memory. So here was Don's dilemma – stay at Rubicon, career stalls – develop relationship with Mary or take the 4 Arrows job (if successful) – career development? – more pay? What was he thinking? Cool down and wait for the letter, – 'you've been offered nothing yet Don, you dope!'

Unfortunately, this timescale was seriously eroded when the 4 Arrows letter arrived the next week. His stomach was in a turmoil as he undid the envelope hoping it was a 'thanks but no thanks' message, but what would it be?

CHAPTER 18

Don opened the letter from the 4 Arrows, hands shaking as he scanned the typeface. He would have to bite the bullet as they wanted him to start immediately as a senior waiter, 2nd only to the maître d'hôtel, in a 4-star operation. It was a seismic move up the chain of command. Don sat down and read through the letter again – they must be desperate, or maybe he had impressed them with his confidence and maturity. The improvements were more responsibility, a notch up in status and more money. It was his chance for a new life but one fly in the ointment was losing the blossoming relationship with Mary. Of course, he might be delusionary in thinking that she shared his future plans but she had given him hope during their tete-a-tete over tea and cakes.

OK, Don made the decision to accept the offer, depending on. A. how this would affect Mary's feelings for him? B. Would the Rubicon make a counteroffer? These unknowns would have to be sorted before his reply, and it was Don's toughest decision.

'That's ze right decision, you know it eez,' Pierre shook Don's hand when he announced the 4 Arrows offer. 'You will do well there Donald, I know. But don't forget we were your springboard to ze future.' Both Eamon and the Manager supported Don's decision and wished him all the best. The Rubicon had offered him an increase in salary and more responsibility but to no avail. Despite the drawbacks Don couldn't really pass up this once in a lifetime offer.

Mary congratulated him but sadly knew their budding relationship was to be short-lived. 'Well done Don. You'll need to watch your back as the new boy because you'll be a target for the old hands. Go with the flow and eventually your personality and resolve will see you through.' Mary said, but near to tears as she had become fond of Don. Two weeks was all he had to cement ties with Mary and then onwards to Cumbria.

'Can we keep in touch Mary because I really want to?' Don asked tentatively holding her hand.

'Of course Don.' Even though she believed it was the end.

*

Elaine, the Personnel Manager of the 4 Arrows was delighted that Don had accepted their offer and informed the manager and maître d'hôtel that he would be arriving in two weeks. She enclosed contract details for Don with the instruction that his employment would commence with a two-day induction programme (copy enclosed). Accommodation would be arranged for him in the staff block for the time being.

'This is a slick operation', Don thought, impressed with the organisation and details. 'I'll replicate their professionalism in my turnout to show they made the right choice.'

*

Mary wasn't surprised he had taken up a better position and their regular tea-time chats had established a belief that they were leading to a commitment although Mary was reluctant to get too carried away with their romance. She came to enjoy their outings to Briar Dean, Seaton Sluice and picnics at the seaside. Don promised Mary to keep in touch by letter and once he was settled in at the 4 Arrows, would arrange visits to Jesmond where Mary lived with her parents. This would give him the opportunity to meet her family and strengthen his commitment.

*

'Welcome to the 4 Arrows Donald.' The General Manager said by way of a greeting, 'I'm sure you're going to like it here as we've much in common with the Rubicon.'

'I certainly hope so Sir and will do my best to fulfil your faith in me.' Don said, hoping he didn't sound too sycophantic.

'I'm sure you will, but if there's anything else you need, Miss Dalrymple is your first port of call.'

He had met the Elaine, the Personnel Manager on his arrival after a problem free, bike ride in fine weather and was able to appreciate the rolling fells dotted with old-fashioned farmsteads, nestling near sparkling waterfalls where sheep and cattle meandered in the lush green fields, protected by ribbons of dry-stone walls which stretched for miles. 'I think I could get used to this countryside,' Don thought as he decelerated and turned into the rear of the hotel, scattering a few hens that the hotel kept for the guests' children.

'Have you had a good run from Shields.' Elaine asked greeting Don's outstretched hand in a firm grip. 'Let's get you settled in first, your room is on the first floor and has a view overlooking the North Tyne and fells. I'll leave you to get sorted then I'll explain the induction programme.'

'Right yes, thank you, I'll just unpack and be with you in a few minutes.'

She had been with the 4 Arrows for four years and was in her late twenties. Smartly turned out in a Harris tweed jacket with a below the knee skirt with a white blouse, not quite hiding a shapely figure. Her hair was coiffured short, framing an oval face, balanced with a dainty nose and hazel eyes above full lips that hinted a resolute character. She was a beauty in Don's estimation and was appreciative of Don's keen examination after handing him a cup of tea and biscuits. She then proceeded to outline his next two days of induction which covered staff introductions and his contract. 'The maître d'hôtel Stefan (Podowski) has asked if you could be around just to observe the dinner service and tomorrow morning after breakfast he'll brief you on the restaurant's modus operandi. Head chef Gordon Stachan will talk you through the requirements of the kitchen and menus.' Elaine continued, 'And finally we'll have what I term a 'Wash-Up' on what has been covered so far.' Don nodded his understanding.

On the morning of day 3 Don was with Stefan who was finalising the staff rotas and explained the system. 'Now we workin a 48 hr five- and half-day week with weekend off every three weeks. Also, breakfast rotates so when on evening you do breakfast and lunch with dinner off, then no breakfast until lunch and dinner so big break from lunch, simple, yeah?' Don didn't think so but he could work it out later. 'You look at menus? Like Rubicon, all French, cuisine francaise. Sometimes we have Polish specials, goulash and gnocchi, you like Polish Don?'

'Oh yes, very much,' agreed Don though he had never heard of either.

'OK for first lunch here I give you easy station only four covers. Most have the table d'hôte at 10 shillings, good value so check with Chef to see what goes yeah? The a la carte is mainly for dinner service including Chef's specials OK.' Stefan looked straight at Don to see if he understood. 'Any questions Don, I'll look after you for coupla weeks then I expect you take over on my day off as you are deputy maître d', yeah?'

*

Don would get used to Stefan's broken English after a while so just nodded his understanding. Who were the other two waiting staff Don had still to meet and hoped he could rely on their skill and their support. Unfortunately, he would be sorely disappointed, at least with one of them.

As he was laying up his six covers for lunch a voice called out testily 'no, no we don't do it that way here.' Don turned to see another waiter with a thin face, aquiline nose and reddish hair, cut short, about 6' tall, pointing to his setting with a superior expression.

'OK so how do you do it, here?' Don asked evenly with a half-smile looking him directly face to face. If he expected Don to be cowed by his presence, he was disappointed. The uncouth waiter then marginally rearranged one of the settings.

'Well thanks very much for your advice. I'm Don Sullivan and you are?' Don smiled and held out his hand which was rudely ignored.

'I know who you are and I'm Trevor Nightingale, the senior waiter here for 6 years so watch your step. We don't want any Rubicon bad habits here.' Smirking as he walked away.

'Excuse me Trevor, as I'm new here so have you any other 4 Arrows tips that might be useful? I'm always willing to learn.' Don said straight-faced, with a questioning incline of his head.

Trevor was at a momentary loss because he thought he'd had the last word and put this upstart in his place. He had expected to get the deputy maître d's job but had been overlooked by Stefan who had been let down by Trevor too often. 'Er yes there's plenty of things you should know about but I'm too busy right now.' Looking uncertain and somewhat flustered by Don's assertiveness.

'Well, I'll look forward to getting those tips Trevor so thanks for putting me straight.' Don said to Trevor's back.

*

Don approached Stefan after the lunch service. 'What's the story on Trevor because he told me he's the senior waiter?' Don asked.

'Oh yeah, Trevor, he has the idea above his station, yeah! Don't mind him. Sometimes he can be difficult so just work with him, OK?'

'Whatever you say Stefan, but I won't take any nonsense. I'm a team-player and expect everyone to work together. He needs to lighten up and forget he has been overlooked for the job; don't you think?' Don hoped Stefan would sort out Trevor.

'That's good, we work as a team yeah, that's what I expect, no arguments eh? It's early days yeah, so we see how things go for a while Donald.' Stefan smiled but coldly, his brow puckered – was it a warning for Don to take it easy?

For a while they Don and Trevor worked together as Stefan hoped but the truce didn't last long. One evening during the dinner service Trevor substituted Don's meal check for his own when the chef was distracted. When Don asked about his order, he was told it hadn't been received. After a short search, the check was found on the floor which meant an unnecessary delay for Don's customers and the subsequent forfeit of a reasonable tip.

Don realised what had happened and this was confirmed to him when Trevor made eye contact later in the service with a grin. For this to happen either by accident or intent meant the system was flawed so Don approached Stefan after the service and told him what had happened, without revealing his suspicions of Trevor.

'OK Don we improve the system with a check board so check can't disappear yeah?' He said with a wink. 'I think this won't happen again, OK?' Don didn't share his optimism.

'Let's hope you're right Stefan because customers come first and everyone should buy into that rule, whoever they are.' Don replied tight lipped. 'If something like this happens again then Trevor will have me as his problem.'

*

Three weeks later Trevor did the same thing again by taking Don's check off the board after the order had been given to the kitchen. The kitchen didn't know who's order it was when it was ready. Only when Don queried his order did the kitchen realise the error, by which time the food was spoilt.

'Your improved checking system works Stefan but not when someone is determined to disable the system, and you know who that is. So where do were go from here Stefan?'

'Is not good this thing with you and Trevor, and customer complains yeah. I talk to him, but you must make peace for good of 4 Arrows?' Stefan insisted.

'Alright Stefan but I've tried to improve relations but Trevor is determined to give me a hard time and get me sacked. My armistice last time changed nothing.'

'What's this 'armistis' Don is a new English word?' Stefan's brow wrinkled.

'No, it just means a cease fire, like in the war.'

'Good we both do what we can and see what happen yeah?'

CHAPTER 19

Trevor confronted Don in the car park the next day.

'I hear you've been telling tales again like a big schoolboy because you're not big enough to man up to me.' Trevor said angrily, his face flushed close to Don.

'As usual, you're wrong Trevor. Stefan says you're letting the side down, so stop acting like the school bully as though you've been hard done by. Don't you see that your feud with me is affecting the customers and the reputation of the hotel and it'll end only one way if you keep this up, you'll be out of a job.' Don tried to keep the anger out of his voice to get Trevor to see sense.

'And it won't be me. I'm not the new boy here and so far, all the complaints have been on your pitch, so any more cockups and you'll be on your way, so don't make threats you can't carry out.' Trevor responded, his face thrust into Don's.

'Any complaints I've had have been of your making and you know it. You're not a clever Trevor you're just a low-level waiter and frustrated you weren't good enough to get my job.' Don's annoyance at Trevor's intractability broke through with anger in his voice and stance, inches from Trevor's face.

Like most bullies, Trevor was confident when faced with inferior opposition but in this case, he was about to make a big mistake.

'Think you're so clever moaning to Stefan, well I can take care of myself.' Trevor's voice raised, his face contorted and pushed Don roughly with both hands, who fell over at Trevor's unexpected aggression, landing heavily.

Don was now in fighting mood and remembered his uncle's Clifford's advice 'stay cool and watch their eyes' as Trevor bent over his fist clenched for the denouement. Don arched his back for leverage, his arms spread out for support and his right leg swung around catching Trevor's left leg just below the knee knocking him off balance. Now Don was on his feet, and an even contest. Trevor was bigger and taller and thought he would teach Don a lesson he would never forget as he swung a right fist and had it landed would have meant curtains. Don easily swayed back and Trevor's fist whistled past leaving him exposed to Don's hard left hand jab to his solar plexus leaving Trevor gasping for air. But instead of following through with a right cross to Trevor's exposed jaw Don stood back to see if Trevor was finished – he wasn't.

Trevor's dented pride gave him a surge of strength to use his superior weight and he rushed forward to crush Don against the brick wall. But instead of backing off Don stepped forward, grabbing Trevor's jacket front to swing him around where his forward momentum sent him crashing into the wall. It should have been the end but Trevor realised that to be beaten in such a manner would put an end to his status so he picked up a two foot piece of wood, left over by the hotel chippie and advanced, smiling in anticipation of a quick victory. Trevor hadn't learnt anything and again misread Don's response, expecting him to backoff and as he swung Don ducked under the baton as Trevor's arm was raised and rushed head down into Trevor's chest, sending the wood flying from his grasp. Trevor was against the wall and badly shaken, his head shaking in puzzlement at the turnaround. This time Don wasn't finished and stepped forward using all his weight as leverage to land a crushing right to Trevor's jaw, knocking him to the ground in a dishevelled heap, clutching at his lacerated face and knew he was beaten.

'If you want a rematch Trevor, you know where to find me but be warned, from now on any more of your attempts to sabotage my service, I'll be looking for you – *is-that-clear*?' Don spat the words out as he hauled Trevor up, eye to eye.

'OK, OK, I get the message,' Trevor's mumbled assent was barely audible as Don turned and walked back to the hotel passing some of the hotel staff who had seen the action. No doubt the grapevine would circulate with Trevor's comprehensive humiliation.

Don returned to his room to tidy himself up and prepare his uniform for the dinner service when there was a knock on the door. 'Come in' he called out and in walked Elaine, the Personnel Manager.

'How are you Don?' She asked with some concern. 'My office overlooks the car park and I saw what happened, after Trevor pushed you over, I was going to intervene but realised you could take care of yourself.' Then added conspiratorially. 'It's about time Trevor was given a lesson, he's such a bully and has been warned about ill-treating the younger waiters. If he tries to blame you for the fight, and he might, I'll be a witness for the defence.'

'That's good of you, Elaine. I just hope Trevor wises up because I've warned him of the consequences if he continues to sabotage my orders.' Don hoped his warning would be transmitted to the manager and hopefully defuse Trevor's belligerence.

*

Stefan approached Don, later that afternoon to say Trevor would miss tonight's service.

'He's not well so can you cover for him, yeah? We're not busy tonight. I think you damage his pride, yeah, but that's not too bad?' Stefan winked as he turned and walked into the kitchen to check on the menus with Chef Gordon.

The dinner service went like a dream without Trevor's distraction. That evening the menu featured expensive dishes like lobster Newburg, Whitstable oysters and Dover soles which were a bonus for the restaurant staff because the bigger the bill the better the tip. Another bonus was the surprise visit of one of the senior members of the Rubicon Club, Lord Sheffield, whose party was in Don's section.

'Good evening, Lord Sheffield, it is very good to see you again.' Don said smiling as he slid the dining chair under Lady Sheffield's well-nourished derriere.

'And it's good to know you have progressed since leaving the Club, despite the unfortunate incident with the porridge.' The Lord said grinning but loud enough for his guests. 'That was quite an evening wasn't it Cybil? I'll have to tell you about it later, he said to his guests,' Cybil shuddered at an evening she preferred to forget.

'It was a difficult decision to leave the Rubicon sir, but it gave me the best training for my career.' Don got down to business. 'But let me tell you what the special is tonight; your favourite, Beef Wellington or perhaps the lobster?' I'll leave you the wine list and come back when you are ready to order, but I can recommend the Chateau Latour '28 as an accompaniment to the beef? Don's icing on the cake was the sale of a bottle of 1938 Chateau Neuf de du Pape for £65.00, one of the most expensive wines – the Sommelier was over the moon!

The Lord ordered all the most expensive dishes including the 'Wellington' to impress his guests. The denouement was the order of crepe suzette, remembering Don's 'faultless' performance at the Rubicon. Naturally Don obliged, and the party was duly impressed with the flambe light show.

'Well done, Donald, you put on big show tonight for the VIPs, yeah and the tips from your section were the best.' Stefan grinned as he clapped Don on the back.

CHAPTER 20

Two days later Don phoned Mary from the box near the hotel to see if they could meet up on his day off with a trip to Blackpool as he'd always longed to ride on the Big Dipper at the Pleasure Beach and watch the famous Blackpool Rock being made. His brother Sidney had told him it was a 'not to miss' spectacle.

'That would be lovely Don, thank you.' Mary hugged herself that their romance was surviving the miles apart. 'I'll organise some time off with my deputy and ring you tomorrow. How are things going? Are you enjoying the higher echelons of the restaurant business and making your mark?' Mary was a tease but that's what Don loved.

'I'm making my mark but not necessarily in the dining room. I'll tell you all about it when we meet and I'm really looking forward to seeing you again – I do miss you, Mary.' Don's eyes misted up as they said they're goodbyes. Mary had been resigned that Don would be a fleeting if pleasant liaison but now she had a renewed hope they still had a future together. Mary felt the sun had just reappeared.

*

Don negotiated with Stefan for an extra night so they would be able to have a night in Blackpool, giving them almost a full day to see the sites, sand and sea. Their hotel was the Imperial, a magnificent seafront edifice that hosted all the great and good with one of its primary functions, the hosting of political party conferences. Their room had a sea view and although expensive, Don had been generating an increased amount from tips and this was an extra special occasion. He had other plans involving Mary but their first visit was the Blackpool Tower's summit.

'You can almost see the Isle of Man on a clear day.' An excited Mary said, standing on tiptoe to get a better view.

'OK Don what other Tower was this one supposed to replicate?' Mary asked as she consulted her local guidebook.

'Let me think, was it by any chance the Eiffel Tower in gay Paree?'

'That's an easy one, so what is its height in feet I'll give you 50 either way?'

'That's a tough one but I think about 450 give or take an inch.'

'A good try but not close enough – it's over 500 in fact 518 and was built in 1891 so it's about 40 years old.'

'Enough questions Mary, my brain hurts, so what's next on the agenda?'

'What about the Winter Gardens for some lunch and after that we can catch the tram down to the Pleasure Beach for a ride of our lives on the little Dipper – I want to keep my lunch down.' Mary replied, as they took their three-minute descent to the promenade.

The Winter Gardens was Blackpool's pride and joy, predating the Tower by 13 years and designed as a tropical refuge from Blackpool's inclement weather. Spread over six acres it embraced a conference hall, two restaurants, a theatre and at its centre an enormous glass covered conservatory. It was a spectacular boon to the town's residents and tourists and just the place for their lunch. A post-war meal of shepherd's pie, carrots, peas and a spotted dick set them up for their busy afternoon which included a visit to the Rock Shop, claiming to be the *'largest in the world.'*

In front of a glass screen, an enormous 'cement mixer' machine moulded a gigantic piece of cooked sugar, sections of which were moulded into giant letters spelling 'Blackpool' which were encased in white toffee and rolled into the traditional red casing. Two technicians tended a machine which extruded the enormous sugar barrel into one inch diameter sticks. These were snapped off in one-foot lengths and wrapped in cellophane with 'Blackpool' lettering all the way through – amazing!

'What an amazing process, I wouldn't have believed if I hadn't seen it.' Mary said in awe as she paid sixpence for two sticks of rock. As they meandered along the prom. on their way to the Pleasure Beach for the ride of their lives, they licked the orange sticks, hand in hand, contented in each other's company.

George Formby had made Blackpool rock famous with his music hall rendition of *'With my little stick of Blackpool Rock,'* which was banned by the BBC because of the thinly disguised double entendre; nevertheless, he was the darling of the seaside entertainment industry. Originally born George Hoy-Booth, Formby was a superstar for plucking the banjolele, a larger instrument than the ukelele with an added sounding board which gave better projection for the enormous music hall theatre audiences. George was not handsome by any stretch, with overlarge teeth, a bulbous nose and slick backed hair which didn't stop him from a stella film career where he was routinely paired with very attractive young ladies. In most films, Formby played a gormless, gullible but indefatigable hero who always came out on top. His working-class anti-hero image making him a darling with the largely working-class cinemagoers with his catch phrase – *'Hey, hey, turned out nice again!'*

'My favourite film of George was *'Come on George''*, Mary insisted; he was so funny and always had the better of the baddy and got the young lady.'

*

High picked screams assaulted their ears as they paid their shillings for the little dipper which operated under and around the big dipper towering above them with twenty or so carriages screeching around the bends filled mostly with youngsters shouting and waving, high on adrenaline.

'I'm so glad I decided on the little dipper otherwise I would have had a heart attack.' Mary said, holding tight onto Don's arm as they boarded the two-seat car and told to grasp the security bar, lowered by the attendant. 'I'm not sure about this Don,' as Mary panicked with second thoughts but too late, they were on their way. The ride rattled, dipped, swung them from side to side, careered downwards almost vertically, leaving their stomachs at the bottom as the car shot upwards again to repeat the process until Mary thought it would never end. 'Never, never, never again.' She vowed, eyes shut and clinging like a leach to Don who was enjoying every minute.

'Oh, Don I don't feel well.' Mary complained as she stepped shakily out of the car. 'Let's sit down with a cup of tea until my insides settle.' She implored, as Don steered her into the Pleasure Beach café.

CHAPTER 21

After a rest and recharge Don suggested they might end their stay to see one of the many pier shows which attracted some of the top entertainers such as Arthur Askey, Gracie Fields and Flanagan & Allen. They would perform twice nightly during the holiday season, entertaining thousands of holiday makers.

Don had checked the listings. 'At the Central Pier there's a variety show with singers, jugglers with the main attraction, Flanagan and Allen. They're the tops so I'll visit the box office for tickets and if they're sold out we could check later for any returns but it'll be worth a visit.'

As expected for the Crazy Gang duo the sign announced 'SOLD OUT' as they stepped off the tram and were about to drown their disappointment at the Winter Gardens when Don asked Mary to wait while he approached the box office. Their luck was in with two returned tickets for the stalls at three shillings with the show was about to start. For two hours they laughed, clapped and applauded a helter-skelter of entertainment and thrills. The supporting acts featured a magician who made people disappear, an aerialist and a young lady who defied gravity with their routines and a lady with three terriers who cavorted around the stage jumping through hoops on fire and working a seesaw. Each act had the audience mesmerised and applauding in equal measure. Finally, Flanagan and Allen topped the bill with their hilarious jokes, amusing stories, dance routines and ended with their signature song 'Underneath the Arches' to bring the house down.

*

'I've never enjoyed myself so much Don, it's been a wonderful break.' Mary face was still flushed from the non-stop action after they returned to their hotel.

'Can I tell you Mary when I first saw you, I thought 'that's the girl for me' and so it has proved. I know we haven't known each other that long but would you consent at some time to consider changing your name to Mrs Sullivan?' Don said, down onto his knees in front of Mary, holding both her hands in his. Wide-eyed with shock and surprise Mary just stared, cheeks flushed again and unable to take in the life-changing significance of what Don was proposing. Recovering slowly, she responded, her voice a little shaky.

'Don, let me get this clear, are you asking me to marry you or is this another one of your jokes?' It was the only response she could muster as she knew exactly what he was proposing. Would she want more time to think about life changing implications. She knew in her heart that Don was someone she loved but his proposal had come out of the blue.

'Mary I've never been so serious. I've been thinking about asking you from the first time I met you. In my case it was *'love at first sight'* and this was a good time to ask for your hand. You don't have to tell me now and spoil a lovely weekend, but will you think about it?' Don felt he had blown it as they had never got close to talking about their future before. He hoped he hadn't ruined their relationship.

'You're right Don it's been a showstopper for me and honestly, I don't really know what to say except that you are the one for me. Yes, I do want to marry you Don. I suppose I've known that since the first time you confessed your feelings towards me in my office which now seems ages ago.' Mary smiled, held his hands and kissed him. 'Hmm…, Mrs Sullivan, it does have a ring to it.

*

Their first night together was in a very large double bed which stifled close intimacy. They had kissed and fondled on the dunes and beach but stayed the right side of consummation. Don felt he should take the lead but after Mary's noncommittal response to his earlier proposal he didn't want her to feel they had to go further. There would be many opportunities for him to get relief so he stayed his side and thought of England, hoping his ardour would subside.

Mary's even breathing suggested she might be asleep, so Don turned towards her just to hear her, be a little closer and inhale her body perfume. This intoxicating combination lulled Don into a doze but immediately his eyes widened as a little hand crept under his pyjama top and onto his chest and moved tantalisingly downwards. She had taken the initiative and now Don was in a quandary. If he stopped the wandering hand Mary would be insulted and if he didn't it would only lead to one thing. But was this the right time Don wondered? His raised expectation (literally) intimated he should allow Mary to continue as she was in charge and Don always deferred to the ladies as the weaker sex. The tiny hand continued down untying his pyjama bottoms cord, easing the cloth aside to place her fingers on his standing ovation.

'Is that good Don? Do you want me to carry on?' Mary whispered snuggling closer, placing his hand on her breast and erect nipple to provide Don with his response in case he wasn't sure.

'Yes, please!' Don coughed and croaked a reply being a true gentleman. Never refuse a lady in situations like this, as it was his first time.

Mary pulled Don towards her still caressing him, her nightie opened to provide Don an opportunity he had long waited for. It was all too quick for Don. Nevertheless, he had an enormous sense of fulfilment as Mary kept him in a tight loving embrace until he fell asleep. In that moment Mary knew that Don would be her life partner.

CHAPTER 22

'I'm please for you Donald and with Trevor sacked we have to find replacement yeah. Everything is better now in restaurant so let's get going, we have full restaurant tonight.' Stefan explained with a sheepish expression knowing he should have disciplined Trevor much earlier.

They were approaching the holiday season and urgently needed replacements. Stefan acknowledged he would have to appoint relatively 'green' applicants and train them up as experienced waiters were hard to come by. Two adverts in the Caterer succeeded in engaging two twenty-one-year-olds, keen to improve their restaurant skills and prospects. Two days were set aside to bring them up to speed, and in the process negate any bad habits developed in their previous employment.

Stefan and Don devised an on-job training schedule that would provide them with the basic selling, social and technical skills and transfer some of the heavy lifting from them. Stefan would take Chris for training and mentoring, and Don would do the same with Penny, with Don taking the initial induction.

'You will address us at Mr Sullivan and Mr Podowski whilst on duty and remember you are actors playing the roles of sales personnel. Your primary aim is to ensure that the customer has an enjoyable experience and looks forward to returning, whatever you think of them personally. You must acknowledge that the customer is always right no matter what you may think. We'll come to complaints handling later.' Don noted the trainee's quizzical expression. 'Now, important things first, let's see you smile – no Chris that's a grimace, look at Penny, now that's a smile, so try again. OK, that's better. A smile does two things – it makes **you** feel more confident and makes the customer feel they have come to the right place. Any questions?'

'But what if they're wrong and their complaint is unjustified?' Penny frowned as she queried the rule.

'Find out what complaint is first and sort it, yeah? If not, see me or Mr Sullivan but 90% of the time it's something you can handle such as cold food, slow service, the wrong order or warm white wine.' Stefan explained, 'but when in doubt *always* assume complaint is justified, yeah?' It's an important area so we cover in detail later, okey?

Don interjected, 'another important thing. You need to be alert to customer needs even when you're not serving or writing a check. Scan the room when there's a lull to see if a customer needs something. You help the customer and what do *you* get? Chris? 'More tips', possibly, but certainly a happier customer and one who is more likely and pass on the good experience to others. Remember an existing customer is likely to return from a bad experience if handled well. Does that make sense?' Don handed out a checklist for the later Q and A session.

Don and Stefan covered silver service, buffet service and butler service during the next fortnight, questioning them at every opportunity to review good and poor practice at the end of each service. The training sessions on silver service generating plenty of laughs in the process with the restaurant floor decorated with an assortment of rolls and vegetables. With Don and Stefan's positive guidance, repetition and encouragement Penny and Chris quickly became adept and started to enjoy demonstrating their new skills during the service. Role plays after each section were used to underline the key features. 'Gaming' was another technique Don developed involving incorrect table setting with each trainee in turn spotting what was wrong. Product Knowledge was another key part of the training with Chef Gordon involved to test them on the content of each dish and garnish; 'What is Sole Veronique Penny?' (poached fish with white grapes in a mornay sauce chef). In these sessions Penny and Chris became competitive and, in the process, reinforced the messages.

'Well Don, what you think of our trainees? They comin on good, yeah?' Stefan said, drawing a hand across his damp brow.

'You're right Stefan it's a good sign that they're enjoying themselves and asking a lot of questions and looking more confident and at home during the service. Did you see Penny chatting to that party earlier about the chef's specials?'

'And Chris making that family laugh at something he say? It's a good sign yeah.' Stefan said approvingly. 'The next training is the wine list so hav you another game Donald?'

'Wine recognition is next and yes games are always a good way to cement learning.' Don agreed, thinking what he owed to the Rubicon's Sommelier.

Don was settling happily into his new role and relishing the challenges after those early harrowing months and wondered what would be the next test the 4 Arrows would throw at him?

*

'Yoo-hoo Don? Don?' Mary called out and waved a gloved hand as she stepped from the 3.45 from Newcastle, partly shrouded in the wispy engine's steam as she clutched a small leather suitcase.

'Oh boy Mary you do look so good, and that perfume is very alluring.' Don's compliment made Mary blush, as he added a quick embrace to the whistled amusement of a school group boarding a bus. 'Our trainees are coping so well with our training that Stefan has given me some time off knowing you were coming, so I've booked the bistro at Low Bales for lunch.' Don said leading her towards the taxi. 'The forecast is good and I don't have to be on duty until dinner service so I've booked you into the restaurant so you can see how the expert behaves. Naturally I'll expect 10/10 for customer feedback.' Mary's response was a dig in the ribs.

'That sounds just ticket Don especially as I've brought some brochures on wedding arrangements to give us some ideas and costs. I don't think we should have a big wedding; we couldn't afford it anyway, but it would be nice to have family and friends to help us celebrate. We're only going to do it once after all?' Don was happy to let her loose with arrangements as it would be her big day. The question was where to have the wedding and they hadn't even decided on a date.

'Well, I had this crazy idea of a wedding reception at the Rubicon.' Mary said with a hint of a grin.

'It's a nice thought Mary but I was talking about realistic options, not dreams. Maybe somewhere in Shields perhaps The Harbour Hotel on the Strand, I know they do weddings.' Don suggested, 'I'll do a list.'

'Yes, but listen to this Don and maybe you can start dreaming.' Mary paused for dramatic effect. 'I told Stuart, Rubicon's manager that we were thinking of getting married and asked him if he could suggest any venues as he had trade connections. As he owes you and me a favour, he offered the Rubicon's facilities, provided permission was approved by the CEO.

'That's incredible news Mary, well done. He must feel he owes us big-time to even consider it.' Don was ever cautious at Mary's initiative but could imagine how impressed his mam and siblings would be, so Don's fingers were crossed.

*

'Is a pleasure to meet you Mary, Donald told me you were very pretty yeah!' Stefan smiled and kissed Mary on both cheeks as she coloured with embarrassment at Stefan's compliment.

'I've heard that your restaurant is the best in the area Mr Podowski and that Don is learning a great deal from you.' Mary returned the compliment to cover her embarrassment.

'Please call me Stefan, yeah. Donald has brought some good ideas from Rubicon, is a fine place. I give you good restaurant place, so you watch the Donald in action?'

Mary hadn't seen Don in action at the Rubicon and was truly impressed by his confident, professional manner, always conscious as to how the new staff were fairing; quietly monitoring their performance. It was obvious they respected him as the boss. Stefan's manner by contrast, was a little brusque at times if they were slow taking orders or picking up from the kitchen.

'That was a delicious meal Don. I had the potted shrimps and the Chef's Special of beef burgundy but deferred on a pudding, must watch my weight you know.' Mary said demurely but those petit fours were mouthwatering. Don was pleased that Mary had seen him in action and arranged to meet in the bar after the service.

*

The next day was but fine and sunny as Don had predicted with only a moderate breeze to rustle the tree leaves as they started their walk along the North Tyne as it bubbled excitedly over the rocks and around banks. Pouring from the high Cheviot fells, the river was a dark brown and chillingly cold despite being late Spring. To the side and up and over the fields the dry-stone walls wound their way, aimlessly, it seemed into the distance and through the pastures where the lambs had lost their early spring and calves were turning into heifers, adding a white and brown brush to the grassy fields that unfolded up and away into the late morning haze.

'Isn't this a beautiful part of the country Don, I could certainly live here.' Mary sighed, resting her head on his shoulder.

'It certainly is Darling. Why don't we have our picnic the chef organised here?' Don indicated a small clump of conifers close by the river.

'This picnic is fit for kings.' Don said approvingly as he unwrapped roasted chicken drumsticks, boiled eggs, small tomatoes, buttered home-made rolls, a bar of Cadbury's Dairy Milk, and a bottle if Tizer. Linen napkins and a checkered cloth completed the feast.

'What a spread.' Mary said, setting the meal out on the gingham cloth. Don hungrily bit into the chicken leg as Mary shelled a boiled egg. 'Is there any salt Don?'

Replete after their meal they lay in each other's arms talking quietly about their future until more urgent matters took over and it was Mary who took the initiative, again. Turning over to smile suggestively into Don's eyes she moved her hand under Don's shirt. His response soon followed as he unbuttoned her blouse and slid his hand under her silky bra, slowly caressing her erect nipples and creamy breast. Mary's response had Don breathing heavily as she unclasped his trouser belt and button then slowly pulled the zip down to reveal underpants that only just covered his manhood which she just encompassed in her tiny hand.

'Are you ready for me Mr Sullivan?' Mary asked innocently as she stroked him to its full length.

'You know I'm always ready for you Mary.' Don replied huskily as he removed her under-garments, stroking his hand down her milk white thighs, eliciting an excited gasp of desire and feverishly moved onto him pressing her lips to his as she was filled, moving slowly then more urgently. Their tempo increased until two simultaneous cries of release echoed through the trees scatter the alarmed woodpigeons.

A flurry of Kite's wings jerked them awake as it zoomed a few feet above their heads to dive into the undergrowth yards away to emerge seconds later with its lunch, a wriggling rodent firmly grasped in its talons. Mesmerised by this example of nature in the raw they could only marvel at the bird's manoeuvrability and accuracy. It was as though the performance had been arranged for their lunch-time entertainment. With the remains of their picnic packed in the hamper, they turned away from the river as the scent of new mown hay wafted over them from the harvesting of fallow fields as they strolled blissfully hand in hand, dreaming of their future together.

CHAPTER 23

Finally, they agreed on Saturday 26th June for their wedding at St Peters Church where Mary had been Christened. The Bans had been called and a further meeting with the vicar, Sebastian Charlton had been set up for Don's Day off. Mary was given more good news by the manager that their wedding reception could be held at the Rubicon.

Now the deadline had been set, a clutch of support activities was set in train with the designation of Sidney as the best man and Mary's best friend Marjorie as the maid of honour with her niece as one of the bridesmaids. Sadie did cartwheels when informed she was the second bridesmaid. Mary's wedding dress and those of her maid and bridesmaids gave her the biggest headache whereas Don had the easier option of ordering his wedding attire and that of Sidney's from Moss Bros in the town centre.

'I'll give you the opportunity of deciding where to go on our honeymoon.' Don said as he looked through some brochures of photographers and florists.

'I've already decided,' Mary said turning Don's head to get his attention. 'I'll give you a clue there's a large tower in the middle of the town.'

'I don't think we can afford Paris, but I'll give it my vote.' Don replied, grabbing Mary as she tried to hit him. 'No? Ah yes, I remember now, it was where had your evil way with him wasn't it? I've never been the same since,' Don admitted as Mary burst out laughing.

'Now Don let's be serious for a minute and sort out a photographer and some carnation buttonholes. What about these two, Country Photos and Pretty Polly Florists, I'll see what their prices are as they're local.'

'Good idea, what about this afternoon and then I have to get back to Cumbria for tonight's dinner service?' Don suggested and Mary agreed.

*

The BSA performed sweetly on his return journey to the hotel but as he approached the turnoff leading to the 4 Arrows, he could see thick smoke swirling away on the breeze. His approach was blocked by four fire engines, two engaged in dampening down the still glowing roof timbers over what would have been the kitchen and staff quarters. Don quickly parked the bike and approached a fireman wearing three shoulder pips.

'Excuse me, I work here what's happened?' Asked Don through gritted teeth.

'And who are you, young man?' The fire Chief asked turning from his notetaking.

'I'm the deputy restaurant manager, Don Sullivan, is everything ruined?'

'I'm afraid the kitchen is gutted, and we won't know about the restaurant for a while but smoke damage will have made that area unusable. You won't be serving any meals in there tonight.' His gallows humour fell on deaf ears.

'That's terrible but was it deliberate?' Don was tearful and frustrated beyond measure as his career at the 4 Arrows seemed over, almost before it had started.

'I can't give you any more information as we're at the early stages of the investigation. A member of your living-in kitchen staff made the call after the smoke alarm was triggered. It's strange that the sprinkler system failed. We're keeping an open mind on the cause and we'll know more once we're in the building, sometime tomorrow.' The Chief explained in detail because he could see how much Don had been affected; tears streaked down his cheeks.

The hotel's entrance, offices and bar had largely escaped, as Don entered to find a group of staff milling about in the foyer. Among them was Stefan, chef Gordon with Graham, the manager in the centre of an anxious buzz. Staff were peppering him with questions he couldn't answer as Stefan disengaged himself from the group when he saw Don and hurried over.

'You know what happen Don? We don't have jobs anymore and the hotel is ruined yeah.' Stefan's teary enquiry was a desperate cry of anguish at the loss of his livelihood.

'Yes, it's terrible Stefan. I've just talked to the fire-chief and he won't know how the fire started until tomorrow at the earliest. I suppose the insurance will pay to repair the damage but that will take months. Maybe, the 4 Arrows will rise from the ashes like a phoenix.' Don declared, grim faced as an icy hand gripped his chest at the prospect of a bleak future for all the staff.

'You're right Donald but who is this feenix you talk about?' Stefan's troubled expression made Don smile despite the calamity.

'Just an English expression Stefan that means the 4 Arrows will open again. You know Stefan, if this fire was started deliberately, I have a very good idea who might be the culprit. It's just the sort of thing that might have appealed to Trevor, as retribution for being dismissed.

'Is lucky no one was hurt. So, we wait to see what the fireman finds out yeah, then is up to Mr Singleton to tell what happens to us. Maybe we get compensation?'

'We'll see, but I wonder if my belongings survived the fire?' Don turned to ask the manager, but he wasn't hopeful.

Elaine the Personnel Manager confirmed that the staff rooms and kitchen had been gutted. Don was relieved to hear that the insurance would cover his losses and that temporary accommodation was being arranged at local hotels for the half dozen living-in staff. The emergency arrangements would be announced at a 4 p.m. staff meeting that afternoon.

*

'Firstly, can I thank the fire services for their speedy and professional action in limiting the fire to the kitchen and staff accommodation. Graham said looking downcast as he addressed most of the staff. 'Elaine has already arranged rooms for the live-in personnel so please see her after this meeting. You'll be pleased to know wages will be paid as normal and none of the staff will suffer financially from the fire. Now, will we be back in business? I cannot say until the damage is assessed and a restoration plan is in place but if I have any say, the 4 Arrows will be back in business as soon as!' Staff applause greeting his statement. 'Thank you for your patience and before you leave, please have a drink on the 4 Arrows.' Graham then summoned the managers to his office. Don thought it wise that Graham had given an upbeat tone to his talk, but he knew the 4 Arrows was doomed, and his comment to Stefan about the 'Phoenix rising' was a forlorn hope.

'Apparently, the fire service arrived from the local station within 10 minutes and contained the blaze to the kitchen area and outhouses.' The manager explained. 'Depending what the fire service finds, my plan is to see if and when a reopening is feasible but it will depend on what the owners think best, we're all for getting back into action as soon as, because once we lose customers it's not going to be easy to coax them back.' Gordon and Stefan nodded in agreement.

'I'll inspect the restaurant and banqueting with Donald for damage and see what is needed yeah?' Stefan said with a sad head shake.

'That's a good point Stefan, now I'm sure you have much to do now so let's meet again tomorrow at 10 a.m. and see if the 4 Arrows can be saved.'

Don bid goodnight to Stefan, Penny and Chris and left for the Plough & Harrow pub for a pint at his arranged accommodation. Don was irrationally consumed with guilt over the fire. Had he not come to blows and been the cause of Trevor's dismissal he would have had no reason to seek revenge on the hotel. 'Wait a minute' Don thought, 'Trevor could have nothing to do with the fire. I should be concentrating on my priorities as deputy maître d' and nothing else.' But the restaurant's smoke damage rendered any early return unlikely. 'Will this catastrophe have any bearing on our wedding plans?' Don wondered, 'I can't see Mary agreeing to a postponement as so much preparation had been done already.'

*

Don called Mary at the Rubicon about the fire and its effect on the survival of the 4 Arrows. 'Oh Don, I'm so sorry, that's awful and everything was going so well for you and the hotel, you must be devastated and I'm not there to give you a hug.' Mary said, her emotions clearly travelling the wires.

'Yes, we're all pretty down as you'd expect but no way will it affect our wedding plans Mary.' Don replied, pre-empting her response.

'If you're sure Don. I've booked the flowers, photographer and have agreed with Chef Stuart the buffet selection. So, everything is fine here, so when can I expect you?' Mary concluded with a kiss, which made Don ears sting.

'Probably two or three days once I've tidied things here, I'll let you know, OK?' Don returned the kiss as he hung up.

CHAPTER 24

A bombshell by the fire chief was reported to the manager two days later. Firemen had discovered a corpse in the embers that was unrecognisable except for a signet ring on a skeletal finger. The police's subsequence enquiries indicated it was probably that of Trevor Nightingale as his parents had recognised their son's ring but had no idea why he had been found in the fire. Accident investigators called in by the fire chief indicated that an accelerant had been used to start the fire and that Mr Nightingale was thought to be the arsonist and had unintentionally locked himself inside due a self-closing fire door, his only escape route. A fire investigator commented drily, 'hoist by his own petard I think'!

After hearing the news, Don was mortified to think he could be the related cause of the fatality, the fire and the hotel's closure although it was Trevor's twisted act of revenge that was the cause, pure and simple. This reasoning did little to lift Don's black thoughts and led to sleepless nights, tossing and turning as he tried to square the circle of his doubts and anxiety and relieved to be engrossed in the clearing up as it pushed his self-flagellation briefly out of mind. He couldn't wait to pour out his concerns into Mary's sympathetic ear and was relieved to be roaring back towards the East coast on his BSA.

Although the wedding plans were well advanced and in the capable hands of Mary, several things could go wrong to threaten their nuptials. In addition, the 4 Arrows restoration was becalmed on the back of health and safety concerns and those of the police investigators. The owners were also reluctant for a quick resumption based on insurance delays. This sad news only accelerated Don's search for alternative employment now his 4 Arrows career was in the dust bin.

News of the renovation of the 4 Arrows hit the buffers once again. After the fire department had found the body, the police took over and taped off the building as a crime scene. They had established that Trevor had purchased a gallon of paraffin two days before the fire and the remains of the can was found under the charred embers which suggested he had acted alone. Until the police left and the site declared was free of asbestos it would be a 'no-go' area. Don was again in the dole queue yet couldn't stop blaming himself for the catastrophe!

'So, Don what's the bad news?' Mary asked, keeping her sense of humour intact. 'You must have been shocked to the core when told who was responsible, but you can't blame yourself, you mustn't.' Mary added, realising she had been totally insensitive to Don's situation and the effect it must have had on him. 'I'm really, sorry but this doesn't have to affect the wedding, does it? You have your insurance pay from the hotel, I still have a job and our savings are quite healthy too, so let me tell you where we are with only three weeks to go.'

'No Mary, let me tell you. You've no idea what I've gone through the past three weeks. Do you realise that rightly or wrongly I'm indirectly responsible for someone's death and the loss of a first-class hotel restaurant, not to mention all the jobs that have been lost. And all you can do is make a crass joke of it. The way I feel now is that having a big celebration on the back of this disaster is not on.' Don had never been this angry with Mary who recoiled from the verbal onslaught as though she had been assaulted and was at a loss what to do. Now in tears, Mary attempted to claw back some dignity from her faux pas.

'Don, I'm really sorry. You know I'm not like that and I was just trying to make you feel better and honestly didn't realise what you've gone through, so will you forgive me, please?'

Rarely had Don been surprised at Mary's response to any criticism which normally was a case of meeting fire with fire, but on this occasion, it was a complete reversal in drawing the sting out of Don's anger.

'On one condition, that the wedding is scaled down to a minimum.' Don responded, still trying to make sense out of Mary's capitulation. Or was this another tactic for him to ease up on his injured pride?

'OK Don, I still want to marry you and I take your point about the wedding but what do you mean by 'scale down to a minimum'? Mary was worried that her 'big day' would be remembered by all the wrong reasons. After all, the time and effort she had put in to make it a special occasion she wasn't having a damp squib wedding.

'The minimum possible to get us married with an invite to family members and a few close friends. Or would you prefer to cancel the whole thing until I'm less troubled and know what's happening with the 4 Arrows?' Don explained, thinking he would really prefer to cancel for a few months.

'You're not using this as an excuse to abandon our marriage are you Don, because I'd rather you came straight out and tell me you're having second thoughts.' Mary was back to her combative best.

'No second thoughts Mary, you know I love you but you have no idea what effect this problem has had on me and hope you never will.' Don was uncertain what he really wanted so he improvised. 'Let's have a honeymoon as planned then maybe we could get ourselves back to square one again and have your grand wedding but not for a few months until things have settled down.' Don suggested, realising for the first time he was unloading his frustration and ill-conceived guilt onto Mary

'That's a big decision for me, considering what I must undo if it's the second option and the first option is something that is straight out of the blue. So, let me sleep on it – nothing is that critical to change – and see how we both feel.' Mary was really upset having to decide something she never envisaged would happen and was at a complete loss at what decision was the best.

'Fine by me darling so as it's the weekend why not come with me to Alston as they've arranged comfortable accommodation until the insurance has been agreed?' Don said, hoping to mend bridges in their relationship over the next couple of days, and he knew just the place to take Mary if she agreed.

'OK Don. You're in the driving seat and I'm on pillion.' Mary agreed, sensing Don was trying to resolve the breach after his uncharacteristic outburst.

*

After their first real argument which was still nagging at Don as to whether they were really suited he decided that a break from each other might for a few weeks show that they were really suited for the long term. He had seen an advert in the Caterer for experienced waiters required for a short-term contract at St Annes on Sea near Blackpool and decided to apply. He phoned the Personnel office and after giving them his background and reasons for his availability was accepted for four-weeks provided he could produce evidence of his qualifications and experience. Wages were a meagre ten shillings weekly, but they said the tips were not shared and, he could live in for only £1 pound a week all found which sounded a reasonable offer, so a start date was agreed a week later.

Mary was not happy when Don revealed the details of his month away and covered it by saying the extra money would be helpful towards their wedding costs, in addition he would gain more valuable experience and keep his hand in while waiting for a permanent job. She was not convinced at Don's reasons for their enforced separation and felt he wasn't being completely honest, especially when she felt they had resolved their differences over the wedding plans. She was determined to know Don's real intentions.

'Is this parting to test our commitment or is it just your excuse to end our relationship Don?' Mary didn't really think this was Don's reason but his flimsy reasons for leaving needed to be properly resolved.

'No, of course it's not a ruse darling but maybe some time apart will give us breathing space, think about our future and test the strength of our relationship, you know the old saying 'absence makes the heart grow fonder?'' Don knew he was skating on thin ice with these additional reasons, but it was the best he could do on the spur of the moment.

'I don't need any breathing space, nor do I need you to leave me for four weeks to test our future or our relationship so come off it. You know better than to kid me.' OK Mary thought, get out of that one if you can with any degree of honesty.

'OK, I agree with you on all accounts, but I haven't got over the 4 Arrows arson and fatality, and your initial reaction in dismissing it so lightly. I know the fire and aftermath is not my problem, but maybe I should have walked away from the confrontation. That's the kind of person I am Mary. I need time away to get my head straight and I thought this was one way to do it. The last thing I want is for you to think I want to break up.' Don took Mary's hands in supplication hoping his effort to come clean might work this time. 'But if you don't really want me to take the job I won't.' It was Don's last throw of the dice.

'I won't stop you going Don, if that's what you want to do but be warned. I don't like being treated like an idiot. So have your four weeks and come back more experienced, richer and with a straighter head. Maybe absence will make the heart grow fonder – we'll see.' Mary did feel sorry for a contrite Don with his troubled frown taking his face between her hands and gave him a kiss.

With a packed case and a sharp suit Don took his leave with Mary waving him off from the Central Station with a sad face, not able to hold back the tears as Don shouted 'see you see in a month darling' as the train puffed its way out of sight in a cloud of steam, chuff, chuff, chuffing wanting it seemed to get away from away from the grimy Tyne River, spotted with loaded coasters, empty trawlers and reconditioned liners, but Don wasn't on it.

Don sat on the platform seat head in hands wondering how to resolve his major indiscretion and fall out. Mary was the best thing that had happened to him so he had to put things right and quickly.

CHAPTER 25

'Hello Miss Macdonald, can I help you?'

'Mary, its Don will you forgive me?'

'What's that? Where are you Don, aren't you in Blackpool?' What are you talking about, you're not making much sense?'

'No, I know, I'm sorry I've treated you shamefully and apologise sincerely. So will you meet me?' Don asked, fingers crossed.

'And where would that be Mr Sullivan?' Asked Mary, hugging herself with relief at Don's change of heart.

*

Don and Mary's reunion at the Central Station looked to any observer as though he had just returned from four years at the front. The extended embrace on platform 10 continued again when they were back at the Rubicon, and all was well.

During their Cumbria weekend Don said it might help her understand what he had gone through to see the devastation of the 4 Arrows. 'I can't imagine what you must have felt when you returned to see the whole place in flames. And that was before you knew the whole story.' Mary held tightly onto Don's arm as she tried to put herself in his place.

'I'm not sure I felt much at the time. I was just numb looking at my own career in ashes. Anyway Mary enough - the manager has called a meeting tomorrow morning to provide an update. It's possible they'll have some idea as to whether the hotel can be rebuilt, we'll see. After the meeting we'll have the rest of the day to ourselves and I've a special treat in store.' Don knew of somewhere that would remind Mary of happy times.

*

'Good morning, ladies and gentlemen,' announced Graham the 4 Arrows manager, 'and thank you for coming. I'm afraid it's not good news from the owners for a possible reopening, but you probably knew that anyway.' Graham paused to look around his senior team to gauge their reaction to the news. 'We're waiting for the fire insurance to be assessed before any decision is taken on a rebuild and the fire department in conjunction with health and safety officers are still working on the asbestos problem. I'm sorry I can't give you any better news but you'll know what's happening as soon as I do – any questions?' Graham's open palms and grim expression said it all.

'How long will the insurance be paying our salary?' Asked the Chef evenly.

'I don't know the extended period but it has been guaranteed for the next two months.'

'Do you know when asbestos will be clear?' Stefan asked.

'I've been reliably informed by the safety people that the green light for clearing the kitchen and rooms should be a couple more weeks.'

'I know you're doing your best to sort everything out and I think we all appreciate that. You've answered two important questions but what we really want to know is, are the owners intending to reopen the hotel?' Don was being devil's advocate because in his heart he knew the answer.

'Thank you Don I would like to know too. The state of play vis a vis the rejuvenation of the 4 Arrows,' the manager shuffled a sheaf of papers. 'Nothing has been finalised but this is what's planned.' He coughed and took a sip from his glass. 'Once we've been given the all-clear to return to the hotel site, we'll prepare the area for a rebuild of the kitchen and rooms, which could take a year or more. If we go down that road, Gordon will be involved to research the feasibility of the mobile kitchen option. I'll know more about this once the surveys are complete, probably in the next couple of weeks.'

A more optimistic air purveyed the group now that the management seemed to have a detailed plan in place for the reopening. Once back in the manager's office Don asked a supplementary question. 'Until the hotel reopens what is the status of your management team?' Don asked, mindful of his career prospects if he was no longer employed.

'You all remain in place in your current roles and after two months the situation will be reviewed, pending a decision by the Board after the insurance is sorted. If the management considers your contracts should be extended while the hotel is closed, then you'll be informed in good time. This will allow you to seek other employment in the interim. That's as much reassurance I can give you now.' Graham apologised that he couldn't be more positive.

*

Mary was all ears. 'I'm OK for the next eight weeks then I'll have to start looking for a job. So, what have you decided about the wedding my true love?' Don accepted that Mary's decision would be final.

'I'm only going to have one wedding Don, so I want it to be an occasion that is memorable for myself and for everyone involved. Based on what you've been told about the 4 Arrows it's best we postpone it until you know more. The Rubicon understands your situation and they will still provide the facilities for us with a new date.' Mary said without any rancour at having her wedding plans put on hold.

'Well Mary, when the time is right you will have a wedding to remember even if it costs my last penny, you can bet on it.' Don stated, delighted to be able to concentrate on getting alternative employment. 'If you can get some time off let's celebrate with a few days in Blackpool, where we had such an enjoyable time there. What do you say?'

'Celebrate the postponement of our wedding? I don't think so Mr Sullivan. But if you're enticing me away to have a dirty weekend in Blackpool now that's a totally different proposition. Fortunately, I do have some days owing so you can book the Imperial for a weekend. I could really look forward to it after all the trauma of the past few weeks.' A confirmatory kiss sealed the deal.

A message had been left for Mary at the hotel to get in touch with the Rubicon manager urgently and Don had received a letter and a message from Stefan to ring him back as he had some important news. It was with some feelings of foreboding that Mary rang the Rubicon to be told that the manager had been taken to hospital with an unidentified illness and that the deputy manager was with him so the reason for Mary's call would have to wait. Don opened his letter to reveal a reply from the Blackpool Tower company to which he had applied for a supervisor's position in their world-famous restaurant that hosted famous cabaret acts like Gracie Fields and backed by the Geraldo orchestra. That reply would have to wait until he had found out what Stefan was so anxious about.

'Donald, we have changes of plan for restaurant yeah,' said Stefan looking anxious, 'and I don't think is a good thing for us now.' He motioned Don to follow him to a quiet corner of the bar which was still the sole operating part of the 4 Arrows.

'Graham tells me the board of directors have a new plan for the hotel to sell to entertainment company for big profit. The fire insurance won't cover costs of major renovation they planned so have decided to cut losses and sell. A new restaurant they say would be 'down market' so no more 4 stars or super staff, they say. They have given notice of six weeks to all staff who can apply to new company.' Stefan was almost in tears as he gave the news.

Don thought his Blackpool applications could be a life saver as he took in the sad news of the 4 Arrows demise. 'Well Stefan, it's a pity that the board have decided to jump ship, I thought they had more resolve, but I suppose that's business. What will you do now my friend?' Don felt sorry for Stefan who would find it hard to find a suitable position after his fifteen years at the hotel.

'Maybe I go back to Poland, but things are not good there at moment with Germany. I'll see what's on offer and maybe go to London. I used to work at Connaught Hotel, very posh place and exclusive before getting better pay at 4 Arrows, long time ago but we see, yeah. You will be alright Donald with your good training and qualification. You're young and fit for anything and I help you with good reference if you want?'

'Well, I wish you all the best Stefan and a reference from you would be very helpful for any job applications so thank you.'

'But we should keep in touch, yeah?' Don smiled at Stefan's oft used emphatic and gave him a supportive hug as they said goodbye.

Don broke the news to Mary about the Blackpool offer to find her in some concern about her mysterious message from the Rubicon, but unable to get any further information as the manager was in hospital.

'It looks like we've both landed in something nasty, but at least I'm clear about my options with regards to jobs. Have you any idea what might be happening at the Rubicon Mary?'

'No, I've been racking my brains all afternoon and no one else has any useful information. Is my job on the line, again? Has the Rubicon been taken over by another company? Until I know more, I'll stop worrying as there's little point, right Don?'

'You're right, let me reply to this offer in Blackpool first and see if I can get an interview because if I can, we can use that occasion to have our mock honeymoon while I'm there for the interview?'

'You're thinking on your feet which is a good sign Don.' Mary tweaked his arm smiling, 'I'm looking forward to having a few relaxing days at Blackpool while I wait to find out what's up at the Rubicon.'

'OK that settled, in fact I think I'll contact Personnel at the Tower rather than write and see about that interview now the 4 Arrows is finished.' Don asked for Stephanie Bowers the Personnel Officer, gave his name to the telephonist and was put through.

'Hello, my name is Don Sullivan. I received a letter from you regarding the position of restaurant supervisor.'

'Oh yes, Don Sullivan I remember, just hold on a second and let me get your details. Here we are. You have had some experience supervising staff at the 4 Arrows Hotel so could you attend an interview within the next couple of weeks. How much notice do you need to give?'

Don explained what happened to the hotel and said he could attend an interview in the next two weeks at their convenience.

'I'm so sorry it must have been a terrible shock.' Stephanie commiserated and said would Tuesday the week after next the 15th at 11 a.m. be convenient, after consulting her diary. 'I'll have you meet our restaurant manager who will give you a tour.' She added, thanking him for his interest and to bring any relevant documentation.

'Well Mary it looks like we'll have an early honeymoon in Blackpool.' Don announced after confirming his interview. 'We'll go even if your Rubicon issue hasn't been sorted.'

'Those chambermaid rotas will have to wait until later. It's a thankless task and you can never please everyone so in future I'll post them on the notice board and that's it!' It was one responsibility that Mary loathed, because it was time consuming and fraught with complaints. 'With Sarah (chambermaid) back tomorrow we will have our full complement and Sharron, (Mary's deputy) will make sure there are no hiccoughs while I'm away.'

CHAPTER 26

Newcastle Central was a hive of activity with travellers scurrying here and there looking for the right platform or for family and friends swallowed in the melee. The busiest station in the North East had belching locomotives chuffing in or grinding slowly out, bellowing clouds of steam as they waited like gigantic leviathans for the green flags to York, London and Edinburgh.

Anxious passengers craned necks and scurried up and down the platform to find their carriage and compartment. First Class passengers followed baggage porters with loaded cases on packed trolleys tut-tutting at all the confusion while bouts of coaly steam wrapped them like a shroud. It was all organised chaos thought Don looking nervously up and down the station entrance for signs of Mary, checking the gigantic green clock high above the bustling throng that ticked over to 10.15 a.m..

'Where is she? We'll miss that train and the reserved seats if she doesn't get here soon.' Don worried needlessly but he hated leaving things to the last minute, but Mary was a serial offender. How she could be so good at managing her job and yet was regularly within seconds of missing an appointment, picture show or in this case a train. He could only conclude that leaving things to the last moment gave her an excited buzz that he would have to live with.' He groaned in frustration, raising his eyes to the clock for the umpteenth time.

'High Don, Don over here.' A shrill call cut through the leaden air like a sharp knife as Don saw his vision of beauty and immediately forgot her tardiness.

'Glad you made it - cow's tail as usual!' Don's comment was smothered by Mary's lips. 'Mmm….ph. Platform 5A, carriage C about halfway down, let me take your case – wow that's heavy how many weeks are you going for Darling?'

As they hurried down platform 5A the conductor was calling 'on board' to energise the late arrivals. 'Women require many more items than men. You might take me out to a posh restaurant or another evening to a night club so a gals got to be ready for all eventualities, unlike men in their boring suits and anonymous jackets.' Mary chattered nonstop as she boarded the carriage.

'Our seats are just down there in the middle compartment.' Don explained, checking the tickets twice, only to find a young couple in their seats.

'Excuse me, but you're in our seats.' Don said showing the young rather scruffy male his tickets. 'So, if you don't mind, we'd like to get our suitcases on the rack.'

'I do mind,' the man replied aggressively, we're in the right seats,' pulling out two tickets which he showed to Don.

'No, your tickets are for carriage D the next one down', Don pointed out the error, returning the tickets, 'so you need to move.'

'I don't think so Pal we're quite cosy here so why don't you go to carriage D and have our seats then we're all happy right.' He said, standing up aggressively to face Don.

The young man like most bullies expected little resistance and for Don to back down, *big mistake*; he was now uncertain what to do but realised he either had to back down and lose face or stand his ground with his girlfriend looking embarrassed.

'Are you sure you want to make a meal of this because I'm not moving until you've moved out. So, it's make your mind up time Pal.' Don replied in like manner eyeballing the man inches from his face and seeing the uncertainty in the interlopers eyes and took the initiative. 'Let me help you with your luggage, this is the one OK,' taking the case off the rack and into the corridor.

'Hey, you can't do that,' the man cried out lunging at Don who, anticipating the move turned to his side, pulled the man towards him by his lapels; out into the corridor, using his momentum to push him up against the window.

'Now are you going quietly like a good boy, or do you want more trouble?' Don whispered in his ear, his hands gripping the man's collar tightly.

'OK we'll go, can't you take a joke.' He replied feebly calling for his girlfriend from the carriage. 'I'll see the conductor about you assaulting me.' He blustered, straightening the rumpled shirt and jacket.

'You do that and enjoy the trip.' Don replied smiling as the pair shuffled away down the corridor to carriage D.

'Well done, Don, my hero.' Mary said, clapping. 'What a nasty piece of work and for what? He obviously expected you to back down, but what if he'd refused to move, what would you have done? Mary asked expectantly.

'Well, I did have plan B but fortunately for him he saw sense. So, no problem, Mary. 'Now, did you bring anything nice for our on-board lunch?'

Just as they finished a filling lunch of cheese and ham rolls, hard boiled eggs, tomatoes, an apple, and a bottle of water Mary nudged a dozing Don and pointed out of the window.

'Look Don that's Durham cathedral, isn't it impressive,' as they took in the towering twin spires overlooking a dark and brooding river.

'Yes, remember we visited the Town Hall where there was a special feature on the DLI (Durham Light Infantry) which included a section on their battle honours around the World. They were Queen Victoria's go to personal army, keeping the Commonwealth alive by the subjugation of its territories and killing thousands in the process.' Don had found the exhibition absorbing and eventually Mary had to drag him away.

'You are an old cynic,' Mary replied, having studied history for her school's certificate, 'the British army did bring much needed stability, order and organisation to these places and stopped all the infighting among the tribes.'

'OK Mary, you can carry on the lecture once we've boarded the cross-country train to Blackpool, but I think we have to change again at Crewe for the branch line.' Don said, as he took the suitcases from the rack, narrowly missing an elderly lady who was staying on the train.

'Here we go again, platform 3 and we've only got 10 minutes to spare so no time for a cuppa – maybe there'll be a buffet on the train?'

'No problem Don, I brought a flask and some biscuits just in case.'

'You're a star Mary. I knew there was a good reason for selecting you as my girlfriend.' Don said narrowly avoided a slap.

'I just love travelling by train for all the evocative sounds – the whoosh, whoosh, whoosh and the clickety clack, clickety clack of the wheels and the hooting as it passes other locos. I even like the smells of burning coal and steam from the engines. I should have been an engine driver, but women weren't allowed on the foot plate.' Mary laughed and Don grinned at the imagery of Mary in a boiler suit, face blackened with soot.

Don there's something important I must tell you when we get to Blackpool but only when we're on our own. It's good that we'll have a few days together to decide what to do if you're offered that Tower job. I don't want to give up my job at the Rubicon as there's a possibility of promotion.' Mary laid out her position to sideline any ideas Don might have of living in Blackpool.

Don is left to wonder what was so important that couldn't be aired then and there? Was the wedding off permanently? Could she be pregnant – God forbid. Waiting wasn't something Don was particularly good at so best put it out of mind.

CHAPTER 27

What was Mary's big announcement that made Don so nervous? Once they had checked in again at the Imperial and retired to a bar that was lavishly decorated with mirrors engraved with names of previous prime ministers – Stanley Baldwin and Ramsey McDonald among them as they settled into an alcove. Mary took Don's hand, looked him in the eye and smiled as she dropped a bombshell.

'Don, I have to tell you something special,' Mary paused to increase Don's concern. 'You-are-going-to-be-a-Daddy!' Mary emphasised triumphantly.

'Whaaaa …t,' Don spluttered, 'you're surely joking, how did that happen?' Actually, he did know but couldn't think of anything else to say. 'Mary are you sure? It's another of your windups, isn't it?' Deep down he knew this time she wasn't joking.

'Yes, I'm sure Darling but is that all I get? What about a 'well done', 'marvellous', 'amazing', 'I'm over the moon Darling' and other sweet nothings?' Chiding Don, although she could see he was thrilled with her news.

'This is the best news I've ever had Darling,' Don embraced Mary, oblivious to some reproachful stares from the other bar clients. 'And what stage are we at,' enquired Don, 'when can we expect a little Donald or Mary to arrive; is there enough time to buy some baby clothes?'

'Don't worry, we have enough time to organise the nuptials, but we will have to bring the wedding forward, next month might do it. This means I'll have to get my skates on and check the Rubicon is on board for the reception.' Previously, the demise of the 4 Arrows had put the wedding on hold but Mary's bombshell had thrown out that option.

'Let's hope I'm able to impress the Tower restaurant management tomorrow to be offered the job so can you help me role play some Q & A considering your delicate position?'

'I'm not too delicate to give you a smack if you keep that up Mr Sullivan.' Mary said, 'C'mon Don let's get to that restaurant I'm starving and don't forget that I'm eating for two!'

*

The tide was on the turn, with infant waves breaking into a foaming surge and an early sun sparkling off the grey oily Irish sea as Don strolled alongside the Blackpool tram tracks to his 11 a.m. appointment at the Tower, pointing its tip to a royal blue sky. He whistled *'Oh I do like to be beside the seaside'* with a jazz beat and couldn't be happier. He was going to be a daddy and soon to be married to the most beautiful girl in the world. 'How did I get so lucky?' Don wondered, the 4 Arrows disaster briefly out of mind. 'In only a few years I've a career, a bright future, a special bride to be and soon to be a dad.

Maybe in an hour of so he might be offered a prestigious position in a top restaurant but what would Mary's reaction be? He couldn't expect her to give up the job she loved and move to Blackpool and commuting from Tyneside wasn't an option either.

*

'Good morning, Mr Sullivan and thank you for attending the interview. Can I get you a tea or coffee?' Stephanie Bowers the Personnel Officer asked, smiling a welcome.

'Coffee please, milk no sugar.' Don replied, taking in a rather attractive young lady who had everything in the right places.

'Denise, two coffees please, milk on the side.' Stephanie asked her secretary. 'Our restaurant manager will be joining us in about half an hour so before that we'll look through your CV and application.' She looked up from Don's CV into his eyes with a half-smile, challenging him to keep his experiences factual. 'So why don't you tell me briefly what qualifies you for this position?'

Don composed himself, took a deep breath and described in detail his Rubicon training and responsibilities and then his promotion to the 4 Arrows as a deputy to the maître d'hôtel, Mr Padowski including his training role with restaurant recruits.

'It was an enjoyable place to work and if not for the fire, I would still be there.' Confided Don. 'Your position would be promotion and your dining quality and service is not dissimilar to the 4 Arrows except on a much larger scale. I did in fact, dine in your restaurant last year.'

After Don's response, Stephanie proudly described their revolutionary checking system to eliminate cash based 'fiddling' by service staff. 'Cash transactions are minimised whereby tickets of varying denominations are 'bought' by the waiters from the restaurant cashier from their cash float and exchanged for food and drink. At the end of the meal the waiter presents the customer with the bill and retain any surplus as tips.' Stephanie paused as Don's brow wrinkled.

Don realised that their system of vouchers just added another level of control and considered the systems flawed but kept his thoughts to himself.

*

Herman the restaurant manager was introduced to Don as they entered the 300-seat restaurant which was almost five times the size of the 4 Arrows. The art décor theme was lavish in the extreme with ceiling high drapes covering windows that provided a sea view on one side while on the other renaissance prints and 10' tall mirrors covered walls around a stage where nightly Geraldo and His Orchestra would play for diners and dancers. Luxury was clearly the watchword, complimented by five enormous gold leafed chandeliers adding illumination to the baroque wall prints. Carpeting reflected the lighting's cream and gold and must have required an army of Hoovers after each service with a central area removed for dancing.

'It must be a pleasure to work in this restaurant Herman, it's truly magnificent.' Don said to underline his interest.

'You are right Donald and it needs ze right staff to make it verk, ja.' Herman's chest puffed up with pride. 'I take you bek to Stephanie and she will tell you vot vee do next.'

Don thanked Herman for his time as they make their way through a maze of corridors back to personnel and hope he had sufficiently impressed both to be offered the job.

'How was the tour Donald, I assume you were suitably impressed as Herman is rightly proud of his restaurant and its reputation?' Don agreed and added more superlatives.

'You're younger than we normally take for a senior position but your background clearly suggests you could grow into the position which we hope you would see as a long term commitment. Are you staying long in Blackpool Donald?'

'We're at the Imperial until Friday before returning to Newcastle.'

'Well maybe I can let know before you leave – I'll either call you or leave a message, will that be alright?' Don readily agreed as he said goodbye.

CHAPTER 28

Don scanned the café in the Winter Gardens and caught sight of Mary who was having a drink and hadn't noticed him. As he stood there looking at all the good-looking stylish woman, he felt immensely pleased with himself that Mary was the one who clearly stood out as the most attractive. Maybe he was a little biased!

'Don, Don, over here.' As she stood up for the expected embrace, oblivious to the turned heads. 'So how was it? Did you get the job? Come on out with-it Don.' Impatient and keenly interested as ever.

'Don rush me Mary,' As he signalled a waitress and ordered a beer. 'It was a good interview and I seemed to have impressed the personnel officer and the maître d'hôtel, but I won't know whether I've got the job for a few days.' Don explained, still buoyed up by his good showing. 'Herman, the maitre d' seemed to like me, especially as he was a pal of Stefans at the 4 Arrows. What do you think if I get offered the job?' Don doubted he wanted to be so far from Tyneside and it wouldn't be right to take the job until he found a position nearer home.

'It sounds like the job you've been waiting for, it's a pity it's so far. Let's wait until they've decided and concentrate on our most important priority – the wedding. Don, tell me honestly, do we tell the family about our little secret or wait until we're married?'

'First things first Darling; our wedding is the top priority. As regards our little secret, my view is to leave any announcement until your condition is obvious, which could be well after the wedding. It's your decision whether you let the cat out of the bag earlier.' Don knew Mary would make the right decision. 'What's the latest on our wedding announcement, I suppose we'll have to manufacture some excuse for the protracted timescale?'

'Well, the Rubicon are still on-board with the catering, but they'll need to know guest numbers soon, maybe 40 as a maximum?' Mary suggested. 'As we agreed, I've booked the Newcastle Registry Office – they have a nice garden at the back for photos. Thankfully, I'm organised with my dress and the bridesmaids.'

'That's good news. Sidney will be my best man and I've made a list of guests from my side but even with friends and family it won't be more than 15 – 20 at most. Perhaps you could organise our buttonholes when you see the florist and what about ………?' Mary stopped him short - Don had forgotten all about their lunch.

'We'd better order lunch Don, before they close!'

'I know Darling you're now eating for two, but he or she isn't that big yet.' As the waitress tapped her order tab and looked at her watch.

*

On their return to the Imperial a letter had been left for Don at reception with a Tower Restaurant post-mark which he was reluctant to open.

'Go on Don, open it – you'll have to sooner or later and it might be good news that you've been rejected.' Mary joked nudging him. Don ruefully took out the letter slowly and opened the single sheet.

Dear Mr Sullivan,

Thank you for attending the recent interview for the position of deputy restaurant manager, we were very impressed with your presentation and are sure you will have a successful career. Unfortunately, we have decided you are not experienced enough for the present role we have in mind but wish you all the best for your future in the industry.

Yours sincerely

Stephanie Bowers, Personnel Officer.

After reading the letter twice and handing it to Mary, Don's reaction was a sense of relief as he would not have to decide between Blackpool and Tyneside but also surprised as he had expected to be offered the job.

'You know Mary, I think the real reason I wasn't offered the job was my reaction to their waiter's ordering system.' They wouldn't want someone in authority who wasn't sold on the present system which I think was flawed.' This thought made Don feel doubly pleased that it wasn't his skills or experience that he had been rejected.

'It's all for the best Darling, and you can move on to the next application.' Mary said philosophically. 'It was good experience and a chance to study another restaurant system. So, what now?' Mary's question was posed to ensure that Don didn't stand still, not that he needed the reminder.

'It's back to the Caterers' sits. vac. column: now let's see if there's an earlier train to Newcastle, don't want to let the grass grow you know.'

Mary gave him a look that said, 'yes Don I do know.' 'Good idea and I'll see if the Rubicon is still standing.'

'You're the boss Mary,' Don hailed a taxi. 'Blackpool North station,' he told the cabbie as he helped Mary with the cases.

Just in time they boarded the LNWR (London North Western Railway) as the guard's whistle blew and the steaming juggernaut lurched into motion.

'I hope we'll be able to get some victuals once we've boarded the connection at Preston, my tummy's rumbling,' Mary complained, rubbing her barely discernible bump.

'Mmm..mh this pasty's just the ticket' Mary said tucking into the hot mince pasty that Don had obtained from the train's buffet. 'I'll have the orange later,' she added looking across Cumbria's rolling fells and farms dotted with livestock and a snow-capped Pennine Mountain. They were jolted awake as the train gave out an exhausted series of hisses and case to rest on time at Newcastle Central at 9 p.m. Don to his old pal Butler Eamon had secured him a room at the Rubicon for a good night's sleep as he considered his next move on the job market.

*

A few weeks later Don saw a news item in the Caterer which revealed how the Tower's much vaunted checking system had been severely compromised by a scam that had been devised and installed by some of the waiters. 'I knew that system was open to abuse.' Don noted with a self-satisfied smile.

TOWER WAITERS ARRESTED AFTER THE SCAM TO DEFRAUD BLACKPOOL TOWER RESTAURANT.

The famous Blackpool Tower Restaurant failed to realise that a small group of waiters had developed a plan to subvert their 'infallible' restaurant ticket system by printing their own! Ringleaders of the scam approached a company in Oldham who printed dozens of ticket rolls which were bought by a few waiters at a discount who had agreed to participate in the scam.

On the day, the corrupt waiters wrote their checks, bypassed the cashier and received their food and drinks as normal. The scam hit the buffers when the cashier raised the alarm and a check of waiters who had not bought official tickets were apprehended. The miscreants and ringleaders were escorted from the restaurant and the police informed. A subsequent search of the waiter's lockers uncovered dozens of counterfeit rolls. The waiters were arrested and charged with fraud with the ringleaders given jail sentences and the participating waiters heavily fined. A Tower Restaurant spokesperson said, 'We can confirm that an improved ordering system had been installed for future security.'

*

'Good morning Don, did you sleep well?' Chirruped Mary looking as fresh as a daisy. We have a small problem with the wedding arrangements. Chef

Stuart's pastry chef is sick and will not be able to decorate the wedding cake, but he knows of a specialist in town, Gillies in Eldon Square, you know just off the Bigg Market?' Mary explained in detail, 'so get yourself down there pronto Don, as there's a lead time for wedding cakes and we're close to the wire.

'Incidentally that emergency call from the Rubicon manager concerned one of my room-maids who had been accused of theft. The police subsequently arrested a sneak thief after a tip off and the manager was unable to contact me having been rushed to hospital with a suspected appendicitis – what a relief!'

'Good news is always welcome' Don replied. OK Darling, I'll check it out for three tiers pronto and see you later.' He wondered what other hiccoughs would they get before the great day? Don wondered, 'par for my recent record with jobs and closures.'

When he explained the reasons for their convoluted wedding plans, Mr Gillie, the owner and cake decorator moved some non-urgent orders and confirmed the cake's details as a 3 tier, traditional 12" diameter cake, sufficient for 50 persons from the base tier. Don hired the silver stand and knife, paying a deposit of £1.00 on the total cost of £5 to be delivered to the Rubicon the day before the wedding.

Just around the corner from Gillies's on Grey Street was a branch of Moss Bros where Don had ordered the morning suits for himself and his brother Sidney and then remembered one job that required immediate attention. The rings! In his excitement over the wedding and Mary's pregnancy an engagement ring had slipped his mind. On the next block in Newgate Street, the Northern Goldsmiths was Don's last stop. The glittering array of rings of all shapes, sizes, occasions and prices had him in a whirl of indecision. He had allocated £10 or less, for both rings so the salesman took control and removed 10 rings from the wedding and engagement sections for Don's inspection. He was assured by the salesman that if the bride-to-be wasn't delighted with Don's choice, they could be readily substituted. The wedding ring was an 18-carat gold crenelated design and the engagement ring had a raised diamond centre with a sapphire on either side which stood out proudly from the others on display. Mary's finger sizes had been written on a scrap of paper for the rings to be adjusted so Don handed over the £8.17.6 for both rings which were boxed and wrapped, and a sigh of relief. He'd completed a trio of jobs within a few dozen yards of the city centre so things were looking up but would he be as fortunate with his job hunting?

*

Don returned to 33 Dakar Street where his mother Gracie, sister Sadie and elder brother Sidney were having tea in the kitchen and received a raucous Geordie welcome from his siblings and a crushing bear hug from his mam.

'It's so good to see you again Donald, it's getting to be a habit,' Gracie's maternal approval was underlined despite his previous tardiness since he left the Rubicon. They were all wide eyed as he recounted his adventures at the 4 Arrows and Blackpool. Don left the best news to last, that he was about to be married! Cue a stunned silence from his adoring fans.

'It's true really, and we're having the reception at the Rubicon, compliments of the management. Of course you're all invited.' Don declared, adding you'll be my Best Man Sidney and Sadie will be one of the bridesmaids, she'll be cock-a-hoop.' I've already hired your outfit Sid, although some adjustments may be needed. 'Mam, I want you to choose a lovely outfit, no expense spared, it'll only happen once! To put their minds at rest Don revealed that his generous release and compensation from the 4 Arrows would cover all their expenses for the wedding including overnight accommodation at a hotel in Whitley. He made sure his family had sufficient resources for a proper turnout. Sidney's morning suit had already been taken care of and Mary was arranging Sadie's bridesmaid dress. An hour later Gracie called a halt to Don's interrogation to announce that supper would soon be on the table which gave Don a chance to secure his BSA in the backyard and prepare for another barrage of questions over the meal.

*

Before returning to the Rubicon, Don made sure they were briefed on the wedding arrangements. Don felt a little guilty that Mary's pregnancy was still a secret from Gracie who would soon become a grandmother. He would make a diversion to call on his pal Jimmy with a wedding invitation that would be well received. Don still felt a measure of guilt for Jimmy's mangled hand in the rail accident as he was unable to get any meaningful employment, but Don was resolved to help his friend when he got the opportunity.

*

'Let's go through our check list again Don I don't want to miss anything out.' Mary laid the list out on her desk and proceeded to tick items off. 'We've the marriage licence from the Town Hall but it needs to be signed by a GP and a two more signatures to state we're sound in wind and limb or something like that.'

'I had the vicar down as one of the signatories although wasn't too pleased he wouldn't be officiating but I explained our dilemma and said I'd be making a significant donation to church funds in lieu of our absence. I also promised to attend church services more in future when my work commitment allowed.'

'I glad you didn't use the royal 'we' with your promise as an ex-choir boy, because I can't remember the last time I attended. I think it was Aunty Millie's funeral. Right, back to the list, we're nearly there – photos, flowers, incl. buttonholes for you and Sidney and bouquets for the bridesmaids. Don confirmed Sadie's delight in being chosen and handed over her measurements. 'Thanks, I'll organise her outfit, and that'll be one less job. My friend Kyla will be the other bridesmaid and my parents have also confirmed.'

'I've also sorted out two cars with Turnbull Bros., one for you and your bridesmaids and another for myself, Mam, and Sidney. They'll take you straight to the registry office and then back to the Rubicon for the reception. Should I book another for your parents?' Anxious to include his future parents-in-law.

'Yes please, it's the least we can do, I'll give you their address and will let them know the pickup time when I see them.'

'I'll triple check on everything in a couple of days because there's no 'plan B'' Mary was an efficient organiser, relishing in the role she enjoyed as head housekeeper. 'Yes Mam,' Don sprang to attention and saluted to Mary's amusement as she realised that maybe she was being a tad sargeant-majorish. 'OK Mr Sullivan very funny, I think it's time for tea don't you? Then I must return to the day job otherwise my manager Cyril will think I've disappeared. 'I'll leave the loose ends to you, darling, so let's go!' Mary commanded as she strode to the canteen.

'Talking of loose ends, how is the mother-to-be bearing up under the strain?' Don was keenly aware that Mary was taking on more than her fair share of arrangements.

'At the moment not too much of a problem, but a little more care and attention from hubby-to-be wouldn't go amiss. I wouldn't say no to a visit to our favourite trattoria in Whitley if that could be arranged.'

CHAPTER 29

On his return to the Rubicon, Don flicked through the Caterer and found a very attractive advert.

EXPERIENCED SENIOR WAITER REQUIRED FOR LUXURY HOTEL.
4* hotel in Whitley Bay requires an experienced waiter with all round silver service skills and luxury restaurant or hotel experience, supported by references and qualifications. Excellent salary, uniform and conditions of work plus living in accommodation provided. Write or phone for an application form to the Personnel Officer, Cliffe Hotel. Whitley 3257

'This is more like it.' Don thought, and nipped to the phone box to call for an application form.

Mary couldn't believe he had sorted so much during the day when he popped into her office during her afternoon break. 'Well done Don, maybe your Tower rejection was written in the stars for a job nearer home. I knew you were the business when I agreed to take you in hand, metaphorically that is,' As she poured Don a cup of tea and wondered why Don was on his knees. 'Have you dropped something Don?'

'No Mary, I'm on my knees to ask if you will marry me.' Don gazed up at her beautiful, surprised face as he'd never had the ring to complete the engagement ritual.

'Well Mr Sullivan it's a bit late and this takes a bit of thinking about but as you've already tarnished my reputation with a little addition, not to put too finer point on it I'd better consider your proposal seriously.' Mary replied and a second later added, 'I have, and I accept.' She was overjoyed as Don slipped the ring onto her slim third finger, helping him to his feet for a confirmatory embrace. 'And what a beautiful ring with my favourite sapphire stones in place. Thank you, darling you've just made my day.'

*

Don's application to the Cliffe Hotel was returned promptly and two days later he was offered an interview by Martine Hindley the Personnel Officer. She welcomed him into a spacious office, overlooking the promenade now thronged with holiday makers and day visitors from the North East and further afield. 'I see you trained at the Rubicon and the 4 Arrows in Cumbria, both with a 4 AA star rating and come recommended from both establishments.' Martine confirmed reading Don's CV. You must hand been distraught when the 4 Arrows was destroyed?'

'Yes, it was a disaster for such a renowned restaurant especially as I had envisaged a long stay, having developed a formidable restaurant team. Our last year was a sales record for the restaurant.' Don stated proudly.

'All very laudable and a great credit to you but how would you handle restaurant and banqueting numbers in excess of 200?' Martine question was designed to expose Don's Achilles heel.

'It's a question of organisation, preparedness with everyone knowing their job and having the commitment. There were times at the Rubicon when we had Association buffets and special event prize-giving occasions for over a hundred. On those occasions we had to rely on agency infills who needed to be brought up to speed and acclimatised in a hurry.' Don explained confidently.

'Thank you, Donald, that was a response our restaurant manager would have been pleased to hear. He is returning today, so can you come back this afternoon at 3 p.m. to meet him, after which we could decide on your application?'

Don decided to kill the three hours strolling into the seaside town centre and treated himself to some fish and chips at the Panama Café situated just off the links with picture windows providing a grand view of the beach and North Sea, calm for a change. As he salted his chips and tucked into his battered cod he soaked in the sea view, casting his mind to a previous occasion many years ago on a day visit from Shields as a seven-year-old with his parents and siblings – a rare treat. Don shivered at the memory.

*

It was late summer and the North East wind had a cutting edge with overcast sky and the grey sea an icy edge as he paddled briefly in the shallows, returning to the family with blue toes to be rebuked by his mother Gracie. 'Come in you silly sod, you'll get chilblains.' He could almost hear an echo of his mother now. Sidney, his elder brother and his sister Sadie, hardly out of nappies helped him build an imposing sandcastle which the tide washed away leaving him crying in frustration as the crenelated castle melted back into the waves. It was the last time they were together as a family. Soon after, his father was called away into the forces in WW1 as a medical orderly and rarely returned home, except for the occasional two or three-day furlough but rarely spent any time with his young son.

Don often wondered in these moments of reflection how different his relationship could have been when he saw how much time his friends' fathers spent with them. Ordinary things like going to Shields on market day or having a picnic on Roker sands. His pals were always telling Don; Dad said this, or Dad did that, or look at what Dad bought me. It made Don realise just how much dads meant to his friends and by contrast how little his dad was part of his life. Gracie was too busy to assume that role, bringing up three children on the meagre budget as his father's forces pay was insufficient and irregular. It was a blessing that Sidney's contribution to the household finances from the coalmine was a blessing. On the street the Sullivan family was felt sorry for because they were to all intents fatherless. This emptiness in Don young life had, even at that age fired a resolve to be self-sufficient above all and if he ever had a son, he would be a proper father, and a good one.

Don shook off these sad reflections to return to the Cliffe along the links and past the Spanish City, a place he remembered fondly for the all too infrequent visits with his family. He was nervous about the interview because he desperately wanted this job to get back into harness, but especially to prove to himself that his career ambitions were still on track. A position at the Cliffe would be a long-term commitment, and an excellent appointment,' Don hoped as he approached the Hotel for the make-or-break cross-examination at the top hotel on the coast.

*

Known locally as 'The Cliffe', the hotel was built during the Edwardian boom. Its glistening white façade fronted 100 superior rooms, most with a sea view. It towered over the 50' high cliffs that butted on to the rocks below forming a natural barrier of sea defences that protected the coastline from the ravages of the North Sea. The hotel's wide frontage extended onto the promenade, enclosing a cultured garden that featured a colourful array of flowering perennials interspersed with evergreen bushes which help shelter the scattered wrought iron seats from the wind. At the centre was a fountain with a blue marble surround, in the centre of which was of a mermaid spouting a sparkling jet which would catch the afternoon sun in its spray, falling into the mosaic base. Don was briefly mesmerised by this demonstration of wealth as he entered through the revolving doors, into the expansive reception area replete with palms and chesterfield sofas for guests and visitors. He straightened his back, adjusted his tie and entered the personnel department with a confident smile, tapping on Miss Hindley's glass door.

'Come in Donald, have a seat; our restaurant manager Dominic Talbot will be here shortly,' Martine announced, brushing an errant curl from her forehead. 'He has read your CV and application so is briefed for your interview. A drink, tea, coffee?' Don declined as he appraised Martine's slim figure, wearing a lime green suit, buttoned down and set off with a strand of malachite beads. Her blond hair was short and flapper styled around a pale face, light blue almond eyes and little makeup. He estimated her age in the early 30's and was very easy on the eye. His brief appraisal had not gone unnoticed or unappreciated by Martine's sexual antennae.

The restaurant manager Dominic entered the office with a wave and an Italianesque 'good afternoon', smartly turned out, a Southern European demeanour Don thought and in his mid-forties. A tanned face was framed by dark wavy mid length hair, streaked with grey gave a confident aura to his 5' 11" lithe frame as he extended his hand to Don. His welcome had just a hint of an Italian accent with English that had been improved maybe with elocution lessons.

Dominic had been at the Cliffe for over fifteen years, first as a junior waiter and was a member of the regional Hotel Restauranteurs Guild (HRG), an organisation Don had heard of through Pierre, his maître d' at the Rubicon.

'Well Donald, or is it Don?' Dominic asked, to be informed it was usually Don. 'Ah so it could be Don and Dom eh?' He smiled conspiratorially at the linkage, 'but I like Dominic in recognition of my Italian father. 'By accident I see, you are unemployed so does that mean you could start within a few days?' Dominic's department was suffering a shortage of skilled restaurant personnel, it would appear.

'Yes, I am available at the moment although I'm due to be married in two weeks,' Don said, quickly adding, 'although that wouldn't be a restriction.'

'What Dominic is saying Don,' Martine explained, 'is that he would be pleased to offer you the position of senior waiter and would like you to start as soon as possible.' Martine was obviously anxious to conclude the interview with an appointment.

'Well, thank you for the offer which I'm delighted to accept, provided my wedding doesn't affect a start?' Don was amazed that the offer and acceptance had been concluded in record time and was not too concerned that things like pay, hours and conditions had not been addressed at that point. The important thing was that he was now employed and wouldn't Mary be overjoyed he thought smugly.

'That would not be a problem Donald once we have the start date confirmed.' Martine took control again and said she would draw up a contract for Don to agree and sign and confirmed that accommodation would be available, for a limited period. 'So why don't you take Don on a tour of your restaurant while I conclude the admin., Dominic?' Martine's tone brooked no argument as Dominic escorted Don from her domain and into his.

And what a restaurant! On a par with Blackpool's Tower in terms of its lush furnishings, grand picture windows overlooking the beach, sea and far beyond, with opulent seating for 100 guests. Don was almost weak at the knees in anticipation of working in such luxurious environment.

*

'What do you think Don?' Dominic's question jerked him into the present as he nodded approvingly making a favourable comparison to the Rubicon.

'I'm going to enjoy working here Dominic, it's certainly a beautiful place with, I imagine customers to match.' Don soaked up the good feelings he had about his fortunate application, and that they seemed to be on the same wavelength. But would Don's joy at landing this 'job in a million' turn out to be another false dawn and Don's glass remain half full? His career so far hadn't been problem free.

Returning to Personnel, Martine presented Don with his contract which included a 40 hr, 5 ½ day week and a remuneration of £6 weekly plus tips. 'You can work out with Dominic on your days off and shifts once we have a start date. However, you need to be aware that before you sign the contract.' Martine warned. 'As part of your trial period of 3 months you will spend two weeks in the kitchen.' Martine paused to see Don's reaction. Don just gave her a nod but remained silent. 'As you know the kitchen is the powerhouse of the hotel and the waiting staff need to be conversant with how it operates and to be mindful of the issues therein.' Martine paused again expecting some response. Don just nodded an assent again but remained silent. We don't expect you to become a chef or even a 'commis' in that time, only to be cognisant with its operation and develop a harmonious working relationship with the kitchen brigade. Does that make sense Don?'

'Absolutely,' Don agreed with some feeling, 'Anything that helps to oil the wheels between kitchen and restaurant must be good. Is there a programme of objectives to be achieved in the two weeks, or are we just kitchen helpers?' Don raised his eyebrows with his question.

'No, not as such but we'll get some feedback on your experience from the Head Chef as to how you've fitted in. You'll be provided with suitable clothing of course. Have you any further questions?' Don demurred and duly signed the contract asking if it would be in order to confirm a start date once he had discussed his appointment with his fiancé. Martine readily agreed as they parted with a congratulatory handshake and a warm welcome to The Cliffe.

Don counted himself a very lucky boy as he walked along the seafront whistling a popular melody with a spring in his step taking in the expanse of the North Sea dotted with cargo ships on their way or coming from the nearby River Tyne. He had been a pupil at the nearby Rockcliffe junior school where the English teacher, Miss Sweet would have them recite John Masefield's famous poem; 'Dirty British Coaster,' *with a salt-caked smoke stack, jutting through the channel in the mad March days, with a cargo of Tyne coal, road-rails, pig-lead, firewood, iron-ware, and cheap tin trays*, and found himself stepping out to that poem's meter, dum-de-dum-de-dum-de-dum-de. That's all he could remember but with fond memories and wondering whether Masefield had ever been on a '*dirty British coaster*'?

Mary was overjoyed to hear Don's news. 'I didn't think my day could get any better, and now it has so well done. When do you start?' She was thinking ahead with the wedding plans reaching fruition.

'Well, with the wedding over a week away, I could confirm with the Cliffe to start in two weeks and that will give us a short honeymoon. Is that enough?' Don looked anxiously at Mary for confirmation. After all it was the biggest day of her life and he didn't want his new job to have priority.

'OK, but will the Cliffe be happy about that? After your speedy interview and offer they seem very keen on getting you in harness.' She didn't want anything to jeopardise his unexpected appointment.

'It won't be a problem; I'll confirm a start in two weeks as there's plenty to do Darling.' In the event Martine was delighted that Don would shortly be in place and made a note to give Dominic the good news that a star recruit would be joining his team.

CHAPTER 30

The wedding day was a blur of activity that worked like clockwork. Cars arrived on the dot at all three locations, the sun shone on the registry office as the family, friends and colleagues of Don and Mary gathered. Most of the Rubicon staff who were not on duty turned out in their summery attire alongside curious shoppers. Sidney's morning suit fitted to a 'T' and little Sadie's bridesmaid outfit lit up the proceedings. Mary's parents rose to the occasion with a fashionable turnout to grace any wedding. Gracie turned heads with an assembly that the Queen would have admired. So what could go wrong?

Mary, not surprisingly was the main attraction and as becomes a bride she kept the growing crowd waiting for ten minutes before alighting from the gleaming Daimler to explosive applause from the expectant onlookers. Mary's wedding dress and bouquet was a revelation of swirling white taffeta, silks and satins with her hair curled up into a sparkling tiara like crown. Don just saw a vision that he could hardly believe was going to be his wife. He had never been so much in love and almost burst into tears of happiness as she was escorted by her father, resplendent in a morning suit, shiny grey cravat, gloves and gleaming top hat to finish at Don's side. He turned to Mary, took her hand and whispered.

'You are my dream fantasy Mary,' Don whispered, as the official in charge silenced the wedding march music as Mary blushed to her roots by Don's comment.

'We are here to witness the marriage etc. etc. as the official read off the transcribed sheet all the officialese necessary to join a man and a woman in holy matrimony. 'Do you take Mary Tearse Macdonald etc.. etc.. and do you take Donald Bernard Sullivan etc.. etc.. till death etc.. etc.. until the fifteen-minute service was concluded with a ring and a confirmatory kiss for Mary, now Mrs. Donald Sullivan. After signing the marriage certificate they exited the registry office to the cheers of the assembled crowd, as a storm of confetti buried the happy couple with the photographer snapping away, shouting over the mayhem to gather in an orderly fashion for the group photos. Herding the proverbial cats would have been an easier option.

A semblance of order was at last established with every combination of bride, groom's best man, bridesmaids, bride's mother and father, grooms mother and finally friends of the bride and groom were all permanently recorded on celluloid at the rear of the registry office. Anyone else who wanted to be photographed with the bridge and groom, were included in the celebrations, and why not?

Despite the limitations imposed by post-war austerity in the 20s and 30's the buffet displayed by the Rubicon chefs would not have been out of place at the Ritz for its quality, variety and culinary expertise. All manner of hot and cold dishes were on display with the coup de grace a glistening black boar's head galantine; a whole decorated salmon side by side with an aspic coated ham on a silver stand. Spread out to the sides of these mouth-watering dishes were salads of all shapes and sizes served by chefs in their pristine toques and whites. Guests were wide-eyed, standing transfixed at such a display of victuals they probably hadn't seen since before the war but their transfixion didn't last long before their stomachs took precedence over their eyes. And, if this wasn't enough, a virtual kaleidoscope of desserts including milles feuilles, tarts, fruit pies and gateaux of every style and content. Finally, a spread of local cheeses, wafted an enticing odour over the spellbound guests.

'What a spread man, why av, nivor seen the like,' was one comment.

'Eee, is that a real boars head pet?' a young man asked of the chef who preceded to carve a large slice.

'Canna have a piece of that salmon, mind it looks too good to eat?' A young lady dressed to the nines asked uncertainly.

'Certainly madame,' a young chef smiled, 'will that be enough?'

'Why aye hinney, an canna have some mixed salad t'gan with it?'

Away from the melee Don looked at the buffet spread and marvelled at the job Stuart and his team had produced. Don held Mary's hand tightly, still bursting with pride that she was now Mrs Sullivan. 'You must have made some impression on the chef to get him to produce this spread. It's just out of this world.' Mary squeezed his hand, gazing adoringly at this young man who had captured her heart.

'Absolutely, it's been a chance to show off their skills to a wider and a more enthusiastic audience. The guests will talk about it for a long time,' as Don was quick to notice Mary's tearful reaction. 'Come and have a look at this Mary,' Don guided her away through the excited guests to a table where a tall, glistening piece de resistance in royal icing took centre stage.

A round three-tier cake topped with two decorative figures sat on a mirrored silver stand with each layer intricately decorated with piped whorls and lattice corniches and finished in gold leaf.

'Oh my, that's too beautiful Don, it would be a shame to cut into it.' Mary's hand went to her mouth in disbelief as she peered closely at the bride and groom figures. 'They're quite a good likeness, don't you think Don.' As she squeezed his arm and pecked his cheek, whispering something that made Don blush.

'Not really, I'm much handsomer than that little effigy,' joked Don. 'Yours is near the mark though but!' As Mary's elbow found its mark.

She stood back and took his arm and lead him onto the dance floor. 'Can I have this first dance with you Sir?' Doing a twirl as the small combo played a popular tune in waltz time. This encouraged some of the early-bird guests to applaud the newlyweds as they made their way onto the floor's centre as the announcer called 'let's hear it for the bride and groom – Mr & Mrs Donald Sullivan,'

'What a lovely couple, I didn't know Don could dance,' Gracie turned to her daughter, 'he made a very good choice with Mary, maybe I'll be a grandmother soon.' Little did she know how prophetic her comment was. 'Sidney hasn't even got a steady girlfriend.' Gracie sighed as her eldest raised his eyes.

Sidney was chatting to Jimmy to find out how his mangled hand was progressing with the skin grafts. 'It'll never be right ye nar but the sargon's said to keep up the massages and it'll improve.'

'It's good to hear it's getting better Jimmy, and can you check with Don he wants to have a chat.' Sidney added and then excused himself to ask Mary's bridesmaid for a dance - he'd been eyeing her up since she arrived at the registry office and was clearly smitten.

'Phew, I don't think this dress was designed for dancing Don, let's have something to eat before the locusts devastate the buffet, but it's good to see,' Mary added quickly with a grin as Don handed her a plate. 'That ham and salmon looks good enough to eat, and don't forget Don ……!

'I know,' he interrupted, 'you're eating for two now,' adding some potato salad and a small chicken vol-au-vent to her plate. 'Can't have my new wife going hungry.'

Don's choice was the boar's head galantine and a slice of quiche Lorraine with a selection of salads, popping a small pork pie to keep him going as he took both plates to his new mother-in-law's table. Gracie and Mary's mother were chatting animatedly, to Don's satisfaction.

*

The afternoon was peppered with an amusing speech by the best man, spilling the beans on Don's various embarrassing mishaps, his BSA accident included. A short speech by the groom thanking the guests, and lauding Mary's achievements and misdemeanours much to her embarrassment.

Finally, interjections by various alcohol fuelled friends and family, all in the best possible taste of course, added a hilarious touch.

A grand finale to complete the celebrations was played in by the combo to the strains of 'we've been together now for forty years' as the wedding cake was wheeled into the centre to gasps of amazement and accompanied by lightning flashes of bulbs. Both hands on the silver blade ceremoniously cut through the icing to applause with Sidney calling for a toast to the happy couple as the cake was wheeled away. Don and Mary mingled with guests to say their goodbyes, finally paying a special visit to Chef Stuart and his team for such a standout buffet.

*

As they lay in each other's arms thinking how lucky they were to have such a unexpected wedding. Hats off to the Rubicon they murmured as they happily indulged in activities that newly-weds were supposed to do and dreamed of an exciting life together.

CHAPTER 31

The wedding celebrations left the happy couple exhausted and thankful for their two day 'honeymoon' in Bamburgh, close to the village of Seahouses that reputedly, had the best fish and chips in Northumberland. Bamburgh had been the home of Grace Darling who, as a young lady rowed through a storm tossed North Easterly gale to rescue the crew of the stricken Forfarshire paddle steamer in 1838 and became a national heroine, her grave protected in the village churchyard. Their too-short weekend ended with a visit to the Castle, an enormous fortified medieval bastion that initially started out as a 5th century Celtic fort and now a popular tourist attraction.

Fortified at Seahouses by the best fish and chips 'in the world' as they sat on the harbour wall they were soon back in harness with a vengeance. Mary's team had been decimated by a bout of influenza necessitating four temporary staff from the Grainger Agency. These temporary staff required some urgent OJT (on job training) and an induction to bring them up to the Rubicon standard as their experience was based on two-star hotels standards. In turn, Don was thrown in the deep end with the designated KP (kitchen porter) fortnight he had forgotten about due to the wedding. It was to be hard labour in the hotel's kitchen so decked out in regulation whites he presented himself at 8.30 a.m. to the Head Chef, Dougal McDonald, a man on a mission.

'Now listen laddie ah don't want ye givin me any bother, yu unerstan? Just cos you're a special waister (waiter). You'll be here forr two weeks an ah expec yu to do your bit or yull git the sharp edge of me tongue.'

'Absolutely Chef I'm here to learn and will take the opportunity to help you out. Just let me know what's involved and I'll try my hardest to gain your approval.' Don's marginal obsequiousness believed that a cooperative chef would be an asset when he was in the restaurant.

'Well said laddie, even if there's a bit of Scotch mist in there too.' Dougal creased a warning smile.

In a quick test of his resolve and cooperation Don was consigned to the kitchen's pot wash under the tutelage of Benny, a KP with fifteen years' service and indeterminate age, although Don's estimate was fifty-five. Benny sported a 5-day growth, a confirmed drinker's nose and pinhole eyes that viewed Don with some suspicion. His attire, fit for the purpose was a full-length leather apron as protection from lugging large copper pots into the elephant sized sinks. His hands were encased in full length industrial strength rubber gloves, a pair of which he handed to Don along with a full-length plastic apron which would be protection for the period he would be a pot-washer's assistant. A PWA sounds better than a KP, Don thought as he wrestled with a dustbin sized pot, sweat beading his forehead.

A brief chat with the kitchen brigade revealed that Benny was regarded in high esteem by all the chefs, commis (second chefs) and kitchen assistants. This seemed a role reversal to Don because in most kitchens a KP was usually bottom of the pyramid and occasionally above the apprentices in status terms. The kitchen brigade was grateful to Benny, labouring on the hardest job that they would avoid like the plague, so on Benny's day off they would draw lots to see who would be KP for a day and usually allocate an unfortunate apprentice to that desperate job. Benny's high status was also due to a much more important role that endeared him to everyone in the brigade. Kitchens are hot places to work, inducing profuse sweating as an accepted occupational hazard, so to help minimise this inconvenience kitchen staff at the Cliffe were allocated a twice daily pint of beer, served from an enamel jug. This was one of Benny's responsibilities, which he took very seriously, doling out the beer ration mid-morning and early evening and this made Benny everyone's favourite KP. Anyone foolish enough to diss Benny or get on his wrong side, and it wouldn't take much, suddenly found the jug empty, or their ration short changed. If they had the temerity to complain to the Head Chef, they would be castigated for annoying Benny and were advised, to make their peace with him for everyone's sake, or the supply of clean pots might suddenly dry up!

Once a week on average and usually on a Thursday afternoon, Benny would remove his work clothes and with great care shave off his four-day growth and from his locker in the pot-wash, take a clean shirt, pressed trousers, brown shoes highly polished, and a smart checked jacket. A cracked mirror on his locker door checked that his pristine hair was neatly combed and his overall appearance up to the mark. This ritual was on account of Benny's weekly visit to his 'lady friend' who might be a different one each week. To cries from the kitchen staff, *'We Know Where You're Going Benny'*, he would acknowledge the good-natured calls, doff his hat and stroll out of the kitchen, totally unrecognizable from the KP potman who came in – a bit like Burlington Bertie from Bow!

*

For two days Don washed more pots than he had ever done in all his years in catering but felt he had gained a measure respect not only from Benny but more importantly from the Head Chef who 'promoted' him to lighter duties. Don would collect supplies for the kitchen from the Goods Inwards checker which included fresh seafood, butchered meat and greengrocery boxes, delivering them to various sections or 'parties' of the kitchen 'brigade'. As a result, he began to appreciate how many products the kitchen relied on every day; their variety, frequency, quality, and who used them. He struck up working relationships with the 'chef's du parti', those responsible for a kitchen section as part of the 'brigade'. Whether it was the 'garde manger' (larder chef), poisonnier (fish chef), entremetier (vegetable/ soup chef) or pâtissier (pastry chef) and so on, Don was a critical observer and stored the information and advice away for another time and opportunity.

Because Don was a good listener and sociable he given a history lesson by chef Dougal in the development of this kind of kitchen structure of which he was totally unaware, being on the other side of the 'hotplate'. According to Dougal, a French master chef, Gustave Escoffier developed this 'Brigade' system, based on the military hierarchy with the head chef at the top of the pyramid and the 'parti' chefs lined below with each responsible for a key part of the operation. At service time the Cliffe chefs all responded to the Sous Chef 'caller' to produce whatever was ordered, with the response, 'Oui Chef' – it was cuisine francais after all.

Depending on the size of the kitchen, sub-divisions might be added such as a bakery under the pâtissier or hors oeuvres under the larder chef. In tandem with this kitchen revolution Escoffier developed hundreds of recipes and garnishes for exotic dishes in a manual entitled *Le Repertoire de la Cuisine*, which in time became the chefs' bible. Escoffier's initiative also developed the concept of the menu into a three and four course format which quickly gained popularity among the dining cognoscente during the Edwardian era. A new world of understanding was Don's reward for his two weeks 'slavery'.

*

The drudgery that Don endured became a source of enlightenment and even enjoyment after Dougal introduced him to the Chef Pâtissier Wally Ladd, and as he was a commis (trainee) chef short Don deputised as a general assistant and was able to observe the production of ice creams, petit fours, varieties of pastry, cakes and desserts of all kinds. On one occasion for a VIP's birthday, he watched Wally make a basket from pulled sugar, filled with an assortment of petit fours which on completion closely resembled a jewellery box. Don was flabbergasted at the skill and dexterity of the pâtissiers as they wove their magic from basic ingredients.

'Well laddie, you've worked out much better than I expected, especially being thrown in the deep end; you'll be welcome here anytime.' Dougal was rarely so fulsome in his praise for a temporary kitchen hand.

'Thank you Chef, I've learnt a great deal and understand the sort of problems the kitchen has to overcome.' Don shook Dougal's hand and said he would be pleased to help again. 'Maybe I could generate some overtime pay in the process.' Don thought as he left to tell Dominic he could resume his duties as a waiter the next day.

'I heard you wowed Dougal and the KP with your pot washing expertise, but I'm delighted you're here to help because we've a mountain of functions and parties in the next week which include two weddings and three birthday parties. Our feet won't touch the ground. In addition, a visit from Manchester United who are playing the Magpies next weekend have a whole floor booked for the team and support staff. You wouldn't think they'd need that much space but football is big business and we must grab the business when we can.' Dominic was realistic about the workload and would find Don doing his best to support their working relationship.

'That's fine Dominic. I've had baptisms of fire before, so you'll have my 100% support. Will you need to get extra staff in to support these one-off functions?'

'Yes, the local agency will provide suitably trained casual staff as they have in the past and our experienced waiters can be seconded to oversee the wedding and parties. We'll keep a close eye on the restaurant with the casuals, some we've used before. Our restaurant is the key part of the hotel's business and a major factor in supporting room sales.' Dominic had his priorities right and showed he had the experience to cope with what would be a testing period. 'Before you go Don, I'll run though our bookings for the next couple of days to ease you into your new role. Tomorrow I've called a meeting of all the waiting, bar and ancillary staff to introduce you as my second in command. There won't be any kickbacks about your appointment from our senior staff as I've already briefed them so when I'm not around you'll be given their full support.' Dominic explained to sooth any nerves Don might have.

'Thanks for that assurance Dominic. Maybe I could say a few words?' Don wanted to state his case so the restaurant staff knew where he stood.

'Of course Don, tell them how you see yourself fitting in. I'm sure they'll like that.' Dominic seemed relieved that Don had made the offer.

*

'Looks like my feet aren't going to get much rest for the next few weeks but it'll be a good time to see where the cracks are and where I can see changes. I'll have to butter up the United manager Scott Duncan with some extra special service as I understand he's quite amenable to improving the team's PR image.' Don explained to Mary as he relaxed with a cup of tea.

'And how's my little KP tonight? I hope all those kitchen pots and pans are shiny now?' Mary teased giving him a welcoming peck.

'Sparkling! Tomorrow I'm back to the coal face with an intro to all the service staff, and an easy ride.' Don hoped.

'So how was your day with all your new chambermaids, I suppose you've already whipped them into shape with your toilet training?'

'Don't mock! A chambermaid is a highly skilled job and requires some expert training over a lengthy period. I'll bet you'd struggle to measure up to their daily regime.' Mary gave him a look with eyes narrowed.

'You're right Darling I'm not about to get involved. At this moment I'd rather wrestle with a medium rare rump steak, so what if I wash and brush up then decamp to our favourite eatery. I've a hard day tomorrow to I'll need to be up for it?'

'You know how to get round me, when you know I'm right Don, so it's a date. And if you're still *'up for it'* after our dinner date, well, you might just get lucky.' Mary pinched his derriere and escaped to the bathroom before he could react.

Don's steak at Giuseppe's was done to a turn while Mary opted for her favourite lasagna al fourno, all washed down with a half bottle of red. On their return to the Rubicon Don did get lucky!

CHAPTER 32

Dominic opened the restaurant service meeting the next morning. 'Many thanks for attending, especially as some of you would have been off duty. I wanted to update you on the next busy, busy, two weeks when we're going to need running pumps with the extra parties, weddings and the visit of Manchester United. Please, please try not to pester the stars for their autographs or ask them to sign anything of a personal nature.' A ripple of laughs greeted Dominic's request. 'However, I might be able to get some players for a signing if I can twist the manager's arm.' Hoots greeted the offer. 'Another reason for this meeting, was to introduce my new deputy Don Sullivan who's already completed his hard labour under Chef Dougal.' Shouts of 'good for him'. 'Don has sterling experience at the Rubicon Club and also a stint as deputy maître d' hotel at the 4 Arrows hotel in Cumbria before it was burnt down, for which he assures me he was not responsible.' Some muted laughter. 'Anyway, welcome to the Cliffe Don, would you'd like to say a few words?'

'Good morning everyone and thanks to Mr Talbot for the introduction. He was right to say I was not responsible for the 4 Arrows fire. I was in Newcastle at the time.' A flurry of laughs eased the tension. 'My two weeks under the watchful eye of Chef McDonald have given me a salutary lesson on what the Cliffe's reputation is based on, a brilliantly organised kitchen, as well as an aching back!' A few informed laughs greeted Don's admission. 'I've known about the Cliffe Hotel and its reputation for many years and must say I was honoured to be offered the position and will apply myself to maintain its five-star standards. I realise I have a lot to learn to fit in but with your help.' Don paused to let his plea sink in. 'I'll try to ensure they made the right decision with my appointment, so if you have been, thanks for listening.' Polite applause and laughter greeted Don's short introduction.

Dominic summarised the upcoming business and took questions so that no one was in any doubt that they would have to be on their mettle for the next few weeks. The meeting broke up as Dominic and Don discussed the specials with Dougal for the lunch and dinner service.

*

The next three weeks were the busiest Don had ever worked and served to underlined the wisdom of the Cliffe management in selecting him. During

Dominic's rare absences Don was given a taste for restaurant management and, at the same time gave staff the reassurance that Don was on the ball.

Manchester United arrived and took over the entire third floor so Don lost no time in contacting Scott Duncan the manager to enquire if anyone had any special dietary requirements. A separate dining area had been organised to ensure they were not pestered. The manager was especially grateful for Don's special efforts for their comfort and in addition to giving Don four tickets for the upcoming match with Newcastle he agreed to have the team provide an opportunity for the hotel staff to meet the players. This additional concession for the staff did Don's popularity no harm at all.

Newcastle United had bonded a special relationship to the Cliffe whereby top national and international teams visiting St. James Park were given priority reservations. The hotel's proximity to Tynemouth's long sands, a short distance away provided a training bonus for the visiting teams.

The hotel's tannoy crackled out an urgent message for Don to contact the Rubicon manager. 'Hello Don, can you get to Preston Hospital as Mary went into labour shortly after lunch. I phoned for an ambulance once Mary's deputy phoned me.' Cyril, Rubicon's manager said Mary seemed calm so told him not to worry. Don ended the call and ordered a taxi to take him to the hospital for the fifteen-minute journey.

On arrival, he was told Mary was in the pre-natal ward and in the advanced stages of childbirth, so Don raced to the second floor, narrowly missing two trollies in the process, one with a surprised patient on-board and took the stairs two at a time, stopping at the theatre door to catch his breath. The door opened to reveal Mary being encouraged by a midwife to breath quickly and push, push, push!

'Ooooh that hurts,' Mary gasped as she spied Don. 'Don, Don, my hand quickly,' gasping with effort as Don gripped her damp hand tightly and looked at his wife's face dripping sweat from her efforts, her lips tight and brows wrinkled in pain.

'You're doing fine, just keep pushing Pet,' the Midwife squeezed Mary's other hand as she encouraged an extra effort.

Don was sweating with the tension and concern for his wife as she squealed again as the pain lanced through her pelvic muscles, stretching and stretching and stretching to ease the newborn into the world.

Don at last found his voice. 'Mary, Mary, push some more, you're nearly there, I can see our baby's head so push for the last time Darling, one last effort,' gasping himself as though he was giving birth.

'Oooooooo....aah!!!! Mary screamed out as finally their baby slowly slid out into the Midwife's experienced hands, wreathed in blood. It was the most beautiful thing Don had every seen as the tiny bundle's umbilical cord was snipped and secured.

'Where's my baby?' Mary cried out, more in relief now with a pain free body as much a demand to see what she had produced. 'Let me see, let me see,' as Don passed the tiny, tot into the mother's embrace with Mary grinning ear to ear as she heard Don whisper that they had a baby boy.

'Darling, you've made me the happiest Geordie in the world,' Don planted a kiss on to cracked lips. 'How is the newest mam in Preston feeling?' Don squeezed her hand and caressed their baby's head with the other, puffed up with an unimaginable pride as what they had achieved.

'Just a little pooped after an hour's hard labour, but I'll recover now the hard works done. This little beggar wasn't due for another week or so, but I suppose he was fed up with the wait.' Mary seemed better as her sense of humour surfaced.

The Midwife announced that the baby's weight was a healthy 7lbs 5ozs, well within the limits. Mary looked relieved and Don laughed and blew his cheeks at the news as they discussed names for another Sullivan. 'I think he's got the black hair of Sullivan senior and my nose, a splendid Roman. What do you think Darling?' Don enquired after a close examination.

'I don't care what he has or what he looks like, he's just the most beautiful thing I've even seen.' Mary exclaimed and burst into tears of happiness and relief as Don responded in like fashion, viewed by a sympathetic Midwife.

'Well done both of you,' the Midwife intervened, 'after all the excitement your wife needs to rest. You'll be here for two days Mary then you can go home with the baby, all being well. We'll check on the progress of both of you after a couple of days, that's the baby, not you Don,' As Don raised an enquiring eyebrow. 'After that there's a post-natal drop-in clinic that will provide information on the baby's aftercare and we recommend you both attend for a few sessions,' the midwife explained as she wrapped the blood pressure strap onto Mary's arm and placed the thermometer under her tongue. 'Good, good, both normal.' She said removing the strapping.

'Wait a minute we can't keep calling the baby 'it' can we?' Mary demanded, having almost recovered from her emotional burst, 'so let's decide on his name.' Mary quite liked Malcolm after eulogising Malcolm Campbell the water speed record holder. After rejecting a few other possibles they finally agreed on Malcolm Preston Sullivan to give the hospital staff some credit for all their efforts. Janet, the midwife was especially pleased with the recognition.

Don kissed Mary and the baby and took his leave to prepare for the Cliffe's evening service, 'no rest for the wicked,' he said ruefully, reluctant to leave his wife and new baby. 'I'll be back to see you tomorrow morning after the breakfast service as Dominic is handling lunch,' kissing his son and now radiant wife. 'Take good care of Malcolm Preston, Darling.'

Don's first job on returning to the hotel was to send a telegram to his mother and family about the birth of their Grandson.

'Mary & Don have a son Malcolm Preston Sullivan – Stop – Will visit soon – Stop – Your loving son Donald – Stop.'

The grapevine quickly circulated among the Cliffe's restaurant staff and management that Don was now a first-time Dad. As the staff lined up before the evening service and sang 'for he's a jolly good Daddy etc. etc.,' then almost on cue, Tristan the hotel manager arrived sporting a bottle of Moet which he deftly popped and filled the speedily delivered flutes for a toast to an embarrassed but appreciative Don.

'Many congratulations Don. How is Mary and son?' Dominic and Tristan asked simultaneously.

'Very well and many thanks for the impromptu bubbly sir.' Don was made up by his thoughtfulness. 'We've named him Malcolm Preston, after the hospital as they were absolutely marvellous, and I saw him born.' blushing slightly at the memory.

'Well, we'll all look forward to seeing the young Malcolm in due course,' Tristan said taking his leave.

'We've not many in the restaurant tonight so take the evening off because I'm sure you've lots to do Don, OK,'

'Many thanks Dominic. Malcolm caught us by surprise being over a week early so were not fully prepared.'

'Mr Sullivan,' a waiter called, you're wanted on the telephone in the reception.'

'Hello Don Sullivan, here, can I help you,' thinking it was a restaurant enquiry.

'Yes, you certainly have Donald,' his mam Gracie cried. 'I've received your telegram and had to remember where the phone box was to find out more about my first grandson and Mary, of course.'

'They're both doing fine Mam, he arrived a week early and weighed in at a 7lb 5oz. We've named him Malcolm Preston after the hospital and Malcolm after the water-speed champ.'

'Oh, I'm so pleased they're fine and how are you? You must be over the moon and a boy too. Is that what you wanted?'

'I'm exhausted, and I didn't give birth, so can only imagine how Mary feels. We're just relieved to have any baby in good health and overjoyed there were no problems,' Don exclaimed, happy for his Mam.

'When can I see Malcom Preston? Maybe we could all come over soon. I'm so happy so give my best wishes to Mary and tell her we'll see her soon.' Gracie couldn't keep the excitement from her voice, she was so proud of her son.

'Mary will be at Preston for another couple of days with the baby and then she'll be back home for a few days so let me know when you can come, and I'll arrange with my boss to have a few hours off?' Don knew his mam couldn't wait to see the baby so would arrange a visit when she'd spoken to Sidney and Sadie.

CHAPTER 33

Don's joy at the birth of their son was short lived with a tragedy that stunned the Cliffe Hotel staff only a few weeks later. Tristan called Don to his office to reveal details of an accident as reported by the Northumbria Constabulary.

Shortly after leaving the hotel two day earlier, Dominic was involved in a three-vehicle accident on the Shields – Newcastle coast road just South of the Jesmond bridge. A left-hand drive lorry loaded with concrete blocks for the A1 extension had moved into the main road with no right of way and ploughed into two cars. The subsequent carnage left one person dead and three others seriously injured, one of whom was Dominic.

As the news filtered through among the hotel staff there was a mixture of shocked incredulity and grief because, Dominic, was a very popular figure across the hotel. Tristan contacted the hospital to be told that although Dominic's condition was serious he was expected to pull through. A long-term period of recovery was expected as he had sustained multiple fractures and a punctured lung so any return to work, even in the long term was unlikely. A bewildered Tristan immediately arranged a meeting of his senior staff to decide what to do.

'Our situation could hardly be worse but at least Dominic will recover although they're not sure when. In the meantime, we must fill the gap and the only person to do that now is Don. So, will you step into the breach?' Tristan asked, a desperate tone to his voice.

'I'll do whatever I can to keep things afloat. You know that Sir, it'll be a tough job to fill because Dominic had everything buttoned down and the restaurant was moving like a well-oiled machine. Don knew not to expect any easy transfer of power, and wondered if he had the ability to manage with less than a year as Dominic's deputy.

'Thank you Don, that's the cooperation I expected. We'll recruit more seasoned staff, but we need someone who knows the system and can also train up the extras we need.' Tristan was quietly relieved that Don had readily accepted the additional responsibility that many would have shied away from. 'You are now the Cliffe's restaurant manager Don. I'll draw up a new contract for you to sign, the details we'll discuss later.' The meeting was adjourned with Don wondering how the service staff would respond to a new regime. Don wasn't too happy to jump in the deep end but would have to learn to swim or drown, that was his challenge. He had been given the opportunity and he would try to make the best of it. He just hoped the tide was in for him with regards support by the restaurant and service staff's because the next few weeks would be tough.

*

'Good morning everyone, and thanks for attending. As you know, the management in their wisdom have ask me to take over for Dominic until a permanent replacement is appointed. Unfortunately, it's unlikely that Dominic will be returning in the foreseeable future because of his injuries. In the meantime, I'll need your support to keep the Cliffe restaurant on track because that's what Dominic would expect. Also, I'm going to need a deputy because I'm unable to work 24/7 even though I'm reasonably fit.' Pausing for a smattering of understanding nods. 'Now if anyone would like to apply for the post of deputy restaurant manager could they please see me after? Whoever is selected their salary will be adjusted accordingly, in the upward direction.' Don intended to keep it light and cheerful. 'With the upcoming surge in functions, meetings and weddings we will also require additional skilled and semi-skilled staff so if anyone has suitable friends or family please see me afterwards to arrange interviews. Are there any questions?'

'Will there be any changes in the rotas?' Asked one of more experienced waiters.

'Well Derek, we're being spread thin, so it is likely but any changes in the rotas will be with the agreement with those concerned.' Don's response was appreciated with nods all round. 'I'd also like volunteers to do extra hours.'

Derek came to him afterwards offering to deputise and that his daughter would be interested in a position having just completed a waiting course at the local Park Technical College.

'Many thanks for your offer, Derek, you may be in a majority of one for the job, but we'll see. Please ask your daughter to see me when convenient and bring any information on her course. I'll give you an application form for her to complete.' Don gave two other staff application forms who had friends with some experience.

*

Tristan, the manager asked to see Don when he had finished his meeting.

'It never rains but it pours Don,' Tristan complained and explained the reason for his anxiety. 'The Great North Exhibition is on next week on the Town Moor and guess who's coming to open it? The most important person in Britain now,' Tristan revealed in a whisper as though conveying a state secret. 'The Prince of Wales! But that's not all; as part of his visit he's involved in a *'meet the people'* at the Northeast major tourist attraction, the Spanish City.'

'Marvellous, and good for the area Tristan, but what has it got to do with us?' Don was bemused at the urgent meeting.

'It's because he has to have a break from all the hand shaking and greeting and as we are the top hotel in the area we've been selected for his afternoon tea break.' Tristan could hardly control his excitement. 'So, no pressure but we've two weeks to prepare during which the hotel will be crawling with security personnel and the prince's attendants to advise on Royal protocol.

'Does this mean we will have to close the restaurant for our afternoon teas.' Don realised he'd probably answered his own question unless the prince wants to eat with his subjects – 'not a bad idea really' Don thought, but unlikely.

'It's almost certain to be taken over for the prince and assorted VIP's. so we better put up notices to that effect.' Tristan said anxiously rubbing he hands over his face.

'Could your secretary confirm the details so we're clear as to dates and times etc.? We don't want to cancel the dinner service.'

'We don't, but I'll check the times with the Royal attendants and let you know.'

*

The date for his arrival in the Northeast was published in all the papers and it was clear that Mrs Simpson, his *'companion'* would not be accompanying him on this Royal visit. The British public regarded the twice divorced American as persona non-grata and children could occasionally be heard chanting an uncomplimentary ditty.

'Look whose coming down the street, Mrs Simpson sweaty feet. She's been married twice before, now she's knocking at Edward's door.'

Despite anti-public opinion and official attempts to dissuade the prince from any permanent association with the divorcee fell on deaf ears as he was completely besotted and determined to marry Wallis Simpson.

As expected, a week before the prince's visit, police and royal officials descended on the Cliffe and on Don with a host of security measures. A Royal tea service was to be used for the actual event and a guest list drawn up to include VIPs of all shapes and sizes. These included Newcastle's Lord Mayor; local MP's; Whitley Bay's Mayor and Mayoress and a film star from the local area made up the prince's tea-party. The protocol and forms of address for the few being personally presented to the prince were put through their paces until word and manner perfect.

'At least we'll be able to trade off the visit with an officially recognised plaque of the visit.' Triston admitted, 'I just hope this carnival will be worth it!' He said grumpily.

'We'll make the most of it because how many hotels can boast a visit by the future King?' Don observed, putting a positive slant on the visit. 'His restaurant table could have a special disk as a memento and customers would be fighting to say they've sat there – we could even charge extra.' Don's light-hearted suggestion was met with a 'hrumm…p' from the manager.

A day before the prince's visit, a mini crisis blew up when the Royal officials checked the dining arrangements to make sure the princess favourite Earl Grey tea was to hand. To Don's horror not a leaf of it could be found anywhere so he checked the area suppliers of specialist teas and located a supplier near Dunstanborough a village 10 miles away. Don handed the lunch service over to Derek, leapt on his BSA and roared off to the village on the edge of the North Sea. An hour later, Don returned with a tin of the precious leaves and the crisis was averted! The royal aids breathed a sigh of relief and gave Don a virtual pat on the back.

CHAPTER 34

Despite booming business at the Cliffe for the rooms and restaurant coupled with the enormous expense for the Great North Exhibition the area was still gripped in crippling levels of unemployment, resulting from coal mine closures and short time working in the Tyneside shipyards and engineering. Because the Government was heedless to the plight of the North East the Jarrow Crusade was organised from the 5th-31st October in 1936 to raise national awareness of their desperate predicament.

Mass unemployment (44%) in the North East drove the Jarrow crusaders to walk 400 miles from Jarrow to London to present a petition to the Government to re-establish industry in the area. The march was organised by the Communist lead National Unemployed Workers Movement (NUWM) but was ignored both by the Labour Party and the Trades Union Congress (NUC) for fear of being associated with Communist agitation. Despite this rejection by the trades union hierarchy, the 'hunger marchers' as they became known was supported by the Jarrow town council and the local labour party and became a *'cause celebre'* for the unemployed nationally. Despite the upswell of public sympathy for the March nothing of any significance was done to reenergise industry or to increase employment in the Tyneside area or the North East region – it was a forgotten area.

*

Against this sombre backdrop the local population were not going to miss an opportunity to celebrate the rare event of a visit by the Prince of Wales and from Newcastle to the coast, bunting and a sea of flag waving enthusiastic groups and Royalists lined the route to cheer their favourite. All around the seaside town of Whitley Bay, Union Jack's sprouted from every house and shop with the Town Council providing bunting to criss-cross the main roads into town. The 45-minute tour around the Spanish City was concluded at the coconut shy where the prince won a coconut with his last pitch, to the applause of the flag waving spectators 'God Save the Prince' echoed around the stalls and switchback rides.

The Cliffe Hotel was royalist to a man with the restaurant decked out in purple and gold and every public area on view sparkling. Tarnished windows had been repainted, the marble fountain fronting the hotel had been scrubbed white and was now sprinkling. Don's staff had been drilled until their places and duties could be replicated in their sleep and a guard of honour of hotel staff in their sparkling attire lined the entrance for the prince's inspection. The VIPs however were peeved that they had to be in place an hour before the appointed time – with late comers denied entry.

The atmosphere above all was good natured with groups singing popular songs of the day such as 'I do like to be beside the Seaside' and 'Red Sails in the Sunset'. As the royal entourage slowly entered the town the prince was clearly heartened by this popular support, smiling and waving at the cheering crowds. The prince was escorted through the guard of honour comprising waiters, chefs and chambermaids, one of whom almost fainted when he stopped to chat. Don had eschewed being part of the lineup to keep a close eye on the increasingly restless VIPs.

Once the prince had been introduced to the manager, the afternoon tea service was signalled by Don who asked a royal aide how long his Earl Grey tea should brew?

'Why don't you ask him?' Replied the aide, adding, 'don't forget the correct address; 'Your Royal Highness'.'

Don swallowed hard and whispered. 'Excuse me Your Royal Highness how long would you like your Earl Grey to brew?'

'Thank you for asking, just a few minutes should be fine. What's your name?' The prince turned to Don smiling warmly. 'Don, Don Sullivan er.. Your Royal Highness.' He'd almost forgot the title.

'Well, Don your team have done a very good job today, well done and keep up the good work.'

'Yes, Your Royal Highness, they will be very pleased to hear, thank you.' Don turned away, not wanting to outstay his welcome.

'What a smart young man.' Observed the Prince to the Mayor, 'he'll go far in this business, will you see he gets this menu I'll sign it; I think his team deserves a memento, don't you.'

'Without doubt Your Highness, they've done a sterling job today and I'll make sure he knows it.'

*

'Congratulations to you and your team Don. The royal equerries have told me of the prince's delight with the afternoon tea arrangements. The staff's guard of honour was a brilliant piece of PR that the press will lap up. I've had the Newcastle Journal on the phone for a quote alongside photos of his arrival.' Don smiled at Tristan's relief.

'I was like a cat on hot bricks until that motorcade disappeared, it was the most stressful time I've had in my management career, but as Shakespeare put it, *'All's Well That Ends Well'*, right Don?'

'Absolutely Tristan, you've come through with flying colours. The board will be giving you a medal, or something suitable, I'm sure.'

'Thanks to you Don, you've done all that has been asked and more, so I'm informing the board that your temporary position of Restaurant Manager be made permanent from today,' shaking Don's hand to underline his promotion.

*

Later that afternoon as the VIP's were departing, the mayor presented Don with the duly signed menu. *'With much appreciation to the Cliffe Hotel staff; (signed) Edward Prince of Wales.'*

Mary had been listening to the broadcast on the BBC and was understandably proud that Don had been at the centre of the prince's visit and doubly so when Don showed them the signed menu.

On his arrival back at Sycamore Avenue Mary was buoyant. 'I can't believe it, Don. I've been pinching myself as they were reporting the visit live and explaining where the prince was and what he was having for his tea etc. etc., it was incredible.' Mary's tears were not far away and when Don looked at her shining face and said how lovely she looked, the flood gates opened. 'Oh Don, I do love you.' Don's hanky was too slow to stem his tears.

CHAPTER 35

A few months later the Prince of Wales became King Edward VIII on the death of his father Geoge V in January 1936 and 10 months later, on 11th December 1936 he abdicated the throne when Parliament refused to sanction his marriage to the divorcee, Mrs Wallis Simpson. A blanket press cover left the population largely ignorant of the reason for the abdication until the foreign press revealed the details, being under no similar restriction. Eventually, an aptly named, Bishop Blunt of Bradford exacerbated the debate by revealing the real reasons for the abdication and a British press clarion call soon trumpeted the facts. Edward's brother, Albert, Duke of York was reluctantly catapulted into the constitutional void left by the short-term King and pronounced George VI on 11th December 1936, the same day of the abdication. The Cliffe staff and management were gravely disappointed that their royal visitor had only been their king for a day.

*

Don's sister Sadie was bubbling with excitement. 'It must have been so amazing to talk to the prince; how did you feel at the time?' She asked in admiration of her big brother.

'Sadie, give your brother at bit of peace after what he must have gone through in the last few days. To have organised a special afternoon tea for the future King must have been some ordeal. Was it an ordeal Don?' His mother wondered with a congratulatory hug. 'We're all very proud of you Donald, especially as you're now a dad and I'm a grandmother. It's all too much,' as she burst into tears of joy.

'It's all been a bit much for Mam, Don, what with your promotion, the baby and talking with the Prince of Wales.' Sidney explained. 'There, there now Mam, have a good cry it'll do you good.'

'Could you hold Malcolm for me Gracie, I have to get the baby's feed.' Mary asked as Gracie's tears dried up and eagerly cradled her minute grandson for the first time.

'What a sweet bundle.' Gracie cooed, rocking him as he locked eyes on his grandmother as though to say. 'Who's this strange person smiling at me, I'll give my best smile in return.' It was probably the wind rather than any sign of affection, but Gracie didn't care - she was in raptures holding the tiny, odorous mite. A Sullivan family get together was a rare occasion so

Don and Mary made the most of the occasion with a special lunch at Tynemouth's Grand Hotel overlooking the beach and open air lido.

*

Mary had been given leave of absence from the Rubicon to care for Malcolm which was good news for Don, allowing him restful nights. The success of the royal visit had helped to cement a feelgood factor with Don and his new team, especially as he had been able to negotiate a one-off bonus for the service and kitchen crew with Tristan. He could do no wrong and the reforms he had introduced, were readily agreed. A new name was given to the restaurant, *The Royal Restaurant*, and an upgraded checking system was part of Don's improvements and bookings as a result had surged due to the publicity.

Yes! Everything was looking good for Don and the Cliffe as 1937 dawned but all was not well elsewhere. Hitler's legions were on the warpath, threatening Europe with the German Jews being persecuted and hounded with increasing viciousness. At home brown shirted fascists under the banner of Sir Edward Mosley 6th Baronet and MP for Smethwick in the West Midlands created the British Union of Fascists who were fermenting increasing public disquiet with Hitleresque demonstrations and antisemitic parades.

*

A year later, Neville Chamberlain's attempt to rein in Hitler with a meeting in Berlin in September 1938, waving a slip of paper, promising '*Peace in our Time;*' a forlorn hope. This was underlined by Hitler's duplicity as German troops surged across Europe and the persecution of the Jews increased with unbridled ferocity occasioned by widespread destruction and looting of Jewish property, businesses and synagogues known as Kristallnacht. This led to the largest exodus of Jews from Germany while the Western allies sat on their hands regarding any direct involvement and Hitler, along with other Balkan countries, proceeded to carve up Czechoslovakia.

At home Sir Winston Churchill was the sole dissenting voice to many Hitler appeasers in the government, indirectly distancing Germany's invasion of Poland which eventually dragged Britain reluctantly into war. While the '*lights all over Europe*' were being extinguished, Britain was still staying calm and carrying on as though it was someone else problem. The Cliffe's new restaurant, now under Don's firm control was the jewel in the

North East restaurants crown and the top place to eat and be seen. Once a month French theme nights would feature innovations as moules frit, escargots a la mode, boeuf bourguignon and a range of French desserts.

Mary's mother-in-law could be relied on for babysitting because she loved little Malcolm and would regularly stay over as Don had bought a house in Monkseaton from his improved income as restaurant manager. Mary too was a great deal happier with her return to her role at the Rubicon and been promoted to Executive Head Housekeeper.

CHAPTER 36

'Don, now we're both earning, in good jobs and with a family should we think about getting a car?'

'Yes, you're right it's a good idea but what with the war, private cars are a bit of a luxury and petrol is being rationed as well.' Don explained, dodging Mary's request. 'But I think it's a good idea for the future.' Don added with a half promise.

She had quizzed Don before, but he always considered the motorbike to be a sufficient mode of transport although recently he had traded his BSA 250 in for a more powerful machine, a 350cc Rudge Ulster which he loved racing along the Coast Road and Beach Road to St Mary's Lighthouse. He knew Mary would pester him unmercifully and to be fair, he had been considering investing in a car as motorbiking was not the safest option for someone with responsibility for a family and an important job. 'Yes,' he thought, 'it's about time I checked out a few dealers to see what I can afford, possibly a Morris Minor or maybe a Sunbeam Talbot although those new Fords might be affordable.' As he was blissfully imagining himself and Mary with little Malcolm in the back seat, Don's phone rang.

'Don, could you come to my office I've had the Rotary President on the phone with an enquiry.' Tristan asked sounding excited. 'It's their annual Ladies Night and a venue they normally use has messed up there booking. He wants to know if we could accommodate them and realises it's short notice but they're desperate.'

'We'll help if we can Tristan, certainly.' Don asked for some details.'

Tristan consulted a scrap of paper with the information. 'It's for 50 guests, an evening function but here's the tricky bit; it's in three weeks' time, midweek.'

'One good thing is that Thursday night is a slow night, but 50 guests would be difficult to section off part of the restaurant, and we don't want to annoy our regulars. Mmmm.........h,' Don scratched his chin thinking, 'what we could to do for one evening Tristan is put our regular diners in one of the meeting rooms?' Don informed a relieved Manager.

'That's a great idea Don, and for the inconvenience, we could charge them slightly more as we're doing them a favour.'

Don's next two weeks went by in a flash, with the new menus to bed down, new staff to interview, and being pestered by the Rotary President with updates of the table plan for the Ladies Night Ball. He had seen little of Mary and Malcolm over this period and was looking forward to a few days off when business quietened down during the Autumn and before the wind-up into the Christmas maelstrom.

'It'll be nice to get away for a few days,' Mary said, looking forward with a rest from the Rubicon. 'You need to book a family room as Malcolm needs a separate bed as he's sprouting up.'

'All booked darling and ready to go. It couldn't come at a better time, now that Derek has develop into a competent deputy. He'll get useful management experience while I'm away.' Don confirmed happy to be spending a rare outing with his family.

A self-satisfied feeling that comes with a job well done was Don's thoughts as he straddled his brand new 350cc Rudge Ulster, kicking down to hear the engine catch, emitting an iconic growl as he eased out of the Cliffe car park and onto the links road towards Monkseaton. The evening had been a long and tiring one for his skilled restaurant team, now trained into a 4-star unit. Congratulation had been fulsome for Don by the Rotary president for a magnificent Ladies Night dinner with the result that their subsequent bi-monthly meetings would now be held at the Cliffe – another feather in Don's cap. He had now been restaurant manager of the Cliffe Hotel for three years after the car accident to his mentor Dominic and had developed French Cuisine within the Royal Restaurant into a place for the discerning diner over the wider North East area. His popularity as the maître d'hôtel, and the RAC's 4-star rating for the hotel meant that reservations were filled a month in advance. His thoughts were concentrated on their well-deserved break in Alston with his family as he roared passed the Crown hotel, heading home along the coast road to Sycamore Avenue in the driving rain, and then, oblivion!

CHAPTER 37

LIFE OR DEATH.

For three hours the 6 strong surgical team with 2 surgeons, the anaesthetist, head nurse, a junior nurse and an orderly worked tirelessly to save Don's life and his leg. It was now 5 a.m. and the exhausted team finally placed Don in a recovery room with a 24-hour watch.

'Thank you, team, we've done all we can.' said Martin Scatelli the surgeon. 'It's up to God and Don's powers of resilience as to whether he'll pull through.'

The bell jangled continuously in Don's head as the pain in his chest felt like a ton weight was pressing on him, but he couldn't stop the ringing.

The emergency bell had duty staff racing for the emergency room when Don's vital signs had flatlined. 'He's in cardiac arrest so help me! Open the gown, quickly now!' The senior locum shouted as he pressed down on Don's chest. The surge forced Don upwards, once; twice; three times as his pulse jumped back onto the monitor screens. 'OK Barry, get Mr Scatelli NOW, and tell him we've a code RED, he'll know what to do.'

'I was afraid the heart couldn't cope with the blood loss, coupled with the shock but well done you've got him started. I'll give him a dose of blood thinners which will ease the heart strain and keep our fingers crossed. I want a 24/ 7 watch on him.'

Don's life was hanging by a thread. The surgeons had battled through the night to save his leg but now they were in a battle to save his life. They had no choice but to amputate the limb just below the knee which would mean the joint would provide some flexibility to the leg once it had healed. Unfortunately, gangrene had beaten them because the tourniquet had been tied too tight and for too long, starving the leg of oxygen and circulation.

'He's certainly a fighter this one. By all accounts he should be dead with the amount of blood he's lost so let's see if we can pull him through – it will be a close one.' Mr Scatelli explained to his colleagues as the nurse wiped sweat from his brow.

Don's leg resembled something from a butcher's slab as they sewed up the wound again and wrapped it in antiseptic gauze after the second amputation and hopefully the last.

'Keep a close eye on him and the monitors nurse and let us know if there's any change in his condition. The sedation should keep him quiet throughout the night and we'll be back tomorrow morning to check on progress.'

Don's pulse and respiration was a little high as expected and beads of perspiration pearled his ashen face. His wife Mary had been informed of his condition but was not allowed to visit at this critical stage. The medical team were doing all they could to pull him through although their private thoughts were not optimistic. As the surgeon gingerly removed the gauze from Don's leg their worst fears were confirmed as they viewed the stump, now black and emitting the foul odour of gangrene once more.

'Let's get all the team together, we're in the last chance saloon I'm afraid. We're going to have to amputate again above the gangrene and hope we can save the leg and his life.'

They operated again to cut away the waste and bone close to the thigh and if that failed then there was no hope and Don would have lost his fight, and his life. His pulse began to race as the operation continued, requiring the anaesthetist to increase the oxygen/ morphine mix. After one and a half hours the exhausted team were done.

'That's it, it's up to Don now. We've done all we can so let's all pray he pulls through.'

Don's feeble cries alerted the duty nurse who rushed in to see what was happening. The pain seemed to engulf his entire body as he struggled to form something coherent that would bring a semblance of relief.

'Don't worry Pet we're here to help with the pain. You're doing well so I'll just increase the morphine dose and you should feel the difference shortly.' Wiping his brow as she tweaked the morphine. 'The surgeon will be along shortly to see you and check on your progress – you've been through the mangle alright, but you do look a little better.'

The waves of pain gradually eased with the increase in painkillers but his leg still itched like mad. Little did he realise there was no leg there – these were *'ghost nerves'* where the nerve endings retain some memory of their position in the leg. Don pulled the sheet aside to scratch the itching and let out a whimpered moan as he couldn't grasp that there was nothing there to see.

'Oh Christ, what have they done? Oh my God what a mess. What will Mary say when she sees this half-man who used to be her husband. How will we manage? I might as well be dead.'

Don was engulfed in self-pity as the promising life he had was gone forever. What was he to do? He just couldn't cope with the hopelessness of his situation. All his skills, training and hard work to land his plum job as restaurant manager at one of the best hotels in the region were laid to waste.

Mentally and physically exhausted, and completely distraught he just hoped this was a nightmare he might wake from of as he drifted back into a morphine inducted sleep.

The Voice startled him awake. **'Self-pity isn't going to help you get through this Don. God, or whoever is up there has given you a reprieve, even the surgeons had left your life to a higher order so snap out of it.'** The voice seemed so close that Don turned his head to see who was talking but he was alone in the ward. **'It's just you and me Don, no one else is here to help so decide what you're going to do because Mary and Malcolm are depending on you.'**

'I must be hallucinating' Don imagined, 'maybe it's the morphine or other painkillers but the voice was loud, I didn't imagine it.' He lay back and tried to make sense of what happened.

*

'It looks like we saved his leg but let's keep a close eye on his overall condition. The shock of that last amputation means he's not out of danger yet. We've got to get his temperature and pulse down nurse, so keep applying those cold compresses. You're doing a great job Sandra, and he certainly looks better than last night. The wound is pink and bright under the gauze, so fingers crossed. Let me know when he comes to, I need to brief him on his condition and it's not going to be easy.' Mr Scalatti and his team had with skill and tenacity managed to save his life by cutting away the last of the stinking gangrene to stabilise the wound.

Two hours later Don took the news of his amputated leg very hard, even knowing they had done all they could to save it. He was perhaps fortunate to still be in the land of the living and Mary was not going to be a widow after all. The surgeon said that once the stump had healed sufficiently with regular applications of surgical spirit he would be taken to London's Roehampton Centre and measured for a prosthetic limb. He would be mobile again – of a sort, but his days as a restaurant manager were over and done! Don wept silently, his throat tight and shoulders heaving at such an avoidable loss realising that his promising career was in ashes, his future bleak in the extreme.

*

While Don's future hung in the balance, he was unaware that the fate of Britain and that of the free world was also hanging by a thread as Hitler's forces steamrolled the Allies towards Calais. What had been called the *'phoney war'* had been a vacuum since the declaration and although there had been a few alerts with air raid sirens, they were largely false alarms with sporadic raids by the Luftwaffe. *'It'll be all over by Christmas,'* was a hoped for but unrealistic expectation by a few super-optimists, and quickly contradicted by news reports of Hitler's rapid advances through Europe, into Belgium and France. The Nazis had met little resistance in the process with their tanks and superior air power, labelled a *'Blitzkrieg'*. Churchill and the British war cabinet was frustrated and angry at France's abject retreat; Britain were now fighting a lone war.

France had capitulated with the collapse of the much-vaunted Siegfried line and on May 6th, 1940, France gave up as a fighting force with the allies running for cover, desperately looking for a way out. Almost 400,000 mainly British troops were stranded on Dunkirk's beaches, hoping for a miracle escape to England across the Channel's 22 miles. They were hemmed in by Axis forces and strafed by Stuka dive bombers with little cover for those waiting to be rescued. Meanwhile the British rearguard was putting up what resistance they could muster by holding back the German tidal wave in a vain attempt to protect the vulnerable beached masses.

A *'miracle'* of sorts occurred when the war department issued a plea for boat or ship owners to head for Dunkirk and rescue as many as they could. Within hours of the announcement a veritable Armada of crafts of all shapes and sizes headed towards Dunkirk and despite being bombed by cynical German aircraft attacking these defenceless heroes, almost 340,000 British and French troops returned to Dover to fight again. The British public celebrated as though the war had been won! But like Britain, Don's fight for survival was far from over.

CHAPTER 38

Dawn had broken over Roehampton in South West London and home of the National Artificial Limb Centre which overlooked Richmond Park, bathed in early morning sunshine after a refreshing downpour. There was with just a hint of spring in the grass scented air as Don awoke from his first day at the centre, hoping to be more mobile with an artificial limb. During his introduction he had been measured and told his new leg would be attached with a harness, clamped onto his stump which was hardening up with surgical spirit. His earlier suicidal thoughts had moderated somewhat to bouts of depression and despair as to his prospects which, on these occasions seemed hopeless, although **The Voice's** appearance had served to remind him of his obligations to his family. Don leant back on the feather pillows, blew his cheeks with hands clasped behind his head thought of the cold, damp, foggy sea frets he would be experiencing at home and sighed. Gradually he was coming to terms with his disability, there was no other way. Mary and his family had been wholly supportive along with the staff and management of the Cliffe Hotel, his former employers who had also been financially generous.

Cream and green made up the colour scheme of his functional room softened by a colourful rug and printed scenes of London parks and the obligatory herd of fallow deer that roamed unmolested in the nearby Royal Park. Mary had also brightened the room with a spray of early daffodils on her visit the day before as she had managed to stay with a cousin nearby in Ealing.

The surgeons had with skill and tenacity saved his life and it was now up to the medical technicians and engineers to construct a workable leg out of metal, resin and leather. Three months had elapsed since the accident but the insurance claim still had not been honoured due, he was told to the car driver being uninsured. As a result, household expenses had been stretched to the limit even with the generous help from family, friends and the Cliffe Hotel, averting what would have been a desperate fight for Mary to support the Sullivan household. Her income from her part-time job at Dobson's grocery, failed to bridge the financial gap and a bank loan was a non-sequitur as they had little collateral having to move to a council house unable to pay the mortgage. Government help in these straightened times of the early war years was limited to military based hardship cases to which Don's situation didn't apply.

*

'How are we today Don, or more importantly how's the leg? Let's have a look.' Gladys Sidebottom the medical technician asked, smiling a lop-sided greeting. She was a buxom lady with a larger-than-life personality to match, born from years of chatting and cheering up difficult patients. Her five years at Roehampton had seen her rise from a standard orderly to a senior technician by the zealous application to her City & Guilds nursing and physiotherapy qualifications and her ability to master the intricacies of limb technology, still in its development stages.

'The stump seems to be less sensitive and getting tougher with the spirit applications, I know, twice daily Gladys, I don't forget. How long before we fit the limb, because my AWOL leg's still itching, will that disappear?' Don asked more in hope than expectation.

'Ooh! Don't get too excited Don you've a long way to go but it's a good sign that you're anxious to think ahead. It's difficult to say as regards the itch, because everyone's different but try to disassociate yourself with some other activity – a lot is mental.' Gladys suggested, 'You're right, the stump is firming up nicely so later this morning we'll get you to the lab. for a fitting with a temporary one. Are you OK to get there on crutches?' Don's agreement was born of his regular practice of haring up and down the corridors to the consternation of staff and the amusement of patients. *'You're not training for the Olympics, are you Don?'* A grinning nurse would call.

*

Don's limb had taken three weeks to construct, based on a variety of measurements of Don's physiology and leg stump. The gleaming piece of metal, leather, resin, studs and straps was ready for action. Don's whole leg had been amputated so the hip joint was incorporated into the limb itself and flexed at the hip and knee with two catches that were either released for sitting or engaged for standing. The stump sat in a basin of soft leather inside a resin form and securely attached by shoulder and waist straps that could be adjusted by the wearer.

'How does that feel on your stump Don?' The technician enquired looking up, gently offering the limb to the recumbent patient, watched attentively by Gladys. 'Now release the catches and slowly sit down, we'll be supporting you.' Don succeeded with help and reversed the process to stand up.

'Not too bad at all considering,' As Don grimaced, the nerves reacting to the limb's intrusion onto the tender stump.

'That's very good as it's the first time, so let's get the straps adjusted.' Gladys said confidently as she wanted Don to see if he was managing the discomfort. She had already recognised a motivated kindred spirit in Don. Now secured by the straps around his waist and shoulders, Don was eased up to a standing position between the parallel bars which he gripped anxiously and too tightly.

'Excellent, well-done Don, just rest there for a minute and flex until you feel comfortable to move.' Gladys encouraged Don with a reassuring hand on his shoulder.

'It feels really weird, almost as though I had my leg back.' Don said smiling with relief at his gleaming appendage. 'Should I try a couple of steps do you think?' Looking at Gladys for a reassuring nod.

'Why not, it's your leg so hold on tight and move the limb forward slowly we'll make sure you stay upright.' Beads of sweat broke out on Don's brow as he clenched his teeth, gripped the bars tighter and with an immense effort attempted to move but he couldn't. He screwed up his lips learnt forward and with another push tried again. Nothing!

'Jesus Christ, I can't do it Gladys it won't move and I'm giving it all I can.' Don cried out in frustration as the technician wiped his brow with a damp cloth.

'Have a rest Don, it's early days and getting you upright is progress. Your body hasn't yet come to terms with the fact it's a leg short. It's a mental thing so let's have a cup of tea and we'll have another try if you're up to it. What do you say?' Giving up so soon wasn't an option. He had given it his best shot and there was no movement so how much pain was he to endure to make some progress – he'd just have to find out?

CHAPTER 39

'OK here we go again Don. Let's try leaning forward on the bars and see if you can drag the limb towards you. Once you've got some movement, however small it's progress, incremental steps, that's how you've got to think.' Gladys' determined smile gave him a boost. Someone once told him you could eat an elephant if you ate small enough amounts over a long period. This was his mantra from now on. *'I'm eating an elephant! I'm eating an elephant.'* Don gritted is teeth as he repeated the mantra.

'I don't think I'm going to be able to walk with this leg, it's too heavy and painful when I put any pressure on it. The joint catches keep sticking. I'll be better off on the crutches, because I won't have the pain.

'Don't be a wimp Don, you've had bigger problems that this,' *The Voice, said pulling Don up short.* **'Do you want to be hopping around like Long John Silver for the rest of your life? All you'll need is a parrot on your shoulder!'**

Don couldn't belief he'd heard **The Voice** responding to his frustrations and wondered if he was losing his marbles and decided to test this unnerving exchange. Don looked around to see if he was being observed. Are you real or is it my overactive imagination playing tricks?' Don whispered to himself.

'OK, if you're right I need to get a grip and give it my best shot. After all these people are doing their best for me so I suppose I should make the effort. It can't get any worse.'

'Don't bet on it Don, it will get worse but you have to tough it out to get back to some sort of normality,' *The Voice* warned.

'Yes! You've got some movement.' The technician cried out as Don moved the limb and grunted in agreement, sweat pouring from his face as he dragged another step.

'That was five steps,' he counted to himself, 'another two and I'm at the end of the bars,' he thought as he heaved in a breath and forced the limb forward again.

'That's enough for today but you can leave the limb on for a while to let the stump settle in.' Gladys suggested, as he relaxed in the wheelchair. Back along the corridor Don was applauded by the patients.

The limb was now part of him, an assembly of mixed materials and a moulded resin foot. Care had to be taken with the catches when standing or sitting otherwise a tumble could result, as Don found out more than once.

The Roehampton technicians and engineers had certainly earned their corn in creating the false leg so Don decided to honour them by giving the leg a name; but what name could do it justice?

*

The Daily Mail's front-page headline covered the allies advance in the dessert where Rommel had been repulsed by a determined masterstroke initiated by the newly formed Special Boat Service and followed through by the tanks of the 8th Army, supremely lead by Field Marshall Montgomery. Don read the piece again and thought 'that's it, I'll call my new leg 'Montgomery' or Monty' for short, in honour of the army warrior. He lay back, grinning with pleasure at his initiative and looked admiringly again at his leg in a new light. 'Yes Monty, we'll do alright together, once I get to know you that is.'

'You've got me now and I'll expect you to look after me.' Don was reminded, *'I quite like the name although I would have chosen a more dynamic one, something with a bit more bite but I suppose it could have been worse.'* Monty squeaked as Don eased the joints. *'You're going to have to put more effort in before I'm fully functional, I can't abide whingers.'*

'Did Monty speak.' Don asked, head in hands, wondering if he was losing it – a talking limb?'

'They can't normally but we're in an unusual situation here and even I can see you're going to need a lot more effort if we're to get through.'

Maybe Monty's been taking lessons from **The Voice** Don thought scratching his head, his brows wrinkled in disbelief.

*

Don continued to struggle because over his recumbent weeks in hospital the left leg muscle had atrophied, and his general fitness had nose-dived so no wonder his initial forays with Monty had been so frustrating. The Centre's physio, Hamid had given him a series of strengthening exercises and now he could see gradual improvement having travelled a length and back on the parallel bars with 3 reps. of 10.

'It's up to you to build that leg because it had to do the work of two. These new exercises will strengthen your upper body and arms. Any improvement in your forward movement with the crutches will depend on your shoulder and arm muscles. You won't get so tired or burnt-out as you did in the first weeks.' Hamid said. 'But you must keep up these daily exercises. 'How much?'' He was asked, ' Your body will tell you when you're overstepped the mark although most patients do too little or short-change the routines and ultimately pay the price. Another procedure that's going to help with your cardio-vascular improvement is swimming. Yes, you heard me right – swimming is the best all round exercise you can get. We'll get you started with Helen the swim instructor for 15 minutes initially – how does that sound?'

'How can I swim with only one leg Hamid? I wasn't that good a swimmer with two!'

'Don't worry about that Don we've had patients with no legs ripping up the pool after a few lessons with Helen.' Hamid laughed. 'And that's the truth.'

Helen was a thirties something stunner with a personality to match and although she was wearing a T shirt and shorts Don could visualise a very attractive set of attributes underneath – as his weeks of forced abstinence sparked a starved libido.

'Now pay attention Don.' Helen snapped as she realised Don's mind was elsewhere and knew his mind wasn't on swimming. 'Let's take the crutches and Bob will help you sit on the edge of the pool. You'll be up to your waist so hold onto the side with your leg on the outside and hop across the width slowly until you get the feel. This will do two things; help with your balance and strengthen leg muscles at the same time – can you try that?'

'Boy, I could try anything with you Helen.' Don imagined. 'OK, I'll give it a go.' Spluttering as he lost his footing and swallowed a mouthful of chlorinated water. After a couple of widths of the pool Don was hopping along like an energised crab.

'A couple more widths Don and then we'll have a go at swimming with a buoyancy aid to see how you go.' The swim aid was a link of cork squares tied together with some twine, wrapped in a waterproof cloth about 5 foot long and worn across the chest and underneath the arms. 'Don, walk with the aid a couple of minutes until you get used to it.'

After fitting the aid Don was able to float forward then kick with his leg and get some movement. It was a glorious feeling suspended and moving in an environment he hadn't experienced for many years. 'I had to lose a leg to feel it but better late than ……..,' as he swung his arms vigorously the endorphins kicked in and a wave of euphoria swept over him.

'Hey that's almost a width you've swum so let's have another 10 minutes towards the deep-end, up to your chin – you'll get more buoyancy there and then we're done.' Helen called out, delighted with Don's excellent progress. 'Maybe we can try without the aid tomorrow,' Helen thought to herself 'this is one motivated individual.'

*

Back in his room Don found a message from his wife Mary that Gracie his mother was in hospital after a fall and was poorly. She was in South Shield's St. Swithin's hospital Ward 410. At five that afternoon Mary would be phoning so Don made a note to get the details. His mother was only sixty but had been troubled with arthritis for ten years and had difficulty walking but declined using a stick because, being a resolute lady didn't want the neighbours to think she was 'soft'. Now the chickens had come to roost and she was going to have to succumb to the indignity of crutches or god help us, a walking frame! This was dependant on her overcoming the shock and trauma of her fall but the signs weren't good.

'Hello Don, how are you? How's the fitting going? I got your letter yesterday and it sounds like you're in good hands there.' Mary's voice was heaven to Don.

'Yes Mary I'm improving, but how are you bearing up? Is Mam going to be alright?'

'We're managing but I'm not sure about Gracie, she's in a lot of pain although she's putting a brave face on it. The surgeon has put a plaster around her leg and they're hoping it'll knit together with the screws they've put in place. It's going to take weeks before she's released and you know what self-reliant person she is. Sidney and Sadie are helping so we're hoping for the best.' Mary didn't want this extra worry on top of Don's incarceration, but family issues had priority in Mary's book.

'The good news is that I'm now walking with Monty, that's my new leg and it's an amazing construction, made to measure. If my progress continues, I might be transferred for the final assessment to a local clinic in Newcastle.'

'Oh Don, that would be so good, I've really missed you, we've all missed you.' Don could hear her sobbing.

'Don't worry Mary it won't be long, and we'll sort everything out when I'm back. I'll chase up the insurance claim as a priority because they're dragging their feet. I'll tell the lawyer to threaten legal action if they don't sort the claim soon. Cheer up it's not like you – listen I'll write you a letter tomorrow after I've contacted the lawyer and you can let me know what progress Mam is making, alright?'

'Alright Don I know, it's not like me but with one thing and another. I can't wait to see you again Don.' Mary swallowed hard her lips pressed resolutely.

With similar endearments Don ended the call and vowed to sort out the insurance and put more effort into his recovery, that way they might be glad to move him out quicker as bed places were a priority, especially as war casualties were building up.

CHAPTER 40

Don couldn't wait for Gladys to complete his release form before his return to the North East. They had already agreed his aftercare with the physio team at Don's local Longbenton centre.

'I'm truly amazed at Don's recovery since his arrival, five weeks ago when he looked like death warmed up and thought we would struggle to get him into shape.' Gladys blew her cheeks and shook her blonde curls in disbelief. 'Now look at him. He's put on over a stone, built up the left leg thigh and calf muscles and can swim unaided a length of the pool.

Not only that, 'Monty' gets him around with only a walking stick, and I'll bet in a couple of weeks he won't even need that!' Helen smiled at the memory of Don discarding the swim aid too early and swallowing a fair amount of the pool.

'You know, on that first day trying to get some movement with the limb on the parallel bars I really thought he was going nowhere and would be consigned to crutches, but his determination and resolve pulled him through.' Hamid recalled Don's superhuman efforts to get some movement.

'I can't thank you enough Gladys, I wouldn't have made it through without your support and encouragement.' As he grasped her hands.

'Don't put yourself down Don, you did the hard work; I was only there to keep your nose to the grindstone.' Replied Gladys smiling. 'Now when you get back home keep up the good work, you've still a way to go. I don't want to hear you've been skipping your physio regime. We'll expect a regular progress report and a visit in due course if Mr Churchill allows. Anyway, have an uneventful journey to the North East and give my best wishes to Mary.'

*

Although Roehampton was marginally outside of the London Blitz zone German bombers would routinely unload their destruction and create craters around Richmond when harassed by RAF fighters and flak. Don's journey home necessitated travelling through these bombed areas into London's Kings Cross for the LNER service to York and Newcastle, and at each stage travel passes were closely inspected either by the Boys in Blue or MPs (miliary police). Even one-legged spies and 5th columnists had to be checked!

*

As Don rattled over the foggy Tyne's High-Level bridge, his hearts sang as the loco screeched into Newcastle Central, then by local rail to Whitley Bay where, waiting expectantly on the platform was Mary, little Malcolm, his sister Sadie and elder brother Sidney waving balloons and scarves, bringing a lump to Don's throat and a tear quickly wiped away. With some difficulty he managed Monty's catches and gave the crutches to Sidney, while Mary's embrace underlined her relief and his love.

'You'll see quite a bit of bomb damage especially near the coast, compliments of the Luftwaffe, and there's been lots of civilian casualties.' Sidney added. 'Those bloody Nazis, I could strangle.'

'Language, Sidney, language,' Corrected Mary.

'Apologies Mary, but I've seen so much devastation and injuries.'

'Why aye, they were after the shipyards, docks and the Reyrolls engineering works where they do a lot of war production – tanks and armoured vehicles like.' Sadie added. 'A friend of mine works on the assembly line, but I shouldn't really talk about it – apparently Adolf has his spies everywhere. Have you seen the posters 'CARELESS TALK COSTS LIVES!'?

'Yes, and you should be setting a better example Sadie.' Mary admonished her with a frown.

Don sat back in his seat letting the Geordie conversational dialect flow over him like a salve. What a relieve it was to be back on Tyneside with his family and to pal up with his buddies at the Cliffe Hotel. Now he was mobile his priority was to resolve the accident insurance claim, as his solicitor had been treading water.

During his Roehampton incarceration Don had decided to contact his local Civil Defence Volunteer office to see how he could help with the war effort. Until he was signed off by the local artificial limb clinic he would have to put in some hard yards with his physio. regime to be considered for employment.

'Don we're home.' Mary nudged him out of his private meanderings as they passed the newly built WD & HO Wills tobacco factory, which had provided badly needed jobs for over 500 unemployed, mostly women. He smiled and gave her a hug thinking how much he had missed Mary's warm body next to his. At times he had given anxious consideration as to how his amputation would affect their sex lives, but Mary's reaction two days later confirmed he shouldn't have worried.

Bomb damage was all too obvious as they neared the coast with rows of houses ripped apart, their private insides of peeling wallpapers and gaping fireplaces that had warmed an unsuspecting family only a short time earlier. Civilian targets were now part of Hitler's plan to destabilize the population and lower morale. His diabolical campaign would only strengthen a collective resolve to survive – how little he understood of Britain's indomitable spirit.

*

The Longbenton's limb clinic was a smaller offshoot of the Roehampton Centre, but nevertheless had a full complement of technicians, physios and specialist advisors, many having been trained at Roehampton. Mable Turnbull had worked there before decamping to the North East to marry a Geordie physio who she had met on a training course and had fallen in love. A receptionist greeted Don warmly with a 'why eye hinnie (how are you)' Geordie welcome and said Mable would be with him shortly handing Don his file with tea and biscuits, without being asked.

'Thanks very much, no sugar please.' Replied Don eyeing the rather attractive receptionist, holding onto his winsome smile a little too long. 'How long have you been at the clinic?'

Before he could pursue the conversation further a door behind the receptionist opened and revealed a lady in her late thirties with auburn hair to her shoulders, full lips undecorated and a nose with a slight upturn at the point. Her most attractive features were her high cheekbones, above which were smiling light brown eyes covered by square red framed glasses. She was covered head to calve in a regulation white coat wearing polished brown mid-heel brogues projecting an aura of a very attractive but efficient operator.

'Good morning Don? I see you've brought Monty with you.' Mabel was obviously a lady who came to the point and had obviously done her homework on Don. 'How are you managing with the limb? I've heard a great deal of your exploits from Gladys.' Don was momentarily at a loss for words by Mabel's initiative and groundwork on his case.

'Er, that is, I'm fine and Monty's working out well apart from a few mechanical issues. Maybe I can show you what the problems are.' Don tried to prise back some control, but it didn't work.

'All in good time Don, first let's go to my office, I have some questions regarding your movement and stability so can you bring me up to speed with your five weeks at Roehampton because in the relatively short time there your progress has been impressive. After that we can go to the assembly room and talk to the limb technician about Monty's issues.

'Well thank you but it was all down to Gladys and her team that got me through some sticky patches, especially with the exercises in the pool.'

'Ah yes, your success in the pool was something of a surprise. In my experience I can't recall anyone who had been able to achieve those distances over such a short time. That must have taken some effort Don.'

'It was only right to make the effort when the team were so committed.' Don replied earnestly.

'Yes, they're a good team. We'll build on your leg muscles over the next four weeks based on the weekly gym programme and once a week at the public baths in Preston Village, which I understand is close your home.' Mabel explained that Don would continue his recovery at 'no nonsense' level. 'Any questions Don? No? OK, let's give you a tour and then to the workshop to sort out Monty.'

The facility included a well-equipped gym with a range of apparatus with which Don was familiar. There was also a small café which provided opportunities to discuss issues with other limb patients and operational staff. The Centre was a breath of fresh air in providing Don with some kind of normality, being with others who had to overcome the horror of lost limbs, some worse than his.

'I'll be in touch with Gladys regarding your progress and she asked me to remind you to get in touch, otherwise you'll have me to contend with.' Mabel smiled as she handed Don a programme for physio and swimming. 'Right, let's sort out Monty before I forget.' The workroom was littered with bits of arms, legs and limbs of all shapes and sizes for all ages and looked like a film set for a horror picture. 'Hi Mark let me introduce to the famous Don and Monty, it seems he has a couple of niggling problems which I'm sure you can sort so I'll leave him with you' Mabel said. 'Could you direct him back to my office please when you're finished?'

'Absolutely Mabel. Now what's the problem with Monty? It certainly looks like a full-on piece of engineering and a credit to its creator down at Roehampton.'

'The catch on the side that engages the knee lock. It sometimes slips out when its locked and the leg collapses. I bit the dust a couple of times but now I always check it's properly engaged.'

'OK, could you take Monty off and I'll check a couple of other parts that could give you problems. With the limb on the bench, Mark soon replaced the catch with a tighter spring and checked the hip catch. 'So, is that it Don? Generally, I'd say Monty's is in good shape overall.' Mark stood back and gave his workmanship a final inspection. 'Anything else?'

'Ah yes, could you adjust the placement of the straps around the stump with more holes as the padding has settled since the first fitting?'

Mark made short work of the adjustment and escorted Don back to Mabel who confirmed the rehabilitation programme and then bid her, 'au revoir,' who responded in kind, 'bon voyage Monty.'

CHAPTER 41

'OK Bertram, you have all the evidence in support of the claim and I'm not accepting anything less than the £2,500. If Fidelity won't play and want to act stupidly, they could be slapped with additional costs by our local magistrates who are not enamoured with these big insurers bullying clients.' Don had the bit between his teeth and Bertram reluctantly agreed to serve notice of court action if they refused to cooperate.

Like many insurance companies they love taking your premiums but when it comes to settling, they're scrooges, as Don discovered. His solicitor had claimed a sum of £2,500 but the company, Fidelity Trust wanted to reduce the amount to £1,900 citing driving negligence by Don that he was driving too fast for the conditions. However, a statement from the car driver who admitted he had not stopped at the intersection and written evidence from the ambulance crew who were first on the scene stated from skid marks it was clear that the driver had been travelling too fast for the weather and road conditions and hadn't stopped at the intersection. Don's solicitor, Bertram Creedy spread out the file for reference.

Fidelity's lawyers weren't in the least worried about a court appearance and were confident of a settlement in their favour but as Don predicted, the magistrates were furious that the matter had come to court in the first place. After seeing the evidence supporting Don, duly added another £500 to the claim as a penalty for wasting the court's time. The chief magistrate added a warning to Fidelity. 'If this company brings to court any future cases with such a lack of cognisance as they have today, I shall hold them in contempt of court.'

*

'What an amazing result Don, it's barely believable but let's celebrate with a bottle of bubbly because I think you deserve it for standing up to them.' Mary said proudly, giving Don a deserved hug and nearly knocking him and Monty off-balance.

'Tell you the truth Mary I had a serious case of butterflies before the verdict especially the way the magistrate's looked at me before their verdict and thought I might have been a little overconfident'. Don felt Monty had played its part in getting the sympathy vote from the magistrates.

Life for Don, Mary and little Malcolm had improved immeasurably with a very healthy bank balance to pay their debtors. Mary was now the Assistant Manager at Dobson's store and the additional income enabled them the luxuries they had been denied since Don's accident. An automatic toaster stood proudly on the kitchen top which Malcolm polished daily while underneath an electric washing machine was the envy of Mary's neighbours.

Don was actively looking for a job while still engaged with Longbenton's physio programme but most jobs at the Employment Centre required more mobility than Don had to offer, other than those that required zero mental effort. The war now was at a critical stage with sirens heralding nightly visits by the Luftwaffe, and speedy retreats to the corrugated iron Anderson shelter in the garden for the family and any neighbours they could fit in. The cramped, damp, cold and malodorous space was dimly lit by a single oil lamp, their only source of illumination. This desperate hiding place was always accompanied by the fear of a direct hit as had happened to a family two streets away. The attending fire-service could find nothing but a large crater that been the home of a family of five. The Stuarts had only recently moved to Tyneside from Dundee where the husband had been employed in a shipyard near Jarrow and this had been their welcome.

Gallows humour was one way of easing the tension but it also to help pass the time. One example involved a Junkers 44 bomber that was caught in the searchlights beam at which point the aircraft dropped a landmine. It was later revealed that the explosion had demolished the church in a nearby village where the organist was said to have been playing *'Nearer my God to Thee'*!

Sometimes it could be up to four hours before the 'All Clear' sirens heralded blessed relief to escape tired, stiff and hungry to find some warmth and nourishment, only to hear the news of another spate of casualties in the area. After one such disturbed night a note had been left for Don to call at the Employment exchange. The job offered was an ARP (Air Raid Protection) Warden whose role was to patrol the streets for any infringements of the black-out regulations and to ensure that the public were safely under cover when the air-raid sirens blared their warning. Although the pay was meagre and part-time the regular exercise would help with his physio programme and his patrol area was close to home. Little did Don realise that all too soon he would be involved in a conflagration, compliments of the Luftwaffe.

CHAPTER 42

'You look quite smart in your ARP's helmet and matching siren suit. But are those shoes comfortable Don?' Mary pointed to Don's two highly polished toecaps.

'Don't you mean 'shoe' Mary, or should Monty have a say?' Don smiled at Mary's faux pas.

'Why not? He as much as part of your life now as anything else.' Mary responded giving him a dig.

'They look just like my football boots Dad.' Chimed in Malcolm.

'That'll be enough funnies from you, young man. This is a serious government issue pair of shoes on important war work, so have some respect. Yes Mary, they are quite comfortable and will be better once broken in. For my first session to-night I'll just take the walking stick as Monty is working well after his maintenance at Longbenton. I can always return for the crutches.'

'Your whistle and nightstick, sandwiches and flask are in your haversack – I put them in earlier. Where are you going tonight?' Mary asked as she adjusted the strap and kissed him affectionately on the cheek. 'Don't go arresting any German parachutist on your first outing will you - that's the police's job.' Mary's impish humour was accompanied by a gentle squeeze.

'I'll be patrolling Sycamore, Maple, Oak, Beverley and Ash Avenues, where I'll be meeting up with Fred at about 8 p.m. and returning via the Quarry by midnight.' Don explained hoping his first night wouldn't be too exciting. How wrong he would be.

*

A full moon dashed his hopes as only an hour into his shift, the sirens wailed, screeching a warning for anyone out and about. Don directed several pedestrians to the nearest public shelters and for good measure blew a piercing blast on his Acme Thunderer turning heads of those scampering home or into the shelters. Within minutes the drone of aircraft engines accompanied a flight of German bombers lit menacingly by the searchlight's glare. Don counted at least a dozen Dorniers and Junkers 88's accompanied by some Fokke-Wolfs for protection.

Anti-aircraft batteries now had good line of sight on the marauders and starbursts of flak soon crackled overhead and caught one of bombers which peeled off to head home. Its payload of high-explosive bombs and incendiary devices were not going back to Berlin, as it jettisoned a reign of death and carnage onto the unsuspecting civilian population below. As the bombs exploded not many streets away Don could feel the percussive shock as the air was suck upwards only a few streets away and close to his home. As fast as possible Don hurried towards the rising smoke two streets away as a fire engine blared it warning and raced past, firemen hanging from its platform. One house had been demolished with a direct hit while its neighbour had a gaping hole at its side, the roof tilted as a crazy angle and in imminent danger of collapse. Don was briefly rooted watching the unfolding devastation until a woman and child emerged from the smoke and dust staggering towards him arms outstretched, their clothes spotted with burn holes and in tatters, the result of the incendiary that was still burning fiercely in the ruins. The woman, in her early thirties had her arm wrapped around the six-year-old girl who was crying 'Where's my Daddy, where's my Daddy?' Don led her to relative safety covering her with his WD waterproof. Acrid fumes from the smoking timbers wafted over the pair making them cough and gag until his flask of tea brought some temporary relief.

'My husband's still in there but I'm not sure he was able to get into the Anderson before we we're hit; can you do anything?' She cried, pleading through the coughs and tear-streaked face.

'Here, take the flask and I'll see if I can find a fireman, I'm a bit restricted.' Don replied surveying the scene from hell. Surely there must be emergency personnel nearby as he gingerly stepped over the rubble and around the bombed house. Some unidentifiable body parts littered the gaping hole where the house had stood, his mind cast back fleetingly to his own ravaged leg after his accident. Don saw a policeman leading an elderly man covered in brick dust, his broken arm hanging limply by his side and blew his whistle as the policeman sat the man on a broken wall.

'There's a mother and child around the corner from the bombed-out house, but her husband is still inside so could you see if he's OK? As you can see, I'm not too mobile. I'll stay with this man and make a sling for his arm.'

'Yes, good idea because everyone from this house is beyond help. I'm Graham from the Hillheads police station and got the call as the sirens started.' He said helping the man to his feet. 'We're just going around the corner to help another casualty.'

The old man, mother and daughter were neighbours so were able to take some comfort in that they had survived. The policeman made his way through the smoke into the ruined house checking with each step on the potential dangers and disappeared emerging minutes later helping a disoriented man to safety. His head was badly cut and bleeding, his clothes in tatters from brick and wood splinters which had pierced his skin as though shot by a 40-gauge shot gun.

Despite his injuries the husband wrapped his arms around his family crying in relief for their safety. 'Oh Gordon, Gordon you're safe, we were out of our minds with worry.' His wife cried dissolving into floods of tears.' Her distressed sobbing set off the daughter in similar vein, 'Oh Daddy, Daddy I love you.' Amid all this uncontrolled emotion Don had a job keeping a dry eye but asserted himself by making the sling and patching up this man's abrasions from his First Aid kit. Maybe you can send someone to escort this group to the local rescue centre – there's one in Maple Avenue.' Don suggested, checking on the family who were still in shock.

'Yes, well done Don I'll send someone asap.' As he set off in a measured stride.

Don did his best to keep their spirits up as they waited for the rescue services with amusing tales from his days as a waiter when he was at the Adelphi Hotel at St. Annes on Sea which had them all laughing and amused, briefly forgetting their dire circumstances.

'One day we played a trick on a new waiter who was full of himself and thought he was the *'bees' knees.''* Don explained. 'The trick was to lay a full table with settings then, holding the tablecloth's edge pull it quickly away and all the table wear remained in place – magic! When the upstart's turn came, the other waiters turned the cloth over when he was distracted placing the cloth's edge upwards so when he pulled cloth away, what happened? Yes, all the dishes and cutlery crashed onto the dining room floor. The young man's face was a picture, eyes wide in disbelief at what had happened. 'Oh dear, oh dear, oh dear sang the other waiters,' laughing out loud, 'that's a pretty penny you'll have to pay and no mistake!''

'And did he have pay for it out of his wages?' Asked the young girl in a voice that echoed some concern for the young trainee. 'Have you any more stories mister?' Now totally absorbed in Don's reminiscing.

'Served him right!' The old man argued, nodding in agreement with the life lesson handed out.

'Do you want to hear another one?'

'Oh yes please came the collective answer.'

'At another hotel, the Grand in Harrogate which is very posh they had a man who served Turkish coffee. It's quite an elaborate task served at the table on a trolley with waiter dressed as a Turk with a turban, baggy trousers and pointy shoes, just like Aladdin. Do you know who Aladdin was?' Don asked the girl. 'Oh yes he was in the same play with Ali Barbour and the Forty Thieves.' She replied confidently.

'That's right.' Replied Don hiding a grin. 'The Turk always served the coffee at the end of the meal and because it's served last, he often got the tips which he should have been shared but often kept them to himself. 'He used a little stove lit by methylated spirits, which heats the coffee so the waiters decided to teach him a lesson for keeping the tips. Do you know what they did?' Shake of heads. 'They diluted the meths with water when he was off duty so the lamp wouldn't light and he couldn't make the coffee so didn't get any tips. The waiters had a good laugh at his expense as they watched him turn red in frustration. He realised what had happened and thereafter always shared any tips he received, and, like Ali Barbour had learnt his lesson.' Don asked if there was any moral to the story?

'Oh yes!' Said the wife after the laughter and warm applause had subsided. 'You should always treat your colleagues as you wish to be treated or you will suffer in the long run.'

'How very true, I was just going to say that.' The old man added disingenuously as two rescuers arrived with a wheelchair.

'Right let's be having you, we've got some warm clothes, tea and crumpets for you all at the centre. Are you alright to walk dear?' The rescuer asked the wife.

'Oh yes thank you I can manage a short walk; I'm feeling much better now we're still a family. Thank you, warden, for all your help and stories – I'll tell my friends how you kept us going. 'Goodbye warden, echoed the little girl, I love you.' As she gave Don a farewell hug.

'I can't thank you enough for what you did warden – you saved my life.' The husband said his voice choking as he shook Dave's hand and a hug for good measure.

Don turned away to finish his shift watching the group slowly vanish out of sight through the drifting smoke and gloom and realised that at last he was doing something worthwhile for his community and took a deep breath.

Don's remaining two hours of his patrol revealed the true devastation of the 20-minute raid with most streets in his area suffering moderate to severe property damage. His report recorded five bombed out houses which included the one where he was able to help, ten partially damaged which were no longer habitable and at least twenty with blown out windows from bomb blasts. It was a sobering account considering how small an area he had covered. How many would be homeless from the wider area he wondered? Being on the fringes of the Tyne River's industrial target areas, they could count themselves lucky as they had sufficient aid stations to cope for the homeless and injured. Don would be glad to get back home, get Monty off and have some badly needed sustenance. All his supplies had been given away to the recued families. Britain's RAF attack squadrons of Spitfires and Hurricanes were thin on the ground in the North East, being prioritised for the London Blitz. Other towns and cities like Hull and Coventry had to rely on anti-aircraft ordnance, barrage balloons and searchlights as their defence which was woefully inadequate and were subsequently devastated by the Luftwaffe.

'We'll just have to muddle through somehow and pray for England's lousy weather to be our saviour.' Said one anti-aircraft gunner to Don as he passed by the battery.

CHAPTER 43

'I was so worried when the sirens went knowing you were out there with only a helmet for protection. I could tell the raid was close by, in fact we heard that some houses near the quarry were hit.' Mary hugged Don with relief. 'Did you see a lot of damage on your rounds?' Mary asked, after hearing Don's account of the bombed-out family.

'Were there any German bombers Dad and were there many, and what kind were they Dad?' Demanded Malcolm tugging on his greatcoat with his eyes covered by wearing Don's ARP helmet.

'There were quite a few Dorniers and I did see one get hit.

'When the sirens started we went into our shelter Dad, with the Fitzpatricks 'cos they don't have one, and Irene read me a Rupert story when the bombing started and I wasn't frightened. And they brought us some tea and cake - Mrs Fitzpatrick did, with icing on it. Wasn't that nice of them Dad?' Malcolm like most youngsters seemed unphased by the raids.

'It certainly was Malcolm, very generous of them wasn't it Mary? Now if you'll excuse me I must see to Monty, he's very tired and needs a rest. 'Don couldn't wait to take off the limb and give his stump a lengthy massage. Gradually, the scarred stump's skin was slowly hardening and developing a durable base.

'I'll come upstairs with some tea and sandwiches Don, you must be starving after that experience which I hope won't be every night.' Mary said over her shoulder as she went into the pantry for the bread and cheese. Don gazed at Mary's cherubic skin, auburn hair, tiny dimples and slim frame and thought, 'I have a wife in a million.'

As Don removed Monty and checked the catches, dripping oil into the joints he suddenly realised his proximity to the devastation; best not to regale Mary with his close calls in future.

'I could have sworn there was some milk in that bottle. Malcolm, have you drunk all the milk?

'Sorry Mam' came the reply. 'I was thirsty after the bombers had left.' Malcolm wasn't sorry because his Mam should have ordered more from the milkman, but he felt guilty knowing he had emptied the bottle.

'I'll see Mrs Heads next door for some milk, won't be a minute, I just hope she has some spare.' Mary gave her son a warning look.

Mrs Heads was a mother of two, Brian, about Malcolm's age and Evelyn with a husband down the Howden pit so they had plenty of coal for their continuous fire in the living room. Sofie Heads was a 35-year-old, big boned, large breasted woman who opened the door, the ever-present Players Full Strength cigarette dangling from her thin lips. 'Oh! Hello Pet, what's up, do come in?' Sofie asked evenly, cigarette smoke curling into a squinting eye. Mary didn't smoke, never had and couldn't understand why someone needed to chain smoke and put up with watering eyes all day long.

'Sorry Sofie have you some spare milk I've run out and Malcolm drinks like a fish. Don has just returned from his patrol and had to give away all his provisions to a bombed-out family. He's had quite a night I can tell you and it was his first outing.'

'Well Andy said bombs landed close the mine during the raid two days ago and they had to abandon operations and get them into shelters. If they'd have hit the pit head and destroyed the lifting gear over 200 miners would have been stuck 400 feet down. Doesn't bare thinking about, does it?'

'No it doesn't, we just have to keep calm and carry on, as the posters tell us? Well, I must get back,' Mary said thanking Sofie for the half-pint of full cream milk. Maybe I'll see you at the club tonight, air-raids permitting, we can't let Adolf have it all his own way, can we?' As she returned a group of teenage lads were singing the latest rude chant to Adolf and his henchmen.

'*Hitler's only got one ball, the other is in the welfare hall. Himmler has something similar while Goebbels has no-balls at all.*' Ha! Ha! Ha! they laughed in unison and repeated the rhyme until the voices drifted away in the damp air close to the municipal rubbish tip at the street's end.

*

Partly to make ends meet, they had agreed to house an RAF Warrant Officer as part of the housing scheme for military personnel on special assignment. Roger Sullivan (no relation) had been drafted in from Leeds to train recruits on the anti-aircraft batteries around the Whitley area. Malcolm slept in his parent's room on a made-up camp bed which he quite liked, being close to his Mam and Dad at night. Roger ate most of his meals at the training base except for some weekends when off duty and his rota of three weeks on and a week off meant he could return to Leeds every month. Malcom was pleased to have an airman in uniform in the house as he had a son about Malcolm's age. Having Roger took some of the weight off Mary for entertaining Malcolm who would tell him stories. The arrangement was good for both parties especially as Roger was about Don's age and rode a Douglas T35 motorbike. They would discuss the merits of Don's previous Rudge Ulster but never agreed on which was the best. Occasionally, Roger would take Malcolm out for a spin down to Whitley Bay, a rare treat for the youngster.

*

The war dragged on for Don, increasing his frustration that he wasn't using his full potential in his fight against the Nazis. Yes, he had rescued several family members, lost children and umpteen dogs and cats, some driven crazy by the bomb blasts but he wanted something more meaningful, given his potential so what could he do to square the circle? Two nights later after another rescue he heard a distressed mewling from a bombed outbuilding and on investigation, a basket of kittens and a mother was revealed under a collapsed wall. The distressed grey kitten was covered in brick dust being the only survivor of the batch. In a surge of compassion for the tiny bundle, Don unlocked the knee catch of Monty and lifted the kitten out of its coffin and into his greatcoat pocket where it mewed its thanks.

His regular forays into the stygian nights away from Mary and Malcolm had brought home to Don how much he cared for them and often during a raid he would be worried sick that one night he might return to find 33 Sycamore Avenue just a hole in the ground and his life an empty shell. How much these feelings were shared by countless individuals and families was of little comfort to Don so he was resolved to do more to help end the war. He had to find work that, for him was directly concerned with the fight against fascism. But what? He had few qualifications that would provide him with work involving war production yet there must be openings with so many of the male workforce on the front-line. But for his accident that's where Don would have been. Crying over spilt milk wasn't in Don's vocabulary. '**Get your thinking cap on Don and find out what's on offer'** **– The Voice** *commanded.*' Don was deep in thought and almost collided with a seated casualty, head in hands crying soundlessly, shoulders shaking.

'Hello there. Can I help?' Don asked touching the woman's shoulder who jumped involuntarily at the unexpected intrusion into her grief.'

'I, I went to the shops before the raid started and couldn't get back in time.' Her voice broke through her sobbing. 'Oh God, oh God what'll I do, my house is gone. There's nothing left of my family. I-wish-I-was-dead!' She cried, tearing at her hair, tears flooding her dust covered cheeks.

Momentarily, Don was at a loss to comfort this stricken woman but couldn't leave her so he had to do something.

'What's your name dear? I'll take you to the centre and get you sorted with a nice cup of tea and some warm clothes; you must be cold in that thin coat. Is that a good idea?' He said soothingly taking her arm and gently lifting he to her feet. 'Are you OK to walk?'

'Yes, thank you. My name is Mrs. Roderick, Elsie that is and I'm able to walk.' Shock had taken over to dry her tears and numb her senses.

Slowly, they made their way to the centre, now crowded with casualties and homeless from the latest bombing, the air thick with cigarette smoke and dusty residue from the broken homes and sweaty, fearful bodies. It was a scene from hell with the strident clamour of the rescue workers, shouting out names and directions for the displaced, trying to make sense of their unfolding nightmare. Don guided the woman to a seat and brought a cup of tea, asking another seated lady to look after her while he made some enquiries.

'Has anyone by the name of Roderick been admitted in the past couple of hours?' Don enquired of a WVS (Women's Voluntary Service) Official who looked to be in charge.

'Let me see, Roderick. Was there a family?' She asked.

'I've just brought in Elsie Roderick who said her house was destroyed in the latest bombing.'

'Ah here we are, Stanley Roderick and two youngsters came in, yes, almost two hours ago. They're over there by the window.' She said, smiling with relief at some good news and pointed towards a man holding on tightly to a boy and girl.

'That is really good news, I'll find Elsie and reunite them – she'll be pleased.' Don grinned at the understatement of the week, returning to the woman still in shock, 'come with me Elsie I want you to meet someone.' Holding onto her arm Don guided her through the crush towards the window.

Elsie followed Don, head down still unable to cope with her reality of a lost family. The husband raised his eyes on their approach.

'Hello Elsie, where have you been we have been looking all over for you.' The husband asked, frowning almost accusingly but then smiled with relief at his wife's teared stained cheeks. Elsie slowly came out of her personal shroud and looked through the smoke in disbelief.

'Stanley, Stanley it's you, it's really you, and the children - are you alright my dears?' Bursting into tears, her voice gagging, catching and choking as she tried to embrace them all at once. Oh Stanley, Stanley I was convinced I'd lost you all when I saw the where the house had been, I thought I'd die, I did really.' Elsie stammered through her happiness; a black cloud suddenly lifted - replaced by a rainbow! Don turned and smiled at the all too infrequent reunions and left them in animated chatter, lost in a warm, carefree world of their own.

CHAPTER 44

Malcolm greeted Don on his return with his usual enthusiasm and barrage of questions then then stopped short when he heard the mewing.

'Dad, Dad what is that, Dad? Have you bought something for me? Can I have a look,' as Don gently lifted out the mewing scrap, 'oh it's so tiny, isn't it? Where did you get it? Can I hold it please oh it's so lovely. Can we keep it?'

Mary came out of the kitchen where she had been preparing a lamb hot pot, a rare meaty delicacy in those days of severe shortages where ration books were guarded as carefully as a bank account. 'What's all this fuss about Don? Now don't get Malcolm all excited, it might bring his cough back and you know how difficult it is to shift.'

'And welcome back to you too Don. Have you had a good night?' Don responded testily at Mary's lack lustre welcome.

'I'm sorry Dear I'm up to my ears with the supper and do not need any more aggravation. So, what have we here?' Gently taking the kitten from Malcolm. 'My you are in some state, covered in dust and I'll bet you're thirsty. I don't know what things are coming to with another mouth to feed. Never mind I'll get a saucer of milk.' Mary huffed and disappeared into the kitchen as Don and Malcolm exchanged smiles knowing that they had a permanent visitor.

With the kitten now contentedly lapping at the saucer with Malcolm kneeling in watchful attendance, Don looked down at his son, happy that the kitten had a responsible parent. 'Now we've enlarged the family by one what are we going to call it?'

'Well, it was covered in dust so why don't we call it Dusty?' suggested Malcolm as he wiped away the dust with a damp cloth. 'Oh, look Mam, Dusty is all black and white underneath, but I still think Dusty suits him, don't you?'

'Yes Dear, now when you've cleaned him up – he'll needs somewhere to sleep so why don't you see if you can find a box, there might be one in the shed.'

'Well, there's one happy boy Mary. Do think I'll get a rescue medal from the RSPCA or a mention in dispatches from the ARP?'

'Don't be silly Don come and have your hot pot before it gets cold. And you can leave that cat alone for five minutes Malcolm, come and eat.'

Mary switched on the radio for Family Favourites, a programme that played popular tunes selected by the Armed Forces but was interrupted by a news announcement. *'British and Allied Forces have made a breakthrough in the desert war under the command of General Montgomery and have captured Tobruk and taken 1,000 Italian and German soldiers and the air force base. This is a major defeat for Rommel, known as the Desert Fox and a bloody nose for Hitler and his Nazis. That is the end of the announcement, and we return you to the studio to enjoy Jean Metcalf's Forces Favourites.'*

'That is one in the eye for Adolf!' Mary with some unaccustomed feeling. 'And hopefully with more to come. Oh, I wish this war would end Don.'

'Well Mary we're on the up now and with the Yankees on board the Nazis have their backs to the wall and will regret they ever started it.' As he settled back, lighting a Players Navy Cut cigarette, Don's allocation of five a day. Flicking through the local paper a Situations Vacant advert caught his eye.

GOVERNMENT WAR FACTORY INSPECTORS WANTED. Applicants should be fit and healthy with a good standard of education and a Schools Certificate. No direct experience required as training will be provided. Meals and accommodation supplied during training. Salary is currently £20.00 monthly paid in arrears during training. Four-week trial period. Successful applicants will be seconded to factories involved in many areas of war production. Application forms can be obtained from any labour office or library quoting ref. Gov.War.Inspection 5.

This was just the thing Don was looking for and a chance to be involved at the sharp end, almost on the front line. Problem! No Schools Certificate! Fit and healthy? Would his disability be a disclaimer? 'I'll complete the application first as I've nothing to lose,' Don decided.

Don passed the advert over to Mary 'I think I'll apply, what do you think?'

'Have you a Schools Certificate and what they mean 'fit and healthy'? Will you have to run and do physical jerks?'

'I'll cross that bridge if I get an interview and won't mention Monty before that.' Don said with some conviction. 'I suppose it depends on how desperate they are.'

When the application form arrived Don couldn't believe how much they wanted. 'Blimey they'll want my inside leg measurement next.' Don was exasperated with the six-page Government application but stuck at it to include the following: -

FULL NAME & ADDRESS, MARITAL STATUS, SCHOOLS/ COLLEGES, EMPLOYMENT, RELIGION, HEIGHT, WEIGHT, SERIOUS ILLNESSES, EDUCATION, POLITICAL AFFILIATIONS, PASSPORT

NUMBER and COUNTERSIGNED BY ONE OF THE FOLLOWING PROFESSIONS. JP, LAWYER, POLICE, SURGEON. N.B. War Factory Inspectors are covered by the Official Secrets Act.

Don signed and dated the marathon size application, countersigned by Mr Scatelli, his accident surgeon and to be sure it arrived in these days of fractured postal services he paid for recorded delivery at the Central Post Office.

Eight days later a reply from the War Inspectorate requested his attendance at the Government Offices in Station Road, Whitley Bay at 2.00, the next Saturday. Charles Leyton, Personnel Supervisor - War Employment, signed the letter, with a reminder to bring his passport. 'Mary, Mary!' Don called out, 'I've got an interview, isn't that great?'

'It certainly is Darling, where do you go and when?'

*

'Good afternoon Mr. Sullivan. I'm Mr Leyton and will be interviewing you for the position of War Factory Inspector, can I see your passport, and have you read the Job Description? I notice you require a walking stick so how does it affect your mobility?' Leyton asked, accompanied by a querulous expression which suggested some surprise at Don's application.

'Yes, I've read the Job Description which I feel capable of handling and I'm able to get around well with no problems. I've had the new limb for four months and have been on patrol, often at night as an ARP Warden and have been recommended for a Rescue Medallion. This involves walking a few miles each night and often over rough ground, as you might imagine.' Don explained with some feeling.

'Indeed, I can Mr Sullivan. I notice your area has suffered quite badly from the bombing. Now tell me a bit about yourself and why you want to become a War Factory Inspector?'

'I've managed personnel in many service situations in the hotel business.' Don recounted his management roles at the Cliffe. 'I stand no nonsense but I'm good with people and since becoming a Warden I've had to keep a clear head and calm demeanour in crisis situations and I've had a few already. I want to do more to help with the war effort as I was denied an opportunity of being in the front line because of my motor-cycle accident.

'Ah yes, your accident. There was quite some coverage of it in the papers and it seems you're very lucky to be with us based on the report. It was a close-run thing, wasn't it?' Leyton asked becoming more engrossed in Don's background.

'So they tell me Mr Leyton, because during the surgery I was either under the anaesthetic or comatose on pain killers. Mr Scatelli, the surgeon and his team pulled me through, so maybe I survived for a reason?'

'Possibly, possibly Mr Sullivan, time will tell.' Leyton replied seeing Don's application in a new light. ' I think that is all for now Mr Sullivan. Do you have any questions?

'Yes. How much travelling will be involved after the training period?'

'That will depend on which factories you're sent to which could be in any part of the country depending on where there is a problem. You'll be notified usually a week before because these factories are blanketed by the Official Secrets Act. Thank you for coming and we will let you know in a few days. Goodbye Mr Sullivan and good luck.' Leyton smiled encouragingly as he shook Don's hand.

As Don made his way home, the sirens blared their 'take cover' warning with pedestrians scuttling for cover into the nearest shelters. It was a false alarm, and with a collective sigh of relief the mixed group were herded slowly back into the sunlit street, wondering just how long before the next siren call. These were nerve-wracking tests on Britain's morale, especially in the high-risk areas.

Mary was already busying herself in the kitchen preparing the supper of braised ox hearts, carrots and cauliflower and carefully placing a jam roly-poly pudding in the steamer. Food supplies of any kind were often unpredictable and in short supply unless you were in a service supply sector such as Dobson's grocery store. However, an effective network between food-based suppliers; grocers, fishmongers, butchers, bakers, greengrocers and even milkmen were part of this 'underground cabal', dedicated to keeping friends and families aware of the fluctuating tide of food supplies and its availability, of which Mary took full advantage.

'How did the interview go Don?' Mary asked, taking the kitten out of the washing basket for the umpteenth time. 'Malcolm, will you come and get Dusty, it's been in the clean washing again! Last warning!'

'Pretty good to be honest.' Don replied lighting up a Players cigarette and sinking thankfully into the sofa with a Bells and soda. Mention of the Rescue Medal and my ARW duties went down well but I won't know for a few days.'

*

A week later Don opened the door to the postman and was handed an official looking letter with a government stamp on it. He opened the flap, hoping it would be the start of an opportunity to give Adolf a bloody nose or would he be left to wander the bombed-out streets of his neighbourhood until the war's end?

CHAPTER 45

Don's heart almost stopped when he read the first line, 'Dear Mr Sullivan, I am pleased to inform you that ....' and blew out his cheeks, overcome by a euphoric sense of satisfaction that at last he could make a personal impact on Britain's war effort. Don read on, his hands shaking with suppressed excitement. He was to report to the Bishop Auckland recruiting centre the War Factory Inspectorate in a week's time for 4 weeks training. After which he would be allocated to a specific factory specialising in various types of production. Recruits were warned that assignments could change dependant on war production requirements for vital products. Don would travel on a government warrant to the training centre and was required to bring suitable personal effects and clothing for the 4 weeks of training.

'Well at least you get weekends off and pay during your training. In a way I'm pleased you're out of the firing line as a Warden because you did have some close shaves Don.' Mary was reassured that whatever happened, Don would be much happier as an inspector and a lot easier to live with.

'Do you think you'll be able to manage Malcolm and Dusty while I'm away in the depths of Durham County?' Don raised an eyebrow, cocking his head.

'Cheeky beast.' Mary replied. 'It'll be a lot easier with you out of my hair. I might even have time to listen to my favourite radio programmes in peace, Forces Favourites and Workers Playtime. Malcom was listening and interrupted.

'And me and Dusty will be able to listen to Dick Barton without you criticizing when Jock, Snowy and Dick are fighting the baddies!' He complained, as his parents hid their grins at his outburst, typical Mal.

Another air-raid on a nearby power plant two nights before Don's departure threatened to scupper his new role, as some of the fallout damaged several houses only a street away, the blast taking out two of their kitchen windows. Roger, their lodger was fortunately on hand the next day to repair the damage, so Don's departure wasn't delayed.

*

His train from the Newcastle had started from Edinburgh and was crammed with troops of all three services, soldiers who didn't look old enough to hold a bucket and spade let alone a 303 rifle; it was an age thing Don realised.

Sprinkled through the military mix were a few GI's and Poles wearing their iconic peaked cap, 'maybe on leave or training in Scotland and well out of Hitler's reach,' Don concluded.

Scotland itself was in the news when Rudolph Hess, Hitler's deputy, had recently ditched a Messerschmitt in the Highlands, masquerading as a Captain Alfred Horn. A Scottish farmer David McLean had found the plane ablaze and escorted the uninjured Hess to his farmhouse for a cup of tea. Hess had parachuted to safety when his plane ran out of fuel! It was reported that Hess had been a Hitler loyalist and in 1920 had been part of the infamous Beer Hall Putsch and served a prison sentence with Adolf, helping with his autobiography, Mein Kampf during their confinement. Hess's deranged attempt to broker a peace deal came to nought and he spent the rest of the war in Spandau Prison, after his abortive Scottish landing. The RAF grapevine finally revealed that part of Hess's Messerschmitt had been recovered and would be exhibited in London's Imperial War Museum.

*

'Durham station, Durham station.' Boomed a station announcement. 'Change here for Bishop Auckland, Middlesborough and Hartlepool.' A mini exodus erupted from Don's carriage as he was ejected with a jostling flood of three services. Don's time at the station buffet allowed him to draw breath and enjoy a mug of tea and slice of Victoria sponge while he waited for his connection. Cigarette and pipe smoke created an eye-watering fog from the assorted militia in the café from which Don made a swift exit into relatively fresh air but immediately into the belching steam and smoke from the waiting locomotive, proudly displaying its title, 'City of Durham'.

'Boarding for Bishop Auckland, Barnard Castle and Carlisle.' Don's obvious impairment with Monty allowed him a boarding priority by the service personnel and a rare seat for the 30-minute journey. The familiar roar, hiss and jerk as the engine gradually gained momentum into the sunlit country air, far removed from the grimy town.

Don sighed as he surveyed the rolling beauty and tranquillity of the English countryside. It was difficult to imagine how quickly things could change under a Nazi jackboot regime where another part of the United Kingdom was already suffering - the Channel Islands. They had been forfeited as too costly to defend against the blitzkrieg but with the might of the United States on board, Hitler and his generals would have to face the prospects of defeat. 'Maybe Hitler had sent Hess on a face-saving mission to Scotland, after all?' Don thought.

Don's carriage companions were in their twenties or early thirties and looking at their earnest faces, he wondered just how many would be still alive in the coming weeks. Don's mission was to help keep these numbers down by an earlier end to the conflict.

'Bishop Auckland, there'll be a ten-minute stop and if you're quick there's a platform trolley serving drinks and snacks.'

Don narrowly avoided the rush to the tea trolley and made his way out of the station to the meeting point where a 10-seater mini-bus with a windscreen notice, 'SHUTTLE BUS – TRAINING CENTRE'. 'Let me take your case young man said the courteous elderly driver, I'll store it in the back.' Don gave his name which was ticked off his clipboard. 'I'm waiting for three more and then we'll be off. My name is Trevor to my friends, and you'll be seeing a lot of me as I drive trainees to various locations around the Centre - it's quite a big place. It used to be stately home 'Hornsby Hall', rented by the War Office from the owner Lord Hornsby. He still lives in one of the wings. You might see him out and about; ah, here are the cow's tails.' Trevor beckoned three smartly dressed middle aged men over and crossed their name off. 'Right, we're all here so we'll get going, it's a 20-minute ride. At the centre you'll be met by Chief Instruction Fred Lainberry, he's a bit officious but alright really.' Trevor said with a grin; a regular mine of information which he liked to demonstrate to the new intakes.

CHAPTER 46

The main building was a baronial hall of Georgian vintage with dual curving stairways to an imposing entrance that a coach and horses would have comfortably negotiated. Four floors high and built to last for centuries with locally quarried stone and windows high and wide to flood the insides with light, the residence was a statement of wealth and privilege, now reduced to housing the proletariat to pay the rent. No more royal visits, Hunt balls or upper-class parties for the privileged. 'War is a great leveller', Don thought, as they disembarked.

'Good afternoon, gentleman my name is Fred Lainberry the Chief Instructor, I hope you have had a relatively problem free journey and welcome to Hornsby Hall, once the pride of North Yorkshire's nobility. Your accommodation is, let's say functional but more than adequate with single rooms. You will have few complaints about the food as we do have a skilled chef on site. Once you have settled in, the evening meal will be served at 18.00 hrs; we go by the 24-hour clock here. The briefing on your training will be begin at 19.30 for an hour.' Fred handed out a folder which contained a map of the site, a schedule and an information sheet containing on-site rules and regulations.

'LAC (Leading Aircraftsman) Grainer, Brenda that is, will see you to your accommodation and show you where the dining facilities are located.' Fred ended his introduction and as if my magic an attractive young lady appeared at his elbow smiling at the entranced recruits. Her diminutive figure was clad in RAF Blues which did nothing to hide an attractive shape, an oval high cheek boned face, improved by some light cosmetics.

'This way gentlemen.' Said Brenda, as she swayed ahead of the fixated trainees.

After a very tasty meal of steak pie, garden vegetables, lemon sponge and custard, the replete trainees made their way to the conference room for their briefing. In addition to the Chief Instructor four other personnel were introduced who covered specialist areas of health and safety, legalities, munitions, and factory personnel. Each of these would be covered in seminars after which each trainee would be allocated to a specific area of war production, based on their employment experience. Don's background with female personnel in the service industry was an asset as most factory workers were women of all ages and backgrounds.

Although he was technically minded Don was surprised at the complexity of producing bomb tails for a range of bomb types, incendiaries, high explosives and propaganda leaflets. It was emphasised that any defects in the tails would affect their trajectory to the target areas, therefore quality control was closely monitored. Similarly with gliders mechanisms, any deviation in product quality could costs the lives of pilots and parachute troops on board. The inspector's remit was to ensure that suppliers and factory managers maintain the highest standards in production, safety and personnel welfare. These essentials were drilled into the trainees at every seminar and in whole group meetings. Weekly assessments of their performance ensured there was no wriggle room in any of these areas of training as lives were at risk.

For the specialist areas of war production, seminars involved detailed plans for each production area, product specification and operational films drew attention to good and bad practices. Special emphasis was placed on accidents and safety as war factories were dangerous places and documentary films showed gruesome footage of the serious injuries sustained because of faulty equipment, slipshod production and ineffective safety training. Trainees were expected to keep detailed notes as tests required an 80% pass in each area. Failure, after reviews would result in the trainee's removal from the programme and midnight oil was burnt by trainees on the eve of these tests. All facets of the training were hotly debated during meal and leisure times.

Occasional light relief was afforded by the occasional ariel dog fights high in the skies above the centre, by Spitfires and Hurricanes against Messerschmitt 109's and Focke-Wolfs as escorts to the Dornier and Junkers heavy bombers on route to Wearside and Tyneside targets. On one occasion in mid-afternoon a Hurricane engaged a Junkers 88, its cannons ripped into one of the engines which caught fire. As the Hurricane turned away a Focke-Wolf came out of the sun and caught the Hurricane which turned away with its superior speed and control. In an instant it was behind the Focke and a blast from its 40 mm cannons tore the German fighter apart as it spiralled down a mile from the centre to the cheers of the centre's personnel. Meanwhile, the damaged Hurricane, smoke gutting from its engine turned turtle, popping the pilot out of the cockpit to engage the parachute which snagged and roman candled as the emergency chute canopy partially deployed. The onlookers' initial cheers turned to gasps of horror as the pilot plunged into a small wood two fields away and out of sight. A Centre ambulance was deployed but the fate of the pilot was unknown. Later that evening a notice was pinned to the Centre bulletin board stating that the pilot had survived but was in intensive care with multiple injuries. The next 24 hours would decide whether he would survive.

CHAPTER 47

The two days granted weekly for trainee's home visits were often forfeit in the interests of improved test scores. Don had told Mary he would take a two-day break halfway through the course to recharge his batteries and ensure he 'graduated' as a WFI (War Factory Inspector). Table tennis was a favoured pastime for the trainee's recreation and Don had been a dab hand pre-Monty but still enjoyed a competitive game despite his restricted movement. His occasional falls served to put off his opponents, usually when he was losing and what he lacked in agility Don made up in technique and sleight of hand serving, which regularly frustrated better opposition. Although betting was forbidden losers were expected to buy the beers and rarely did Don have to dig into his cash reserves.

*.

'Oh, it's so good to see you Don, seems like ages you've been away.' Mary's lengthy embrace made Don tingle. 'Anyway, how are you and Monty getting on with the training so far?' She said, disentangling herself.

'I'm fine, but the course is tough and requires a steep learning curve with the information I had to take on board. Most of it was completely alien but the instructors are first rate and very helpful as they know that most of the technical information is brand new.' Don was helped off with his great coat. 'So far, I've scraped through the tests but they're going to get more demanding in the final weeks. I'll have another in-depth interview, and something called a psychological test before we are finally let loose and allocated a factory. At least we get a week's leave before our assignment.' Don explained as a little whirlwind flew down the stairs to wrap itself around his midriff.

'Hello Daddy, me and Dusty have missed you lots, haven't we?' Malcolm cried as he turned to his treasured kitten, now about twice the size since Don started his training. 'Did you pass all your exams? Mam was telling me you had to do lots and lots.'

'Yes I did, and I can see you've grown a bit since I left, certainly Dusty has, it must be all the good food you're feeding him. He's unrecognisable from the waif I rescued.' Don ruffled his son's hair and gave Dusty a stroke - thankful to be amongst his family again.

'You must be starving Don. I've prepared one of your favourites Liver and Bacon, with Syrup sponge to follow. I suppose you'd like a Newcastle Brown after your meal?' Mary fussed with delight at Don's return.

'I certainly would and that was a very tasty meal, a cut above the offerings that the 'cordon blue' chef produces at the training centre so go to the top of the class.' Don said and 'I'm going to show you how much more I enjoyed it, later on.' Don winked, making Mary blush.

'Actually, I need to talk to you about Sgt. Roger later, when Malcolm's in bed.' Mary said in a meaningful way.

Don's antenna was on high alert at what Mary intimated and would stand no nonsense where his family was concerned. Roger had been in the habit of standing close to Mary in the kitchen when making excuses to help and had taken to paying her compliments on her dress and make-up, perhaps as part of his softening up process it seemed and it was making her uncomfortable.

'Don't worry love I'll have a word with Roger when he returns and tell him to pack his bags. A pity really as I liked him, and he has made himself useful with the chores but he's overstepped the mark and I can't have that.'

*

When Roger returned the next day Don came straight to the point. 'I'll be away on war factories inspections on a regular basis soon and I'm not happy having a single man in the house so I'd appreciate Roger if you could move out before I return to the training centre, that's next Wednesday. Mary's concerned that people might put 2 and 2 together and make 5 so it's not something she wants to risk. You understand her point of view, don't you? We've been happy to have you around and helping with Malcolm.' Don spoke evenly but made it clear his request was final.

'OK, yes Don, I understand, and have enjoyed being part of a family again. I'll contact the depot tomorrow and I'm sure they'll find other accommodation locally.' Roger said conversationally but realised his testosterone had let him down.

A telegram came for Don the next day instructing him to contact the Centre's recruitment officer without delay. A WFI had suffered an injury during a bombing raid that would put him out of action for some time and a replacement was required urgently. Don's weeks leave was cut to three days when the postman delivered his travel warrant and assignment details for the factory in Hull. The city had for some weeks been the Luftwaffe's bombing destination because of its strategic North Sea coastal location and a major centre for war production. In popular parlance it had 'taken a pasting', with hundreds of civilian and war worker casualties from direct hits on war component factories and collateral damage to thousands of homes. Don was on his way to a blitzed Hull.

*

Long before he arrived in a rerouted bus, the result of a derailment on the branch line connection from Sheffield, Hull appeared to be on fire with flames and smoke pouring from factory buildings and the fire service overwhelmed by the Nazis incendiary bombardment. German bombers were having a field day as the paper-thin defences had no respite from the Nazi armada.

The United bus dropped Don off in a residential area and he made his way to his accommodation at 47 Latimer Grove, a three bed semi owned by Mrs Jeanette Gibson a middle-aged lady, petit, attractive and genial in her welcome.

'The local war recruitment office has been in touch, Mr Sullivan so I've been expecting you. Let me take your case; I've just put the kettle on because you must be parched after your journey, from the North East was it, that's quite a way? Come into the sitting room while I get the tea and cake.' She said in a local accent, hurrying into the kitchen. 'I've arranged a room on the ground floor, as I was told about your limited mobility.'

'That's very thoughtful of you Mrs Gibson thank you. My assignment here is for approximately four weeks and I'm to report to the local war recruitment office tomorrow.'

'Oh yes I know, it's not far and please call me Jeanette I'm not one for formality.' She said smiling as she poured the tea into rose decorated China cups. 'Milk and sugar?'

Don's accommodation with meals was more than adequate with the use of the kitchen, if required. His room contained a four-foot bed, a small chest of drawers topped with a mirror, a small table and chair and a voluminous easy chair for good measure. His window revealed a well-kept garden, a section of which had been allocated for vegetables which included potatoes, cabbages and string beans to help with the rationing restrictions. A downstairs toilet was a very convenient alternative to the upstairs bathroom so all in all, Don was relieved his accommodation ticked all the boxes.

*

After a good night's sleep and a hearty breakfast Don was directed to the centre, a leisurely ten minutes' walk away where the deployment officer for the area Simon Parlane gave him a quick rundown on the factory which produced bomb tails and glider connections. The previous inspector had been in place for a month and his file produced assessments of operations and procedures across the board. It was handed to Don and providing an excellent working base as to where the issues were for Don's attention. An overall score of 8/10 had been given for factory operations with variable scores for separate areas and those requiring action. One of these was on accidents and safety as the number of accidents and injuries reported were unusually high.

Don was amazed that the factory seemed to have charmed life, situated close to many bombed out residences and two adjacent factories which had been damaged, one of which was still being attended to by fireman and tenders. Looking around Don compared the damaged area to Tyneside and had to admit Hull seemed much worse off. Recent inclement weather of rain and wind had kept Luftwaffe raids at bay but as improved weather was forecast the blanket bombing would resume.

The factory had previously produced a range of household items and had been transformed into a formidable production line with an output of tens of thousands of bomb tails every week Don was informed by Stuart Tomlinson the factory manager. In addition, about half the space had been allocated to the manufacture of glider release mechanisms which had been calibrated for variable glider sizes and the number of paratroopers. The hook attached to the glider's 'O' ring had to be strength tested along with the quick release lever which was activated once the glider had gained the optimum altitude and distance. The lives of these troops were heavily dependent on these operations working 100%, hence tolerances had no error margin and required the tightest quality control.

The factory's problem was an inconsistent supply of raw materials, according to Stuart so anything Don could do to prioritise that area would be a godsend. The largely female factory population were naturally curious as to Don's disability during a tour of the factory, as Stuart briefly described each operational area. The grape vine conclude that Don must be a government VIP. Last week, production had slipped to 50% because a delivery from the steel works had been diverted to other priority area. Contributing to the factory's poor accident record were defective cutting and milling machines. Stuart lamented that safety guards and equipment he had ordered had not been delivered in support of H & S (Health & Safety) training. There was plenty for Don to get his teeth into.

Back in his lodgings Don made a list of his priorities based on his assessment and tour of the factory. Top of the list was H & S operator training as it affected all areas of output down the line in terms of accidents and labour turnover.

CHAPTER 48

'I'll have your supper ready in half an hour Don, will you be ready?' Jeanette asked as she tapped lightly on the door.

'I'm always ready for a tasty meal Jeanette, thank you.' Replied Don, putting the finished touches to his action plan.

'I hope you like the Cottage Pie, because getting decent mince beef with the rationing is a nightmare so you need to know your butcher. There's apple pie to finish because we have some apple trees and fresh fruit is in short supply as well.' Jeanette explained, serving Don a healthy portion of cottage pie from the Pyrex dish, adding a heap of vegetables to fill the plate.

'This food is delicious Janette and I do appreciate it. The factory's canteen food is basic but they're doing their best.' Don tucked into the tasty food, smiling to himself at the thought of Mary worrying that he might be under-nourished. 'No chance with these meals!' Don thought.

'How are you and Hull managing the Blitz?' Don asked, 'I noticed the number of fires and smoke when I arrived - it must be dreadful for everyone.'

'I'm lucky being just outside the centre but we did have some incendiary fires on nearby houses last week and must admit I was frightened.' She said holding back the tears as her attractive face crumpled. 'When will it end Donald?'

'Not too long, I hope. We've taken back the middle east with Monty, and with the Americans on board with their superior firepower we're forcing the Germans back through France. It's chin up time I think, because Hitler and his generals must realise their error taking on the allies.' Don's positive analysis of the conflict raised Janette's spirits.

'You're right we must be positive and do our best to beat Hitler. It is tough for Hull and I suppose there's more to come – we'll just have stick it out.' She added forcing a smile, 'I'll make another pot of tea!'

*

Don's first job was to gauge staff morale and job satisfaction and chatted to a variety of operational staff in the canteen. Secondly, assessing the factory's bomb tail and glider operations he compared each operation with the production manual requirements and found several inconsistencies. Finally, the H & S manual's training requirements were being disregarded compromising worksite safety.

'I've talked to staff of both sides of production and they feel that many of the accidents occur because safety training is inadequate. Also, I've noticed that in high-risk areas, glider parts in particular, protective helmets and face coverings aren't worn, so who is responsible?' Don asked referring to his notes.

Stuart was now on the back foot and full of excuses. 'I agree, but we've only a part-time training officer and he is shared with another factory. I want to improve on safety but we're under the cosh with tight production targets from the war procurement inspectorate.' Stuart was genuinely aggrieved that his hands were tied in the absence of a full time H & S trainer.

'The wheel that squeaks gets the grease Stuart, so what complaining have you done and to whom?' Don was getting a clear impression that the manager was not proactive in getting support or chasing suppliers.

'I did write to the personnel procurement but that was a while back and haven't had a reply.' Stuart replied lamely.

'Hmmm, here's the thing Stuart. I'll do what can but it's a chicken and egg situation - inadequate H & S training means more accidents and more accidents means lower production through fewer and less able staff. It's a downward spiral with the added effect on morale and turnover.' Don felt the manager hadn't taken enough pre-emptive action for these areas and was paying the price.

'I'll contact personnel procurement regarding a full time H & A training role but until that happens your part-timer trainer must display safety notices prominently and insist on the wearing of safety equipment on the job? Can you also compile a priority list as to which areas of training are most in need?'

'I'll do that with my supervisors as they're going to be involved in its implementation.' Stuart readily agreed, pleased that he now had some support.

'Based on my observations and comparisons with the Q.C. (quality control) manuals you could start with the glider workshop's Q.C. supervisor as the percentage of returns is too high.' Don requested, to get the changes rolling. 'My interim report to the inspectorate will confirm my priorities for action.'

'I'll do what I can to sort these issues and issue a general notice regarding H & S observance to all staff. A full time H & A officer will be a big help.' Stuart explained with some relief.

'It's a start Stuart but you need to walk the walk as a priority. What are the other issues you've prioritised? Earlier you mentioned a problem with the supply of materials; specifically where is this and what action are you taking?

'Right, glider parts for the hooks and lines are unreliable so we cannot provide the glider factory in Swindon with enough finished assemblies and the factory has gliders ready to go and they're being pressurised by the RAF high command for the supply of combat ready gliders.' Stuart complained that his calls to his supplier are never returned.

'Give me their names and their MD's and I'll do some leaning to increase their supply efforts, or their contracts will be forfeit; that might concentrate their minds. Exactly where are these suppliers because if they're not too distant I'll make a personal visit and check their operational effectiveness at the same time.' Don knew he could make an impact on some important areas of war production which was the primary purpose of a factory inspector. The Luftwaffe might have a say on Don's initiatives.

CHAPTER 49

Hull City was increasingly the target of Hitler's frustration and paranoia with wave after wave of Luftwaffe bombers layering the city, unprotected in the main by Spitfires or Hurricanes. Incendiaries coated the houses and factories by nightly waves with the fire services desperate to arrest a losing battle with the wind assisted fires. Herr Hitler had transferred his fury to British cities hoping to erode the public's morale and force the government into a settlement. How wrong he was to underestimate the resolve and bulldog spirit of the British and the tenacity of young Spitfire and Hurricane pilots in the Battle of Britain. Herr Goring's expectations of blasting Britain into submission and Hitler's invasion plans has been seriously derailed by young airmen who had other ideas and were helping to turn the tide of the war in the allies favour. Churchill coined that immortal thank you to the Battle of Britain pilots, *'Never, in the field of human conflict has so much been owed by so many to so few.'*

Don's desire to be more directly involved in the war effort was granted in spades with his assignment to Hull. Despite all the carnage, Hull continued to supply essential war production throughout the blitz with Don in the middle of the action. Into this living hell Don returned to the factory the next day picking his way through the smoking ruins of factories and houses. Their factory was largely intact apart from a few broken windows so production of the bomb tails and glider parts continued at a pace.

'We've had a few close calls but so far fingers crossed,' said Stuart the factory manager, 'and we now have a full time H & S (health & safety) officer in place, thanks to you. Safety training schedules have been circulated, starting tomorrow, with safety notices in both production areas. Training in key areas starts next week.'

'That's good news.' Don said nodding, 'but how much production has been lost with the air-raids and false alarms?'

'We have deep cellars that are used as air-raid shelters so after the all-clear we're back on the job. We've lost some production mainly on the bomb tails due to delayed shipments but, with cloudy nights we'll catch up.'

*

Mrs Gibson had been alerted to Don's late return to his lodgings and had produced a veritable piece of 'haute cuisine' from the meagre ration book allowances. Steaming on the table and emitting a tantalising aroma was a plateful of liver and onions, mashed potatoes, carrots and cabbage and from Jeanette's garden a baked apple dumpling and custard to follow. Don was hardly through the door before he was salivating!

'You're treating me too well Jeanette because when the time comes, I won't want to leave.' Don said smiling as he tucked into the unexpected feast.

'Well, that's as maybe,' replied Doris, 'we have to keep your strength up with all that's going on at the factory.' She had been informed of Don's delay but warned not to repeat anything – German informers and fourth columnist's' were about in war production areas and would take comfort knowing there were production problems in key areas. Numerous posters warned the public, 'BE LIKE DAD – KEEP MUM' and 'LOOSE TALK COSTS LIVES'.

Don was wakened at 2 a.m. with sirens wailing their warning and minutes later came the crump and flash of falling bombs and incendiaries, some far too close for comfort. Jeanette was already up, pouring sweet tea into a flask and ready to depart for the communal shelters in the next street. Once seated amongst the two dozen locals, a local wag was recounting some wartime humour, heard on the radio.

"Where are you going, Mary," asked Dad as his wife was leaving the shelter. *"Back for my false teeth,"* his wife replied. *"Come back here you silly woman, the Germans are dropping bombs not meat pies,"*

Ten minutes later the 'all clear' was signalled and amid all the tut-tutting frustration they trooped out into a chilly, sleep disturbed morning. Don decided to continue with his report writing and take a closer look at the specifications for the glider connections in the testing bay. A separate office was allocated for Don to network all the various strands of decision making which meant burning the midnight oil for over a week, after which production was resumed with better trained operatives and more reliable materials after Don's warning to the supplier's CAO.

CHAPTER 50

Don's factory finally ran out of luck. They had been operating on borrowed time when compared to the devastation of other factories – some had been damaged three times. A daytime raid came with too little warning on a bright sunny day and perfect for the Luftwaffe. Incendiaries rained down accompanied by high explosive bombs one of which caught one end of the factory with the subsequent blast ripping through the remainder as the workers scurried to the shelters. Don was in his office as the siren screeched its warning but as he opened the door the shock wave knocked him over, still inside and Monty's catches buckled as he fell. The door was now jammed tight so with nowhere to go he crawled under the metal desk and curled into a ball pulling in two chairs for added protection. It was a forlorn hope but the only option under the circumstances. The factory's timber construction was now well alight and collapsing all around his office as the sound of more explosions hammered Don's ears. 'This is it, and what an ignominious end,' thought Don, how will Mary and Malcolm manage without him. How would they react to his demise and what condition would he be in when his remains were discovered? A black cloud descended over him as another blast rendered him unconscious. **'Don't worry Don you're in the best place' The Voice** *called***,' rescue is on the way.'**

'Help me, please help me!' a plaintive cry from the young factory worker, her clothes in tatters from the blast as she staggered towards Don's office. Somewhere in his subconscious he heard the cry for help and crawled to the door opened by the blast and took a trembling hand in his and guided her into his makeshift shelter. 'Oh, thank you Mr Sullivan, I'd given up.' As she squeezed into the tiny space as Don passed out again.

*

The factory safety officer did a head count to find ten female workers were unaccounted for, all from the bomb tail section and furthest from the shelter.

'Did anyone see Don?' asked Stuart. 'I was on my way to his office when the alarm went off.' No-one had, so concern for his safety and the other workers was heightened. Rescue operations couldn't be mounted until the fire services had doused the flames and organise a search party although hope was considered slim for those who had been in the factory during the raid. Another half hour elapsed before the 'all clear' sounded and they emerged from the shelter into the sunlight to witness a smoking factory, all but destroyed except for a few sturdy walls. Firemen's hoses finally doused the remaining fires and a search began of the few sections that remained intact.

'That's Don's office,' said Stuart to a fireman pointing towards one of the remaining walls in its shadow. 'Could you check please, he could still be in there?' Stuart pleaded, hoping for a miracle.

'I'm not sure there's much left but I'll find out.' The fireman stepped around some smouldering embers to the charred office door which he levered open by his razor-sharp axe and peered through the gloom to see two curled bodies underneath the desk. The metal desk was covered with burnt timbers and bricks but otherwise seemed intact. 'This doesn't look good,' he thought as his eyes narrowed for a closer examination, he gingerly removed the chairs and called out but there was no response from either body, both covered in brick dust. He lay down his axe and removed his helmet to take a closer look to check for any vital signs. Don was in a foetal position as was the young women. With great care he gently lifted he woman's wrist and felt a weak but steady pulse. Don's head was nearest to the fireman to check the main artery for a pulse, but before that he had to remove brick debris first. Eventually his middle finger found the artery and blowing out his cheeks with the effort was able to sense an erratic pulse and gave a huge sigh of relieve. His priority as he picked his way back over the debris was to get the survivors some oxygen and summon the medics.

The fireman made his way tentatively towards the workers strained and expectant faces and shouted 'they're alive,' over the relieved clamour, 'get two stretchers, and call for an ambulance, we need to get them out of there fast ....' His demands were interrupted by a tremendous cheer who believed they had witnessed a miracle.

A subsequent search for the other nine workers found them in an adjacent shelter as their escape path to the cellars had been blocked by the first blast. All were dishevelled and shaken by their ordeal but otherwise unharmed. It was good news for the workers but bad news for the factory, now a smoking ruin. Adolf would have been delighted with his Luftwaffe.

The events during the bombing were confirmed by the young worker, Penny Faberman who said Don had heard her screams and brought her into the office where they were later discovered. Don had no memory of his incarceration or her rescue, except for hearing **The Voice,** which would remain his secret.

'If it hadn't of been for Mr Sullivan I would have died, truly.' Penny recalled at the memory and sobbed uncontrollably at her narrow escape.

*

Don was taken to the nearby hospital and his condition assessed as serious but not life threatening. His burns and the blast damage to his hearing was not considered permanent or needing surgery although an extended period of R and R would be required before he could resume his inspection duties after a medical assessment.

On hearing the news Mary was briefly traumatised and given a sedative by the doctor and sent home by her boss, Mr Dobson. Once Don's condition had stabilised he was transferred to Preston hospital in Shields and this helped to alleviate Mary's concerns over her husband's welfare. Monty also survived but required an overhaul as some of the catches had been damaged and a charred foot would need replacing. Don was sitting up in a four-person ward at the local Meadowbank hospital when Jeanette his landlady bustled in with a bunch of geraniums and a carton of fruit and a packet of fig rolls, Don's favourite.

'You look better than I imagined Donald but I was worried sick when I heard the factory had been bombed. By all accounts you had a lucky escape, someone up there must like you.' Janette said inspecting him closely. 'You need some fresh air, good food and a bit of sun to get you on your feet – or foot.' She grinned giving Don a reassuring pat on his arm.

'I'll settle for that Jeanette but the takeout service is a bit restricted at present.' Don responded with a knowing smile, 'so many thanks for the snacks and flowers – very thoughtful of you.'

By the time visiting was over, Don was exhausted and fell asleep dreaming of being back in Dakar Street with two legs, chatting with his friends and family. Then in a twist of time and place all his family were with him at the Rubicon until the burning roof fell in on them, waking him with a start, bathed in sweat, disoriented and unsure as to where he was.

'By all accounts you had a narrow escape but considering the factory's devastation you're in relatively good condition. The burns don't require any skin grafts and your hearing will return although it may be a bit restricted for a while.' The surgeon explained, surprised at Don's recovery.

Two days after Janette's visit Don's boss from the training centre came to discuss Don's report on the Hull factory and was mightily relieved by his recovery. This had led to several reforms on materials procurement and safety regulations for which he was given a star performance rating. Another development was that Don had been awarded a Life Saving Medal by the Royal Society based on Penny's confirmation of her recue. Don was perplexed by an award that he knew nothing about but could hardly give credit to **The Voice!**

During Don's three-week incarceration Monty had been returned to Roehampton for repair and an overhaul, so Don continued on his crutches. The following afternoon shortly after the departure of Janette, a trolley was wheeled into his berth to reveal a rejuvenated Monty. 'It's just like the return of a long-lost friend.' he thought, as he struggled out of bed and onto a chair to connect with Monty after weeks on crutches – he couldn't wait to be properly mobile as Monty squeaked his catches in welcome.

*

As the train pulled into the Central Station Don could see Mary and his son looking up and down Platform 5 then waving frantically as he was spotted, carefully negotiating the carriage step because of his period without Monty he could still feel the soreness from the burns around his stump.

'Hello Daddy, are you glad to be home?' An excited Malcolm rushed up and threw his arms around Don. 'We've missed you lots and so has Dusty. 'Can I see your medal? Did you really save someone's life Daddy?' Malcolm fizzed his questions as Don handed his son the Royal Society's Life Saving Medal

'I've missed you too Darling,' Mary whispered as she kissed him tenderly and stepped back to look at Don's drawn face, tears in her eyes. 'How are you? You look at though you could do with some home comforts - you've come to the right place.' She smiled and took his arm as they made their way to the taxi rank with Malcolm taking the other.

'Well Mary I have been worse but much better after seeing you all.' Relieved beyond measure to be reunited with his family. 'I can't wait to get some of that North Sea ozone to clear the tubes of that smoke and dust I took on-board.'

'I hope you're up to a family celebration because we've a few visitors waiting to welcome you. Your brother Sidney, sister Sadie and my folks too. Incidentally, Sidney has a serious girlfriend, and he might bring her along as well.'

'Not before time either, I was getting worried about our Sidney. It will be a real treat, believe me to see everyone again and get acquainted. It's ages since we were all together.' Don relaxed and sat back luxuriated in the view as the taxi sped past Newcastle's Grey's Monument, passing the Haymarket towards Jesmond and onto the Coast Road.

*

'Wake up Don, we're nearly home,' Mary nudged him out of a slumber where he was back on his BSA, roaring along the A46 towards to the 4 Arrows.

His family had done him proud with bunting and balloons festooning the semi and a welcoming committee at the door smiling and waving. His neighbours had heard and joined in the celebrations. His Life Saving Medal, now proudly worn by his son had been presented while he was recovering in Hull and had it stored in his luggage along with a photo and article from the Hull Herald. Mary took his arm, guiding him into the house as he felt a lump in his throat, and tried to keep the tears away. Even Dusty, no longer a dusty bomb survivor, came out and purred a greeting around his leg.

*

Don's war was not finished, and he couldn't wait to get back into harness as an inspector. His next assignment was a small factory producing components for bombers, mainly Lancasters and Halifax bombers, based just South of Gateshead in the Team Valley. A bonus for this assignment was being home every weekend but Don wasn't to have an easy ride!

CHAPTER 51

'I see you've done a great job Don.' James his boss at the Training Centre exclaimed shaking him warmly by the hand. 'It looked like everything that could go wrong, did. I was surprised and relieved my boss Lesley came through and organised a transfer of workers; he doesn't usually get his hands dirty.' James said smiling as he read Don's report. Pity about the factory though. 'I must say it's an excellent outcome overall so well-done Don. I've obviously chosen the best inspector for the job.

'Thank you James, just doing my job to help the war effort and shorten it where-ever possible. What's the latest on the allies' advance? I've been otherwise distracted for a while.' Don admitted, expecting to be provided with progress after the 'D' Day landings.

'It's good to know after all the battering we've had over the past few years. The boot is on the other foot now and about time.' Don having experienced at first hand the wrath of the Luftwaffe's onslaught of Tyneside and Hull.

'I'll drink to that Don. Now, your next assignment might appeal. It's quite different from what you've had so far and not as arduous but it's an important task all the same. The good thing is you should be able to get home most weekends.' James explained, without providing any details of the assignment. Knowing James, this project was unlikely to be a walk in the park.

'I haven't worked out all the details yet, so bear with me. It's a challenging one so have a few days at home first and I'll be touch.' Rarely would Don describe his projects as 'enjoyable'. 'You'll be able to travel straight to the assignment which has a timescale of a couple of months.' James explained, giving little away which wasn't a good sign.

*

'Hello stranger,' Mary said as he awkwardly negotiated the bus steps, walking stick at the ready. 'One day Monty, I'll get the hang of this,' Don winced, as he was engulfed by Mary and Malcolm who seemed to be sprouting like a weed. 'How are you Don, you look tired, so we'll have to give you lots of home comforts, won't we Malc? I've some good news too but I'll tell you about that later. Malcolm also has some good news too, haven't you?'

'Oh yes, I have Dad, do you want to hear what it is Dad.' Malcolm said excitedly, grasping his dad's hand.

'I just can't wait Malc. so you'll have to tell me, otherwise I'll never know.' Don grinned at his son's exuberance.

'Well, you know Dusty who we thought was a 'boy' cat? Well, he's not, he's a 'she' cat and do you know how we found out Dad?'

'I have no idea Malc. just how DID you find out?' Don was enjoying his mild teasing while Mary's raised eyebrows showed she didn't really approve.

'We----ell,' Malcolm paused for effect, 'Dusty's had four kittens. What do you think of that Dad?'

'Frankly my dear, I'm shocked,' Don said, open mouthed in mock surprise. 'And when did this happen?'

'Oh, about three weeks ago and Mrs Fitzpatrick said she'll take one and knows someone who will take two so there's one left. Maybe we'll keep it won't we Mam?' Malcolm explained showing that he was on top of the maths.

'We'll see Malc,' Mary replied shaking her head. 'I must admit Dusty kept things secret until Malcolm discovered them in the basket when he went to feed him, or her.' Mary patted Malcolm's head. 'He's got the makings of a very good parent Don. I'll get your supper, you looked tired and then it's up the wooden hill for Malcolm. I'll have Daddy read you a story from your Biggles book – you can choose your favourite story, alright?'

*

'So, what's your good news Mary, I'm all ears.' Don enquired, relaxing hands behind his head after another of Mary's specialities – lambs' liver and onions followed by bread & butter pudding.

'As you know I've been working at Dobson's the grocery store since the war started, as assistant manager. Mr Dobson, the owner hasn't been well recently and has decided to retire so he wants me to take over as the manager.' Mary said proudly, looking expectantly for Don's reaction. 'Of course, it will mean more money, more responsibility and a few more hours but it's something I really enjoy.'

'That is marvellous Darling, you deserve it for all the times you've managed on your own. How will that fit in with Malcolm's school times?' Don asked wondering whether Mary's exuberance has masked her family duties.

'Malcolm sees himself home now and I've arranged with Mrs Heads next door to look after him on the odd occasion when I'm working late.

Sometimes he comes to the shop after school and he has a snack at the shop before we go home.' Mary explained, 'he sometimes helps to me bag up the loose tea, sugar and biscuits.

'Well, you know best Mary and I'm sure Malcolm enjoys helping you with the groceries.' Don said, looking forward to the end of the war when he would be able to spend more time with his family and guide his son's progress at first hand.

*

Don made most of his short time at home, organising a visit to St Mary's lighthouse a couple of miles along the coast. In Victorian times its light had guided ships away from the notorious rocky outcrops that guarded the Tyne River, named the Black Middens where countless ships had foundered. Now, the Low Lights and High Lights inside Tynemouth and South Shields piers had made St Mary's redundant. The lighthouse was a popular tourist attraction with the promontory providing access to the island at low tide. Tardy sightseers would find themselves marooned for six hours and get very wet if they didn't pay close attention to the tide tables! On their day out a myriad of rock pools contained an assortment of sea life that Malcolm loved to search; crabs, jelly fish, small dog fish were there to worry and winkles to eat later. The lighthouse was a prominent landmark, 100 feet high and coated a brilliant white that allowed access to the top by a lung busting 130 steps, charging a small fee for access. The views over the surrounding coastline from Blyth in the North to the Tynemouth Priory and even Marsden Rock to the South could be seen on a clear day. The custodians were the RNLI coastguard who ran an information centre at the base of the lighthouse.

'Maybe next time we'll climb to the top son when I'm fitter and the weather's better.' Don said in answer to his son's request, although he knew it was a forlorn hope. Armed with his bucket and fishing net, Malcolm couldn't wait to explore the pools and before long the air was punctuated by shrieks of joy as he captured a very angry crab, craws outstretched and a tiny dogfish.

'Can you help me lift that rock Mam it's too heavy and I'm sure I saw a big crab hiding under it?' Mary was regularly roped into the search while Don, ever mindful of Monty's aversion to seaweed covered rocks stayed well clear and watched enviously from a distance.

*

Two days before his return to the training centre Don planned a picnic on the sand-dunes at Seaton Sluice, a couple of miles from Whitley and a rare treat for Malcolm to play on the adjacent beach. The icing on the cake would be to see *'Lassie Come Home',* at the Colosseum picture house featuring Elizabeth Taylor and Roddy McDowall.

'That's a great idea Don.' Mary said she would make a picnic with hot water for the tea from the Cavendish Hotel on the promenade. 'Malcolm, you can take your bucket and spade and we'll make some sandcastles on the beach, if you like.'

'Oh yes Mam that will be grand cos I'm pretty good at building them with my bucket and spade. And can we get an ice-cream as well please, as it's a day out and usually on a day out we get ice cream, don't we Mam?' Malcolm challenged his mother to contradict him.

On the Saturday they took the #8 Newcastle to Blyth bus from Whitley station, stopping opposite the Cavendish hotel twenty minutes later and adjacent to the sand-dunes. Choosing a sheltered spot out of the North Easterly breeze, they had a commanding view of the beach and, for a change a relative calm North Sea. Although the beach was still ringed with barbed wire and anti-tank concrete emplacements to guard against a thwarted German invasion, there was still plenty of beach for Malcolm's sandcastles.

'Come on Mam, I'll show you what to do.' Her son called out racing through the grass topped dunes, waving his bucket and spade like a warrior.

Don had struggled through the soft sand with Monty and gradually subsided onto the side of the dune, content to watch his wife and son at play. It was at times like these when he agonised over his lost limb that had robbed him of opportunities to share his own experiences as a youngster. Don knew it was a futile exercise but ....!

'I'll keep a watch on things when you get the tea.' Don offered as Mary and Malcolm abandoned the castles some of which had been ingeniously decorated with shells, seaweed and shoreline flotsam. 'I'm going to give you both 10/10 for effort and construction quality, and Malcolm, a gold star as the man in charge.' As his son did a little jig to celebrate his 'reward'.

*

As Mother and Son trudged through the sand to get the tea Don was left to consider what lay ahead for him because before long, WFI's would be redundant. The war for the Nazis and Hitler was as good as over and it was just a matter of time before Hitler's generals forced him to surrender. Don's career as a waiter had been cruelly cut short but he still hankered over a return to the hotel industry he loved. Restricted as he was with Monty, the obvious role would be one in management where his organisation skills and front of house experience could attract suitable employers. He was fearful that the post-war flood of young, eager and talented men could see him cast adrift because little was on offer for a disabled ex-factory inspector, already past his half century. But, based on what he had achieved in the years since his accident and against all the doomsters and 'job's comforters', his dream could still be realised if he was resourceful and committed. He was shaken out of these depressing thoughts of life on the employment scrapheap by his son's cries and a tug on his arm.

'Wake up Daddy, wake up we've got some tea and lovely cakes and they do have ice cream that Mam says I can have later. Isn't that marvellous?' His son's infectious demeanour lifted Don's negativity to see a brighter more positive future.

'Ice cream? That's certainly a treat,' Don replied, heartened that his son's response had brought about a more positive demeanour. 'And what flavour have you chosen Malcolm?'

'They had four kinds, didn't they Malcolm?' Mary said, waiting to be contradicted.

'Oh no Mam they'd only one, vanilla.' Malcolm said with a frown as he looked at curiously at his mam.

'No, you'll find there's four Malc. Vanilla or nothing, take it or leave it!' Mary said with a grin ruffling Malcolm hair.

'Oh, that is funny Mam but it's silly too. Isn't it Daddy?' Turning to Don for support.

'Very silly, but clever too. You can always bet your Mam to be funny when it suits her.' Giving Mary a raised eyebrow.

'Next time I'm on leave we could visit Holy Island and stop off where they do the best fish and chips. What's that place next to Bamburgh Castle Mary?'

'Seahouses,' Mary replied, 'they also smoke the best kippers anywhere so we could take some home.'

'I'd like that Daddy; cos I've been told you have to take the taxi and sometimes wait for six hours until the tide goes out.' Malcolm informed them, 'we were told that by Miss Beaton, my history teacher,'

'Now here's a question Malcolm, do kippers swim flat or folded?' Don quizzed raising his eyebrows.

'Oh Daddy, that's very silly. You know kippers don't swim. Everyone knows that!' Giving his dad a disbelieving stare.

'Very silly Malcolm. And you're right, if you were caught by the tide there are towers where you can wait until the tide goes out.' Mary added, 'you have to be really careful.'

Tired but happy they caught the return bus from Seaton Sluice later that afternoon, all with sun and wind-blown faces, each licking a Bertorelli's vanilla ice-cream cornet, happy being together again. Their family day ended as they joined the Colosseum queue where Don paid their 1.6 pence's eventually sympathising with Mary and Malcolm as they cried watching 'Lassie come home'.

CHAPTER 52

'Welcome back Don, how was Mary and Malcolm, all well I hope?' James enquired, 'I don't know how long your next assignment will last with the war in the final stages, but we have to keep up the momentum.'

'They're all fine James. We had a few good days together, so I'm well rested and ready to go.' Don smiled confidently, unlocking Monty's knee and hip catches carefully as he sat down.

'Great, that's the spirit. Our next assignment is a tricky one at a factory that's producing components for a range of motor vehicles, some in the front line and others in support roles such as ambulances and all vital to the allies advance through Europe and into Germany.' James paused thinking how best to describe the assignment. 'Thing is, the factory has a problem with production quality and the owner is a bit of a tyrant, a traditional leader who brooks no questioning of his decisions. Sinclair Beck, the owner, has a good team and skilled staff but he won't delegate and this is leading to staff and management dissatisfaction and higher than average labour turnover. It's affecting morale and ultimately output quality. Beck is in his late forties and needs careful handling to get him to realise there are better ways to get the results we want. You have up to a couple of months to work the miracle if you can.' James concluded, giving Don a file with Beck's background and the factories output statistics which included his management team and the production statistics.

'I'd be grateful if you could contact me after a couple of weeks with an update plus anything I can do to help, not that you'll need any.' James said, smiling with a firm handshake.

Don was again on his way again into the unknown, but it was the challenge he looked forward to and this one was likely to test his patience and resolve to the limit.

*

The Sinclair Beck factory was based in Sunderland, adjacent to Roker Park the home of Sunderland FC. Prior to the takeover, the factory had produced a range of polishes for furniture, footwear and leatherware until requisitioned for war production, and to judge from its pre-war accounts, barely kept its head about water. The family-owned business had been operational for three generations with Sinclair Beck the last surviving member of the family. Accommodation for Don had been arranged at a boarding house overlooking the Strand for his mid-week stay with the intention of getting home most weekends, depending on what issues were revealed in his first week.

*

'Ah, the new war factory spy,' Sinclair Beck announced, smirking at his ungracious humour as he greeted Don. His management team of production, personnel, finance and training smiled slightly embarrassed. 'We saw off the last one in double quick time didn't we Fred?' Looking at his production manager who failed to respond. 'Only joking Don, we'll afford you all the cooperation you need, not that you'll require much because we run a tight ship here, don't we Gordon,' looking at his personnel manager.

'We try to Mr Beck,' was the nervous reply, 'despite all the restrictions and regulations.'

'Well, maybe Don, that is Mr Sullivan can help us through some of the obstacles to our production, 'what do you say?'

As Don listened to Beck's rambling introduction, he realised that the report as to the character and demeanour of Sinclair was spot on. Here was a leader ruling through fear and intimidation; in short, a bully who unconsciously had given Don some valuable ammunition as to his best approach.

'Many thanks for the welcome and introduction to your team,' Don replied smiling but leaving Sinclair Beck to know that he was unimpressed with the obvious slight. 'I've been assigned by the war office to look into some issues here that are seriously affecting output quality and quantity.' He paused but there was no response other than an angry glare from Beck and an amazed look from the managers, 'the War Department's report requires my role to help you resolve these problems, and I mean with the workforce as a whole.' Don paused through the stunned silence. 'My first task will be to analyse in detail the issues with Mr Beck, after which I hope that whatever action is required will be identified in my review. I would imagine that the workforce might also have a view on these issues.' Another pause, another silence. 'Are there any questions?' There were none, except expressions of surprise as the managers exchanged startled *'what's next'* glances. I hope I've given you a summary of my role and reasons for being here?' Don enquired evenly, looking around to see only startled looks although Sinclair Becks face had become more strained and redder as Don elaborated on his role.

'Well, we now know that the war department is here to interfere in our well-run operation so I think Mr Sullivan and I should have a private word or two before anything else?' Beck turned, indicating Don to follow.

'I would welcome that Mr Beck, provided there's a cup of tea on offer at the same time.' Don responded with a grin as he was escorted into the inner office while the management team departed in something of a daze after what they had heard.

Once the tea had been brought by a young secretary Beck immediately went on the attack. 'I don't know why you're here; my production quotas are on budget and we're also meeting the cost of materials targets so what is the problem?' He was a man with a big chip on his shoulder and resented having his business decisions being questioned. It didn't occur to him that the war department had issues with his factory even though two inspectors had already been assigned to investigate. Don's response took the wind completely out of Sinclair's sales.

'If you think the war department inspectorate has no reason to investigate your operation then you need to think again. Your problems have been clearly identified and were included in the report sent to you a month ago.'

'They're always complaining and sending reports which I don't have time to bother with, I'm trying to run a factory here.' Sinclair blustered a half-baked excuse.

'Mr Beck, I'm here to get your head out of the sand and get things back on track. If not, the war department has the power to close you down and transfer production elsewhere and I don't think you want that, do you? It's not an idle threat and what the inspectorate decide will be based on my assessment.'

'No, of course not but what are the issues they're so worried about?' Beck admission of ignorance as to where his management was failing was a revelation that Don now believed was true. He was so consumed with his infallibility and ignorance of the damning statistics that his team was too fearful tell him. They had been cowed into accepting the status quo with the production issues continuing to deteriorate, until the failures had been revealed by the war department's analysis.

'Here's the thing. First of all, your labour turnover is twice the level of other factories and this is having direct effect not only on product quality but also the high number of rejects.' Don observed a puzzled frown on Sinclair and realised he didn't know. 'Are you aware of these failings Sinclair?'

'No, well not really, Gordon my Personnel Manager had mentioned we were having some leavers, but I thought they had just been offered better wages elsewhere, and that he was overplaying the problem to get improved pay and we can't afford that with profit margins so tight.'

'The chickens have come home to roost now and you will have the bite the bullet of change and quickly as the war ministry is not known for its patience.' Don explained, mixing his metaphors for effect and didn't think 'change' was a word in Sinclair Beck's dictionary unless he was the instigator. It was up to Don to kick start the process and there was no time to lose.

'Why yes, of course Don, that's why you're here isn't it to sort everything out until things are on an even keel to satisfy the inspectorate?'

'No Sinclair, that's where you're wrong. I'm here to *help you* and *your team* put things right in key areas because you and your team will be doing the hard graft. I'm here to facilitate the necessary changes. Let's get your team together in a participative atmosphere and get them to suggest solutions to the problems in their areas of management; labour turnover, product rejects and product quality and come up with an action plan. Secondly, find out from the workers themselves what they see as the problems in their jobs and sections and what they see as solutions. After all, they are the ones directly involved, they may even be the problem i.e. potential leavers. You're not in the blame game either, you're to find solutions and the more feedback you get from whatever source, the better.'

'OK, yes, I see how this could work but my managers basically do what I tell them. I don't think they're capable of sorting these problems out.' Sinclair's response showed how little confidence or trust he had in his team.

'Well now's the time to find out because they're all you've got and doing it on your own hasn't worked out too well so far, has it?' Don said with some impact as the time for a softly, softly approach was over. Nevertheless, Sinclair's comments about his team revealed the need for some 'hand holding' and guidance towards a more delegative style of management. A big ask for those who had followed his management mantra of *'do it my way, or else!'* for some time.

'I suppose we could give it a try Don. I'll call a meeting for tomorrow morning and see what they come up with but I'm not holding out much hope.' Sinclair said, resignedly and without much enthusiasm because he was beginning to feel out of his depth.

'First of all Sinclair, you have to come clean with them and tell them your way hasn't worked, and that's going to be tough for you because you are admitting you've failed them and the workforce. You're to blame for the mess you're in and unless you can admit that, and with some honesty, they will still think you're blaming them for the current situation. Can you do that

Sinclair because it's the only way forward?' Don looked at a man facing his Armageddon and wondered whether it was a bridge too far.

'I don't know whether I can face them with that kind of admittance and even if I do, will it work out anyway?' Sinclair's tortured face showed that his previous combative, uncompromising style had been replaced with someone who was now floundering to square his circle of doubt. To an extent Don was encouraged by Sinclair's change of attitude to one of self-doubt.

'Don't you think they know you've failed them; they've just been too cowed by your dominance to tell you?' Don turned the knife knowing more had to be done. 'So, let's have that meeting and start to find some solutions, it'll be hard for you but it's a necessary first step.'

Sinclair Beck's moment of truth had arrived and despite his reservations felt that Don was trying to help him by his no-nonsense approach.

CHAPTER 53

Sinclair recalled his managers the next morning after Don's ultimatum and basically admitted his failure to recognise the dire straits they were in and that he would arrange a meeting of the workforce two days later to explain his culpability and set the changes in motion. His managers could hardly believe their collective ears but were heartened by Sinclair's mea culpa.

'I've called the meeting for 10.00 and arranged to have beverages and snacks on tap. In addition to the management team, I've invited the main production supervisors and will outline the reasons for your visit. I won't ask for any answers at the meeting but will ask them to identify their issues and suggestions. These will be identified at another meeting a few days later.' Sinclair stated with some renewed authority that Don found encouraging. 'What do you think Don?'

'That's a well organised start Sinclair, particularly inviting the wider group of supervisors, because the grapevine will get the message out a great deal quicker that major changes are on the way.' Don nodded encouragingly. 'Also arranging a further meeting to kick start their suggestions underlines your resolve to initiate change. An integrated plan can then be installed from the feedback.'

'Before the meeting Sinclair I'd like a stroll through the factory to get a feel for the place.' Don wanted more of an insight into the factory's grass roots workings than just talking to the owner.

'Certainly, but you won't see much as we've scaled down the afternoon shift due to the staff shortages.'

*

Assemblers and machine operators stubbed their cigarettes out as Don and Sinclair approached, busying themselves heads down. Rarely was there any acknowledgement by either worker or supervisor as they passed down the rows which suggested either they didn't know who Sinclair was or they were too cowed with his presence. 'Establishing Sinclair as a participative owner on this evidence was going to be some ask.' Don thought.

'They're allowed to smoke on the job?' Don enquired evenly.

'Their supervisors should penalise them with a pay deduction if caught but it's rarely enforced.' Sinclair confirmed a little shamefacedly.

'So why not have a coffee/ cigarette break for a few minutes, maybe twice during each shift, it's worked in other factories and reduced associated accidents?'

'Mmm,..I suppose it's worth considering but the supervisors wouldn't like to interrupt production.' Sinclair's guarded response suggested the supervisors were tough opposition when it came to interfering with their schedules.

'You could always have a trial run in a couple of sections to see what the reaction is, perhaps get your production manager to organise a trial? Use the excuse that it's part of your accident prevention programme?'

'I see, yes that might work and if production levels were not affected that would be a justification to extend it to other sections, wouldn't it?' Sinclair was getting quite enthused with the idea. 'We don't have a safety officer as issues have been left to the production manager and he's too busy keeping to production schedules, unless there's an accident and then we have a purge, but it doesn't last.'

'Did you know that accident awareness and prevention, where it's applied professionally is directly linked to improved production, fewer worker absences and lower personal insurance claims?' Don was ramming home the benefits to each area of risk and hoped Sinclair was seeing the positives for him.

'Yes, I see what you're getting at, but we don't have the time or personnel to develop any worthwhile safety procedures or training and our personnel manager hasn't the background.' Sinclair's approach to any changes was to erect barriers and resist.

'What if you transferred the role of safety and accidents to your training manager, presumably he is a qualified trainer and conducts induction, skills and safety training as part of his remit?'

'Well, yes, but with the staff turnover he doesn't have much time after induction and skills training with the newcomers to conduct accident training and prevention.'

'You've put your finger on the problem Sinclair, labour turnover is preventing you from accident training. This problem is all part of the factory's system, so improve one thing; that is labour turnover and hey presto, you have time for accident training. So, how do you reduce labour turnover Sinclair?' Don waited for an answer and received a shake of the head. 'OK, let's find out why staff leave; it's rarely money you know, because if there's one thing they know when they start a job it's their wages, even if they'd like more. It's usually down to other things like job satisfaction, social aspects, supervision or a satisfying work environment.

Let's find out if your workers are happy with these job elements. Do you think they are Sinclair?'

'I don't really know to be honest Don; I've never asked my managers that question. Maybe I've assumed they are reasonably happy unless my managers tell me otherwise and from what you're saying they probably aren't.' Sinclair admitted ruefully.

'At last,' Don thought, Sinclair Beck is becoming aware about where his problems lie and more importantly where the solutions might be addressed by the process of discovery. In short, a factory survey.

'So why not, through your managers have the supervisors organise work groups in each section during work time to find out why they are leaving and have one of your managers sitting in purely as an observer?'

'I'm not sure the supervisors would agree to these meetings during worktime.' More barricades from Sinclair.

'Why not ask them and if they're still reluctant during work time, have them ask for volunteers for a meeting after work. But first use your considerable powers of persuasion Sinclair to convince them that if they find out the reasons and you're able to install their solutions, they'll be the beneficiaries.'

*

Sinclair was feeling he had been unwittingly dragooned into several changes and tasks well out of his comfort zone but at the same time he was enthused with Don's involvement. Don knew that progress had been made by providing answers to all Sinclair's objections. The acid test would come the next morning as to whether Sinclair could admit personal responsibility for the factory's dire situation in a way that his managers and supervisors could believe. That a new inclusive leader had appeared, like a genie from the corporate bottle, and respond accordingly. If not, then all Don's preparatory work the previous evening would be stillborn. A disturbed night for Don was in prospect.

Don's welcome by his new landlady Iona Clayton, was a satisfying start to his assignment but did little to provide him a comfortable night's sleep after and a filling meal of shepherd's pie, carrots, and cabbage, followed by baked rice pudding.

CHAPTER 54

'Good morning, everyone and many thanks for taking the time from your busy schedules to attend. Please help yourselves to the drinks and snacks, all home-made I've been informed by the Eleanor our cordon blue cook - pausing as a few nervous laughs broke out - we'll start the meeting promptly at 10.15.' Don smiled and surveyed the room with satisfaction at what appeared to be a full attendance of managers and supervisors, who were all approaching the meeting in an anxious frame of mind.

Don immediately noticed a subtle change in the atmosphere by Sinclair's announcement, with smiles at his unexpected informality and even a joke. It was an encouraging start and a good indicator. As he toured the room being introduced as the factory inspector, many looking surprised at his obvious disability. Sinclair then tapped the table to get the room's attention and the make-or-break meeting started promptly.

'My friends.' Sinclair Beck announced, 'we are in a crisis situation, and I bear full responsibility.' You could have heard a pin drop at Sinclair's raw admission. 'That is why Don Sullivan is here from the war factory inspectorate.' Don acknowledged his introduction. If things don't change significantly in several areas, we are basically out of business. Don is not here to solve our problems, that's our job, but to help us identify the best ways to do it.' Sinclair paused to let his message sink in amid a hubbub of astonished chatter. 'Let me explain the reasons for this situation which has gradually worsened over the past few months. High labour turnover is creating problems with increased rejects, accidents and ultimately with falling production. Urgent action is required by myself, the management team, the supervisors and finally the workforce itself, because without your cooperation and their commitment these problems cannot be improved. In short, we must identify what these failings are and what is needed to rectify them, and I'm talking about solutions in days and weeks not months. Ladies and gentlemen, these are our priorities, are there any questions before I continue?' Sinclair paused to assess the mood of his supervisors.

'We're already working flat out so what are you saying we have to do, work harder, put more time in than we do at the moment?' A female supervisor arm raised, asked forcefully.

'Thank you, Barbara is it? I'm not expecting more effort, you're doing that already. All I'm asking is for you to help the management identify the reasons for these problems, all of which contribute to falling production levels. Our first task is one of discovery. Why are workers leaving? Why do we have an unacceptable level of returns? Why are accidents on the rise? Why is production falling when, as you say you're working harder than ever? So, let's find out!' Sinclair's clarion call was clearly personal and had an electrifying effect on the meeting. A loud dissenting voice shouted from another supervisor, Clive in charge of distribution and one who was continually chaffing at management edicts.

'You want us to do the job of management so when we screw up you can blame us, as you're doing now?' He grumbled looking around for support which came from a few nods of agreement.

'I'm not in the 'blame game' nor are the managers Clive, but do you know anyone or any group to identify what's wrong with the present system than the supervisors and the workforce? If there's anyone to blame Clive, I'm your man!' Sinclair's admission drew some laughs and applause as he had cleverly drawn Clive's sting who could only mumble his agreement. 'So, what is required is for a representative group from each section, to identify the issues that have led to our present crisis situation. That's the plan. We'll return in a weeks' time with your suggestions and recommendations and agree an action plan. Does that sound like the way forward?' Sinclair enquired.

'Yes, I can see that might be a useful starting point but only if what we suggest is not rejected out of hand?' Barbara's observation was roundly supported by the other supervisors.

'I can put on record that whatever you suggest will be the basis of improvements across the board. Let's face it, who better to identify solutions than those most affected by the problems? You and your staff are part of the solution, and it will be managements job to install those changes with your involvement. Does that answer your concern?' Sinclair was at pains to draw out any major reasons for them to reject the move forward. A wave of nodding heads and a bubble of chatter greeted Sinclair's offer.

CHAPTER 55

'I can hardly believe what I've heard over the last half hour.' Graham a moderate supervisor confided soto voce to a colleague. 'It's a revelation that management wants our help with the factory's problems and I for one would like to see if he can *'walk the walk'* because talking about change is the easy bit.'

'You're right Graham, walking the walk will be the acid test for Mr Beck.' Lionel agreed doubtfully.

'I believe that with a team effort we can look forward to better times. Thank you all.' Sinclair closed the meeting with the participants shocked at the owner's admission of failure but with a feeling that for once he was someone they might look up to in future.

Don was frankly amazed at Sinclair's turnaround, both in his attitude and behaviour, it was almost as though he had had a personality transplant. 'Maybe the shock of his business's demise had brought about this volte face; it hasn't come a moment too soon.' Don thought to himself.

'That was a successful meeting Mr Beck, and I think the supervisors will cooperate with your suggestions,' the production manager announced once Don and the management team had returned to Sinclair's office.

'Please call me Sinclair, Fred because from now on we're a team for solving problems. I want to hear your take on our next step to help your supervisors organise the work group meetings to develop a questionnaire.'

'Can I say that I'm not too happy being made responsible for Accidents and Safety (A & S),' Said Reg. the Training Manager after Sinclair suggested an additional role, 'first of all I'm up against it with the labour turnover which requires more recruitment induction and skills training.' Looking directly at Sinclair Beck expecting a negative reaction. 'Although, I can see the need for a separate role.' Reg modified his angry outburst. A short silence followed as the other managers expected a put down by Sinclair.

'That is a good point to identify the importance of the A and S role and the relevance to your problems with labour turnover Reg. We have identified A & S as closely linked to our production and quality issues. Question is, how do we help Reg with his Training role if he agrees to take on an additional responsibility?' Another silence followed.

'Well, if it would help, I could take on some of your induction training as I'm already applying a checklist of tasks for their first days on the job?' Gordon the Personnel Manager suggested to Reg whose eyebrows rose in surprise.

'Many thanks Gordon, maybe we can have a chat about that after the meeting?'

Fred in charge of Production also chipped in with a suggestion. 'If you give me your skills training schedule Reg, I'll see what bits I could take off you because our workplace induction replicates some of your induction and that would reduce your involvement. We don't want to cover the same ground twice.'

'It looks like we're making some progress here Reg. so are you willing to take on the A and S role?' Sinclair said, daring Reg to disagree.

'I'm more than willing if it helps with our overall problems, but my knowledge of A and S could be covered on the back of a postage stamp.' He replied, provoking some amusement.

'I'm also in the same situation Reg but isn't it mainly common sense? We can order enough handouts and notices.' Sinclair acknowledged. 'What's your view Don, is it just common sense when all's said and done?'

All eyes turned to Don for a knowledgeable response to the issue. 'I agree with you both that much of A and S is common sense and if I asked you for a list, I suspect you would cover most of the essentials. But, we're talking here of a training programme designed by specialists and supported by all the relevant publicity, posters and training. The war department recognises how important a well organised and conducted A and S programmes is, being closely linked to increased output, improved product quality and even workplace morale.' Don's detailed response had the managers and Sinclair hanging on his every word and nodding in agreement.

'Thank you for that clarification. I'm sure we all agree with what is required but we're short of this high-powered specialist input you talk about.' Sinclair added looking for a response.

'Perhaps the war factory inspectorate might be able to lend a helping hand. If I can persuade the powers to be that your A & S training is a priority, then it's possible they might allocate a specialist to you for a limited period. Would that help?'

Managers and owner responded with one voice *'yes it would'* and laughed at their spontaneous agreement.

In that single moment Don felt a corner had been turned towards their collective salvation. Here was the start of common resolve to kick-start the necessary swath of action across all areas of the factory.

CHAPTER 56

A week later Sinclair called an emergency meeting of his management team with the news that production targets had been revised by the war production inspectorate because a factory in Hull that had been a main source of vehicle parts had been bombed in Hitler's last throw of the dice.

'We're really up against it now.' Sinclair complained, 'just when I hoped we'd gained a bit of breathing space Adolf strikes again. We'll just have to tighten our belts and eke out a little more from our diminished workforce.' He explained, looking hopefully at Fred the production manager.

'There's one good thing Sinclair, Gordon said, the feedback from the workgroups have been collated and several areas have been identified for quick action that could improve production.'

'Yes, good point, the sooner the better. Let's have a quick management meeting tomorrow after we've analysed the findings. We can have copies today if Janet can wind up the Gestetner.' Sinclair was now a man of action as yesterday was today's tomorrow! 'Janet, are you free for a bit of overtime?' He called to his long serving personal assistant and secretary. 'We've got an urgent desire for your technical expertise.'

*

'OK we've all had a good look at what the work groups consider are the contributory issues and what can be addressed as short-term quick fixes first.' Sinclair asked as he peeled back the first page of faded blue Gestetner print.

'Smoking at the workface shouldn't be penalised as it helps with the concentration.' Was a complaint logged by every group Gordon read out.

'Yes, but it also contributes to many accidents.' Fred added. 'So, what about having a smoking/ coffee break which would eliminate the need to smoke on the job?'

'If that's agreed, will you schedule the times with the supervisors Fred?' Suggested Sinclair which was given unanimous agreement. 'OK what next, Reg anything in your area for action?

'Yes, Sinclair two things. Firstly, rubbish build-ups around machines and is often the cause of accidents in production, so in conjunction with Gordon and Fred I can rearrange the cleaners' rotas to increase rubbish collections.

'Well done Reg, and what was the third thing?' Asked Sinclair pleased to hear his managers taking the initiative.

The second is a bit off the wall but it could improve morale and have a knock-on effect on production. The issue was mentioned several times, exclusively by female staff regarding uniforms.'

'What's the problems with female uniforms Reg, they look fine to me?' Sinclair muttered from a male perspective.

Scrutinising the small print, Reg read out one complaint from a work group in the Assembly department. *'They don't fit properly, they're the wrong colour and they're not very stylish.'*

'This is a point raised by most of the work groups and it's clearly linked to job satisfaction, especially if they don't feel comfortable in what they're wearing for eight hours.' Don interjected quickly scanning a few pages.

'Janet, could you give me your valuable time for a couple of minutes about a female issue, I don't think the masculine elements can provided any solution worth consideration. Could you have a chat with some of the women concerned about their uniforms and find out what can be done asap, seems it's a widespread issue.' Sinclair asked persuasively.

'I take it from your tone Mr Beck that you would like some idea by yesterday? Fine, I'll see what they want.' Janet said agreeably, I'll just finish those letters to catch the post.'

'Moving on Gordon, have you dug up anything that might help with this turnover?' Sinclair directed his gaze to the head of personnel. 'Anything we can do quickly?'

'A number of comments from a cross section of areas and particularly the machine operatives who had little time for socialising on their lunch break.' *'we only get 20 minutes and 'there's not much to do after work' or 'our supervisors never have time to chat' and 'we're never given credit for a good job.'* The Personnel Manager's view was that social aspects were an important contributor to job satisfaction. 'Perhaps the supervisors could have more involvement with their recruits because many of our workers are young females with absentee families or boyfriends in the forces. Maybe we could look at ways to provide more social opportunities at work and after.' Gordon's contribution was well received.

'Having the smoking/ coffee break will help and is it possible to extend the lunch break to 30 minutes? Fred that's your area so can you see if it's feasible, although I know that you're under the cosh for extra production.' Sinclair asked empathetically.

'Any comment of these areas Don?' Sinclair was getting increasingly agitated to nail down some agreement that they could present to the meeting.

'Gordon's point about social needs is a good one, so maybe Reg could liaise on how to extend social opportunities. Are there any recreational opportunities after work such as gaming, quizzes, dances for example? Also, 'recognition needs' are a major contributor to job satisfaction so the comment about *'never given credit for a good job'* touches on this. Maybe the supervisors and managers could address that one?' Sinclair asked pointedly. 'I'll take that one on board myself with my staff.' Smiling at his managers.

Other ideas for improving involvement were suggested by Don. 'Some factories I visited had things like *'employee of the month'; 'most productive department'; 'best suggestion of the month (productivity, waste reduction, accident reduction etc.).* A trophy or a voucher could be presented to the winner, but the real 'reward' would be the recognition that they received.' Don's contribution struck a nerve and prompted some animated exchanges.

'Thanks Don, food for thought there so now we've a base for some solid action let's draft these into proposals for the next meeting and attach a timescale. I would like to announce these to the whole workforce as soon as possible.' Sinclair realised that he was delegating more responsibility to his managers to perform and would have to live or die by the results.

Before the make-or-break meeting with the supervisors Sinclair scanned the list of proposed improvements and was justly proud of his team's efforts. Each manager had been allocated into a subgroup to determine which area of job satisfaction they could implement. These were linked to issues raised by the workforce in three main areas of job satisfaction.

BASIC – improvement work environment (cleaner); production bonus scheme; improved female uniforms; improved canteen quality and selection; A & S training.

SOCIAL – 2 x 15-minute smoking/ tea breaks per shift; extended lunch time to 30 minutes; increased supervisors/ worker interaction; post work activities.

SELF ESTEEM/ RECOGNITION – job competence recognised; employee of the month; work group of the month; increased job responsibilities.

'Even if half of these proposals are installed it's still a leap forward in terms of work improvements.' Sinclair declared enthusiastically.

The review meeting started full of anticipation as the factory grapevine has been in overdrive with supervisors ready and willing to leak as much information as would guarantee their popularity and status as instigators of 'participative management'.

*

'Good morning, ladies and gentlemen, and thank you for attending a meeting that I hope will move the factory forward. Please help yourself to the fine fare that our cordon blue pastry cook has amassed for your benefit.' Sinclair paused as a round of applause rang out for the 5-star victuals. 'You have all had a summary of the work-group feedback and it is intended to install these recommendations as soon as possible with your agreement.' Sinclair had set the scene and ploughed on with the reforms.

'First of all, can I pay tribute to my managers, supervisors and to the workforce for their ideas and suggestions and acknowledge the sterling role that Don Sullivan, has played in helping us identify the best approaches. In addition, he is in the process of engaging a specialist advisor for A and S (Accident and Safety) to help our training manager Reg Forthright set up the accident prevention initiative to improve workplace safety and help to reduce staff turnover. 'Now to the main meat of our meeting – the action areas. I've given pride of place to the women, and why not, they're in the majority here?' Pause for female cheers. 'What was almost universally identified as a major gripe was ladies' uniforms. Janet, my personal assistant has, in conjunction with supervisor and shop steward Barbara, been working to resolve this issue. Barbara will you tell us what has been agreed.' Whistles and applause as Barbara approached the rostrum.

'Well brothers and sisters, Janet and I met a representative group of ladies.' Barbara answered haltingly to cries of 'speak up Barbara'. Barbara reprimanded the hecklers and continued. 'We have agreed with the management to redesign the workwear and have chosen styles and colours we can all agree on after a catwalk of design options by the uniform company. After this the new uniforms should be available within a month. Thank you, Mr Beck.' Barbara smiled warmly at Sinclair before stepping down to applause and whistles in support of what many considered a major concession by the management.

In order of their seniority, supervisors were asked to comment on the reforms that had been suggested by the various work groups. A lively discussion on the timetable for each of the reforms resulted in some being adjusted such as smoking breaks being reduced to 10 minutes from 15 and canteen menus to be based on a monthly plan. The suggestion box scheme and monthly awards i.e. employee or team of the month etc. would have the details finalised by an employee work group.

Monthly Review Meetings, chaired by supervisors with management observers, would assess the success of the various initiatives. Management monitoring of these effects on labour turnover, product waste, return levels and the overall effect on output would have a monthly focus with related feedback to supervisors after which it was hoped there would be some measurable improvement in labour turnover in particular.

Don looked around at expressions that seemed to reflect hope for a brighter future for the Sinclair Beck factory. Sinclair was in animated discussion with a group of supervisors, an unheard-of occurrence a few weeks earlier when the factory was on the edge of an abyss. Don smiled inwardly as his thoughts returned to that first day when Beck labelled him a *'spy from the inspectorate'*. Sinclair wound up the meeting by taking responsibility for the success or failure of the changes agreed. His clarion call was cheered to the echo at the meeting's conclusion.

Don's job was done as he accepted a glass of bubbly from Sinclair to celebrate the success of the management initiative. He promised to keep a weather eye on the Beck factory and wished them all the best for the future.

CHAPTER 57

As he stepped gingerly from the train at Bishop Auckland, the platform was a heaving mass of soldiers, sailors and airmen cavorting wildly with the locals waving Union Jacks. Don heard the air raid sirens blast again and hoped they could get under cover in time but this time the siren was an all-clear that carried on, and on, and on. 'What's happened?' Don shouted above the racket to an airman who immediately embraced him in a bear hug, teetering on the platform edge. It was a Christmas and New Year celebration rolled into one, with knobs on!

'We won, we won, we beat Adolf and the Nazis – the war's over,' the soldier whooped, dancing and threading his way along the platform, grabbing and kissing anyone within range.

Don brain was in a whirl, after 6 long years of global devastation and untold millions sacrificed, the fighting had ceased, at least in Europe. He made his way out of the frenzy with a porter in tow to a WHSmith's stand. A Daily Mirrow headline emblazed a confirmation of Germany's unconditional surrender. **'WAR ENDS IN EUROPE – Victory Celebration - May 8th 1945.**

Don searched around the station until he found a free phone box and called Mary at Dobson's. 'Hello, Dobson's grocery can I help you? Mary's dulcet tones were like music to Don's ears.

' Hello it's Don and I've just heard to the news. How are you coping?'

'It's like the flood gates have been opened here, we've never been so busy and anything that's not on ration is being taken. We've had to limit certain items like toilet rolls or we'll have none left for our regulars, it's a madhouse. Don, sorry I've got to go – love you.

'No, no, I understand. Ring me later if you can at the training centre. Love you too Mary, bye.' Don finished the call with tears running down his chin and he wasn't sure why. Maybe hearing Mary's voice or the joy he felt at the war's end - it didn't really matter Don thought, wiping his eyes.'

'Hey! Are you finished with that phone? There's a Peace On you know!' A strident voice shouted with a hint of humour.

'Sorry' said Don, smiling, 'I just fought a war and think I won.' As he ploughed his way through the cheering mob to the bus.

CHAPTER 58

'Welcome back Don, you concluded your final assignment just before Germany's capitulation. The reforms you engineered at the Beck factory will serve them as well in peacetime, so well done,' James declared shaking Don's hand with some conviction. All around the centre joyous staff were enjoying a celebratory drink and jig.

'I thought the World had gone mad when I got to Bishop Auckland station!' Don said, relieved that had finished his last assignment in style.

'So, what will you do now Don? You've two months to get your act together.'

It was now post-war so what was he going to do? His notice from the inspectorate would help prepare for peacetime employment. Don could be on the scrapheap with legions of others and competition for jobs of all kinds would be fierce. The past year had worn him down, yet he was sad in a way his war was over and his inspectorate role redundant. Monty had survived and had allowed him to fight the war on two legs in the dark days of the war but now required an overhaul. He was also indebted to **The Voice,** whatever its origin for being there for him in a crisis.

As he said goodbye to his friends and colleagues at the centre and flagged down the station bus for a lift to the station Don felt like a punctured balloon, all meaning had, in an instant been wiped away by the armistice. His war contribution was in the past tense and would soon be forgotten, so what did the future hold for a one-legged ex-factory inspector, now approaching middle age? Maybe **The Voice** would provide sound council and encouragement as it had in the past?

*

Mary, Malcolm and Dusty waved the Union Jacks to welcome Don off the bus to the amusement of the other passengers as the Hunter bus chugged away in a blast of oily smoke on its way to the coast.

'You look like you need a good cup of tea and a meal. Has your landlady been giving you short rations?' Mary took his arm in a warm embrace. 'Oh, it's so good to have you back again Don and hopefully for much longer.'

Malcolm gave his Dad a hug. 'Is Monty alright Daddy? Has he been behaving, I hope? Dusty and me have missed you, you know,' Putting on a serious face.

'That's Dusty and I,' Mary corrected his grammar with a smile and pat on the head.

'And I've missed you as well. And haven't you grown since I saw you?' Malcolm was filling out into a sturdy youth. 'Monty and I have brought you all a little present.'

'Quick Mam, let's get home so we can see what Daddy's brought us.'

*

While at the factory one of the metal workers Don had befriended knew of his young son and had made a model of a Spitfire for Malcolm. Before he left the training centre he had also been able to buy a bottle of Eau de Cologne for Mary.

'That's my favourite perfume Don, thank you so much and what have you there Malcolm?' Looking down as she dabbed some perfume behind both ears, breathing in the heavenly scent.

'Oh Daddy that's the best present I've had for ages,' Malcolm cried as his excited son he ripped off the wrapping to reveal a gleaming Spitfire with British rondels in place and numbers SP 1 on either side of the fuselage. He looked admiringly at the plane and promptly dashed around the room - rrrrh, rrrh, rrrrh, boooom, ack, ack, ack mimicking a fighter in action.

'I can see you've made a hit there Don. It'll keep him amused for some time and be the source of some serious admiration by his friends at school.' Mary said, complimenting Don's thoughtfulness. 'Don darling I almost forgot a letter came for you a couple of days ago.' Mary handed over a large letter embossed BECKS POLISHES and inside was a letter and enclosure which he sat down to read, sipping his tea.

Dear Don,

I didn't get the opportunity to thank you properly for what you achieved for the factory, and me in particularly. If you hadn't made me see myself as the problem, the factory would have slid into a morass. I know it took all your considerable skills and steely temperament to pull us round. We'll be forever in your dept.

The enclosed card comes with our best wishes for your future and was signed by the management team, supervisors and many of the staff who cherished your advice and encouragement.

Could give me a call as I have a proposition that may interest you.

Best wishes to you and your family.

Sinclair Beck

Don read the letter twice, inspected the card with a lump in his throat and dabbed his eyes with his handkerchief as he handed the letter and card to Mary.

'Don, what a beautiful letter and card, Mary cried, bursting into tears as she took his handkerchief to stem the tears and blew her nose. 'You must have done something extra-special there to get that reaction. Do you have any idea what he means by his proposition?'

'I've no idea, but there's an easy way to find out.' Don's brow creased in thought although he had an idea what Sinclair had in mind.

CHAPTER 59

The next morning, hand in hand, Don took Malcolm to Bygate School for the first time since his accident and felt he was part of a family again. Don was immediately surrounded at the school gates, by a group of young mums eager to congratulate him on his Royal Society medal for saving the young worker's life. An article and photo had appeared in the local paper after Don's presentation. 'Tell you the truth I don't remember too much about it,' Don explained, which no one believed.

*

'Daddy, will you thank the man who made my Spitfire? I don't want him wondering whether I liked it.' Malcolm's face was creased in concern.

'I've a better idea Malcolm, when you return from school today why don't you write him a letter and we can go to the post office with it? What do think?'

'W…..ell, my writing is'nt very good y'know or my spelling and I wouldn't want him to be confused with my letter.' He replied lips pursed.

'Oh, I don't think that'll be a problem became we'll check your spelling and I'll add a little note too.' Don smiled at his son's concern.

Deer Mr Parkinson,

Thank you very much for my spitfire which is reely sooper and all my pals are very enveus of it. I play with it a lot and it is the verry best present i have had sins crissmas.

Best wishs Malcolm Sullivan

This was the original version sent to Clive Parkinson with a note from Don to say his Mam subsequently helped him correct the spelling.

*

Don rang Becks from the corner phone box the next morning to enquire about Sinclair's offer.

'Hello Don, it's Sinclair and good of you to call back, how are you?'

'Fine, just fine' Don replied after pushing button A for the connection. 'I'm and enjoying some family life for a change, and how are you and the team?'

'I'm in rude health and we're all in good shape at present, thanks to you.'

'Just doing my job Sinclar. I wanted to thank you for your letter and card, it meant a lot to me and Mary so please thank everyone for their kindness?' Don paused for Sinclair to respond.

'I'll certainly pass on your best wishes and thanks. The proposition I mentioned concerns a position here that I thought might interest you. Gordon our Personnel Manager is leaving in a couple of weeks for a more varied role and I need to fill that vacancy. With your background in the service industry and your intimate connection with the team you would be an ideal replacement for Gordon. What do you think? Sinclair laid out his offer with little preamble, which was after all his style.

'Many thanks for thinking about me Sinclair but at present I'm considering a return to the hospitality industry in some form.' Don replied noncommittally.

'That's fine Don but if you've nothing finalised why don't you come to the factory and we can discuss the deal with no strings attached?' He sensed Don had no concrete plan and knew his deal would be attractive for an unemployed WFI.

As Don had nothing planned, he agreed to visit the following Wednesday. Personnel Management was an area of management that he was attracted to and depending on the offer he could have a flying start.

*

On arrival Don was given a huge welcome back by Sinclair with a tour of the factory. It had in that short time been returned to its previous role of producing polishes of all shapes, sizes and applications. Here was Sinclair's forte and didn't it show as he proudly escorted Don around the reorganised works, being warmly welcomed by many he knew. It was as though he'd never left and during his tour he met Clive Parkinson, the Spitfire maker. 'Here's the letter to prove the spitfire was a hit Clive.' Don shook Clive's hand warmly.

'As Personnel Manager you would have complete control of all Personnel affairs and Fred Shorthouse would answer to you for training as well as accident and safety matters. You would be part of the senior management team with myself, the finance and production directors.

When they returned to Sinclair's office he outlined his offer to Don. 'Your salary would be £20 weekly or £1,040 p.a. reviewed annually and you would be included in our profit-sharing scheme and a non-contributory pension scheme as well. This will all be in the contract.' Sinclair paused looking very self-satisfied with a deal he thought no-one could possible turn down.

'That's a tempting offer Sinclair and thank you for your confidence in me. I'll need a to talk it over with Mary and let you know in a few days.

'To be honest, Don' Sinclair explained, 'I can't think of anyone who would be better especially as you know the managers, the workforce, the setup, and they all love you for what you did.' Sinclair was pulling out all the emotional stops. 'Of course, Don, it's a big decision and I wouldn't want you to rush into it. So, give me a call when you decide and hope we can get things organised, it would be great to work together again.' Sinclair smiled encouragingly as he shook Don's hands to put a positive slant on the offer.

*

'That's it in a nutshell Mary, it's an offer that seems to tick all the boxes and we've a few days to consider so what do you think? I won't take it unless you're sure it's the right decision for both of us' He took both of her hands and looked at the only person he'd ever loved. Don was a lucky man to have such a woman on his side.

'It is a big decision Darling but it's yours to take or not. You won't get a better offer that's for sure and it's in a place you know as well as an area of management you're familiar with. 'Make a decision and go to it Mr Sullivan if you're really sure.'

CHAPTER 60

Out of the blue came an offer from a Leisure Consortium that was headed by an ex-colleague from the Cliffe Hotel which would mean Don could return to a senior management position in the hotel industry. Don opened a intriguing letter from an ex-work colleague from the Cliffe who he had not seen since the war started.

15 Promontory Way, Whiteladies Estate, Whitley Bay.
Dear Don,
Many apologies for not contacting you earlier although I always intended to. I understood from the Grapevine you were a factory inspector during the war and made a great success of it. My reason for writing is to find out whether you would be interested in a business opportunity. I left the Cliffe during the war to create my own company and want to develop in a new area.
Suffice to say I would like to discuss this with you if you're available on Saturday 4th October at 10 a.m. at the Cliffe to discuss this venture.
All the very best to you and your family.
Tim (Spalding)

'Well Mary, that's put the proverbial cat among the pigeons.' Don was nonplussed by Tim's letter. 'You remember Tim, he worked in the bar and came for dinner a couple of times with his wife. 'I'm available the Saturday after next so I might as well see what's on offer, what do you think?'

'Yes, I remember his wife. She was the driving force as I recall and probably the reason for his business success. You'll only find out if you go.' Mary said with an edge.

*

'I'm delighted you could make the meeting Don,' pumping his hand, 'it's really good to see you again, after your accident.' Looking at Don's disability. 'Come and meet my friends and fellow directors.'

'Thanks for the invitation Tim, I've had excellent rehabilitation with the new limb so mobility is not a problem, otherwise the War Department would have shown me the door.' Don walked easily with his stick towards two middle aged, well-built, overweight and expensively suited men who rose to meet him. Tim introduced Godfrey Chalmers and Trevor Bateman as Tim's partners. 'Can I get you a drink Don?' Tim enquired.

'Thanks Tim, I'll have a coffee, milk no sugar.' As Tim signalled a waitress.

After a short reminisce about their time at the Cliffe, Tim told his colleagues about Don's time as the restaurant manager. 'Don was able to develop a really good team in quick time.' Tim's summary demonstrated Don's management suitability to the other directors. Tim then outlined his project. 'There's local hotel up for sale and looks like a good investment opportunity. In brief we would like you to consider running it as the Managing Director. We want you to give us your opinion as to whether is worth developing as it would require substantial updating and renovation but otherwise seems to be in reasonable condition and is still operational.'

'I see, where is it and have you any details?' Don asked.

'It's between Cullercoats and Tynemouth overlooking the beach with a great location.' Tim explained handing over the sales brochure showing a broad, white fronted building on three floors with an imposing entrance and its name over the main frontage, Sands Hotel.

'We could also consider a name change,' Tim added, 'and there's a car park at the rear with potential for adding rooms, so there's options for development.'

Don knew the area but couldn't remember the hotel or its exact location. 'Hmmm..,' Don flicked through the details, which indicated a closer inspection. 'Yes, I remember now, it's a good location. When could we have a look and is there a surveyor's report?'

'No, but I'll check with the estate agents and let you know.' Tim agreed, delighted that Don was tempted.

After checking diaries, Tim agreed to arrange a visit to the Sands and the group broke up for a lunch that Tim had booked in the Cliffe's main restaurant. 'For old times sake Don, I thought you'd like to see how your old seat of power is operating.'

'That's very thoughtful of you Tim,' Don acknowledged some of the staff he had trained, which seemed a lifetime ago. As he looked around his old stamping ground where he had envisaged a lifelong commitment and railed briefly at those few seconds that had extinguished his career and almost his life.

*

Three days later Tim picked up Don from his house in Hill Heads to evaluate the Sands Hotel. The brochure provided all the salient information he required; a restaurant that seated 40, accommodation for 40 – 50 which included family rooms, an unlicensed bar, a spacious kitchen, a laundry room and two meeting rooms for 30 persons and 2 storage rooms.

The present owners were a husband and wife who, after 30 years had decided to retire to Spain as the husband had an arthritic condition that they thought a warmer, sunnier climate would ease. If the consortium decided to buy, the staff would also be available. After a quick tour they enjoyed a lunch of good quality by well-trained service staff and returned to Tim's office to discuss their visit and most importantly Don's reaction.

Don was asked for his evaluation as the specialist. 'It's in need of a make-over as the décor and furnishings are tired and old fashioned. It does have potential and it's in the right place for both the holiday traffic and passing trade for the bar and restaurant, although a drink licence is a must. The rooms we saw certainly needed updating and once it was up and running, an AA rating of 3 Stars should be aimed for initially.' Don's analysis made it clear that any offer should bear in mind the need for a significant outlay for modernisation.

'I agree there's a lot to be done Don, but it does have potential and the structure appears to be sound. It all depends on the sums, and whether success in the long term is worth the outlay.' Let's discuss the options back to the office.'

'On paper the projected outlay on renovations, redecoration and upgrading although significant is manageable if we can negotiate a price of £11,000 and we're in a good position for two reasons. Firstly, there doesn't seem to be anyone interested and secondly the couple want a quick sale to they can sail off to Sunny Spain.' A self-satisfied Tim concluded, hands behind his head as he sat back and looked enquiringly at Don.

'Now you have a clear idea of what's involved, are you interested?' Tim enquired with a hopeful look.

'Yes, Tim I'm interested but at present I've been offered a position at Becks as Personnel Director, where I was a WFI a war factory inspector. Before I commit myself I would expect the same conditions and some long term assurance of my employment.' Don provided Tim with a thumb-nail sketch of his contract at Becks and wondered whether his demands would short circuit their offer then and there.

'OK Don, I fully understand you would need some assurances so let me discuss this with my colleagues now I understand your position and I'll be in touch within a few days.' Tim knew that if he really wanted Don then top dollar would have to be paid for his services. He couldn't think of anyone else that could fill the bill. His project would be still-born without Don's signature.

*

Don explained to Mary how things had developed and was now waiting to see if his demands would be met. Even if they were it would be up to them to decide whether the opportunity would be worthwhile in the long-term.

'I know what you mean, but it's an unexpected route back into the work I love.' Don stopped star gazing and mentally shook himself, thinking he had almost signed on the dotted line before he'd been offered anything!

'And another thing Don, what about my job at Dobson's? I'm good at running the shop and who knows, I could be gifted the shop when Dobson retires.' Mary was at pains to erect as many barriers as possible against the move to thwart this *'pie in the sky'*, offer.

'It would be fine by me if you wanted to keep the job Darling, but it's early days and even if they do offer the job, we still have to decide whether to take it.'

Later that week a bulky envelope was delivered to 44 Sycamore Avenue addressed to Mr Don Sullivan embossed with the logo. *'Leisure Consortium'*.

'Well Mary it looks like they really want me to take the job because I can't imagine a 'thanks, but no thanks' would require this much paper.'

'Well let's find out and get it over with as I'm on the edge of my seat.' Mary knew the package would be a test of their relationship and was a bag of nerves.

In a few short few weeks Don's life had gone full circle with the unexpected offer to return to the hotel industry and as a Managing Director and an opportunity to create a new business from the ground up. 'What a challenge.' He thought and then realised that a more immediate issue was what to do about Sinclair's offer.

Dear Don,

Many thanks for your valuable advice and observations on the proposed purchase of the hotel as this has provided us with the information to proceed with the purchase of the Sands Hotel. Please find enclosed a contract specifying your employment conditions, most of which are based on your offer at Becks. We have left the date for your commencement blank until you have decided whether to join us.

We are obliged to operate the Sands Hotel on a limited basis until the renovations are completed and we would take your advice on how this could be managed effectively. We have left the date for your commencement blank as your employment would start from that date.

I would be obliged if you could confirm your decision ether way as an early response would be appreciated.

Best wishes,
Tim

'The fat's in the fire now Don,' Mary said after examining the contract. 'If Becks job wasn't in the mix, I would have expected you to grab their offer with both hands.'

'They've added a three-year no-fault extension, which means that if the hotel goes belly-up, I'm still employed.' Don wondered whether he'd missed something in the small print to have landed such an opportunity but try as he might the deal seemed gold plated. 'Let's sleep on this and then decide.' Don had been offered the best deal for a return to his first love so he had to go with what was in his best interests. Prior to his call to Sinclair, Don agonised over his decision but he couldn't live with himself if he accepted Becks offer and then let him down.

Don grinned ruefully at the cruel juxtaposition of the two jobs. Although he couldn't really pass up on the Leisure deal.

'Tell me if I'm wrong Mary but it seems they will be paying me the going rate as soon as the hotel has been transferred which could be a year or more?' It was more a rhetorical question for Don, but he was anxious to involve Mary every step of the way.

Mary deliberated. 'Your employment starts as soon as the sale is agreed.' Mary was beginning to warm to the move because she would see much more of him and be a sounding board for Don's problems during the development phase of the project. 'After all,' Mary added, 'I've been a top housekeeper in a luxury operation so my experience would be useful as you develop the Sands.'

'You see some positives in the move obviously and that's good? Locationally and financially we'd be a lot better off but the more important thing is I would be seeing more of you and Malcolm.' Relieved that Mary was now on his side. 'Incidentally, have you put on a little weight while I've been away; you're not pregnant again, are you?' Don enquired with raised eyebrows.

'Cheeky beast, I'm as slim as ever at 8st.4 so watch it if you want your favourite supper later on.' Mary said, smoothing her dress, anxious to change the subject. 'You had become Beck's conscience and go-to person for their development so Sinclair will be devastated.' Mary responded sadly, but felt it was time for Becks to move forward without him. 'We're agreed it's your dream job after all Don and an opportunity you're unlikely to get again. You might want an attractive housekeeping consultant in due course you never know.' Mary agreed smiling, without the qualms she had only a week earlier.

*

Two days later Tim was a dog with two tails after Don agreed to sign and met with the other directors to formally approve the contract. A bottle of Lanson was cracked to celebrate the deal.

'Now you've become our newest Managing Director I can tell you this is just the start. We've almost concluded the hotel's transfer and were able to negotiate a healthy discount on the original price, finalising the transfer at £11,000 which included all the fixtures, fittings and current business contracts, all of which are worth a tidy sum. The owners were desperate to generate enough from the sale for their dream house near Malaga so we're all happy with the win-win outcome.' Tim announced smiling as they now had an asset that would develop under Don's management. He was under no illusions that hard work and long hours would be required for the Sands development but that's what he was looking forward to - the challenge.

*

'Hello Sinclair, I've made a decision about your offer but I'm afraid it's not the one you want to hear.' Don paused for a reaction, but Sinclair response was non-committal, 'I've had some sleepless nights, but I must prove to myself that I can still develop a career in the hotel industry, even though it would have been easier to accept your offer. I would be treading water at Becks because all the things I helped you put in place for a post war transition are there with a great team to take you forward. I would suggest Stuart as Gordon's replacement as he has developed in leaps and bounds during my time with him.'

'You're right Don it's not the decision I hoped to hear but I understand your reasons and I agree that you've given us a solid base for development. I'll have to live with that headache for a while and I agree that Stuart is worth considering as Gordon's replacement. However, would you be interested in a temporary consultancy role, we could use your expertise to advise on our development plans, what do you think?

'I'm not sure Sinclair, I might feel I'm still pulling the strings at Becks, but can I let you know – I suppose it could work in the short term?' Don replied, pleased that he hadn't fractured his relationship with Sinclair.

CHAPTER 61

'What was the reaction from Becks?' Tim asked after Don returned to the Leisure Consortium office.

'Sinclair was disappointed, and not best pleased as he expected me to accept the position which was tempting but the company is in good shape and most of the reforms will be in place within a year, and, more importantly, I've left on amicable terms.'

'Good, I'm glad as I would have hated to have been the reason for any animosity.' Tim looked relieved and Don was pleasantly surprised by his reaction.

Don's weekends were taken up overseeing the repairs and development plans to what was now the renamed the Bay Hotel. Over the next few weeks the hotel and restaurant business had continued at a restricted level but anxious that their regulars would understand that the developments were for their future benefit notices and artwork were displayed describing the future improvements and timescale. Most of the old staff had agreed to transfer and were rewarded with improved conditions of employment. Their presence also helped to ease customer concerns occasioned by the work-in-progress and despite the upheaval, Don was able to create a productive working relationship with his new staff in bedding in the new systems'

Mary however, wasn't impressed with Don's priorities at the Bay Hotel as she expected him to be around at weekends and despite his argument that it was for a brief period, it became necessary to arrange flowers and dining-outs to overcome Mary's objections. 'How about a weekend away in Alston Mary? We never did manage that break before the accident – did we?'

'That would be lovely Don, Malcolm will start to wonder who this strange man is.' Mary said playfully. 'Gracie said she would love to look after Malcolm while we're away.'

'I don't get enough time with my grandson as it is, so your break will be welcome.' Gracie agreed, giving Malcolm a hug.

*

Haltwhistle to Alston is a branch off the main Newcastle to Carlisle line and meanders through rolling Cumbrian countryside for about half an hour. A local ramshackle taxi took Don and Mary to their hotel, The Waterside Inn aptly named as it overlooked a small lake fed by a tiny tributary of the North

Tyne. As luck would have it their window provided a picturesque view of the lake and distant fells, dotted with hardy Herwick sheep and a few Banded cattle meandered under fluffy cumulus clouds. 'Look at that view Don, it's perfect isn't it?' Mary exclaimed drawing the curtain wider. 'It's a lovely hotel, but I'm gasping for a cup of tea and then stretch my legs.'

'The lady commands and the gentleman obeys,' Don gave a mock salute, dodging Mary's playful swipe.

'This is such a peaceful place, I could retire here,' Mary sighed as she linked arms and rested her head on Don's shoulder as they strolled on a well-worn path alongside the bubbling, iron coloured stream. 'Not yet, although it would be a nice place to run a hotel?'

'I don't think so; the season is too short and being the highest market town in England winter weather could easily isolate the place. Don't forget I'm already running a hotel – The Bay.'

'Mmmmh - just the thought,' added Mary, still cloaked in an unreal vision, then back to reality. 'I wonder what to have for dinner, I noticed they had local salmon so what do you fancy Don?'

'Yes, that's worth considering and for starters, maybe the local venison pate.'

'That walk has given me an appetite though. On the way back I wanted to have a look in that dress shop just up the High Street, there's a Fair Isle jumper I liked the look of and it wasn't expensive.'

'You'll have to come back tomorrow, it's after five so they'll be closed.' Don steered her away to the hotel, 'we have an early sitting at 6.30 and I want to smarten up and have a pre-dinner aperitif.'

'Good thinking Don, so let's go. Last one to the hotel's a sissy,' as she broke into a trot, almost colliding with a pram and a young mother in the process. 'Sorry, sorry,' Mary called out over her shoulder as she entered the hotel well ahead of Don, through the revolving door and up the stairs, two at a time, laughing to herself. She threw herself onto the bed, spread eagled as Don appeared, puffing hard and out of breath. 'You're not great shape Mr Sullivan when a young Mum can run you ragged; you need to get in some gym time.'

'I'll loan you Monty and then see how fast you can go,' Don grinned, as he leant on his walking stick. 'Maybe I should go back to crutches, then I'd give you a race.' His crutches were fine to give his stump a rest but little help with his day-to-day management.

*

As they sat down in the light and well-appointed restaurant, appraising the menu a familiar face caught Don's eye. He had met before the war when he was moving up the career ladder and the future looked rosy.

'Talk about deja vue,' Don exclaimed, 'I think you met him when I was at the 4 Arrows and we were a great team until the fire ruined everything.' Don thought back to those halcyon days in Cumbria and what might have been but for a disgruntled waiter.'

'Good evenin Sir, Madam, can I take your drink order?' The waiter asked as Don leafed through the wine list.

'And how are you this evening Stefan? You look well.' Don smiled at his old maître d'hôtel.

The intervening years had been kind to Stefan Podowski, who had the same twinkle in his sky-blue eyes and the bass Hungarian accent still evident as he did a double take at Don.

'Why it's Don, Don Sullivan. I canno believe it. Of course, the 4 Arrows a long time ago, many years yeah? Now I remember, your accident and your leg, so how are you now? It's good to see you and this is your wife Mary yeah?' Stefan came alive as he recalled their partnership.

'Yes, you remembered Mary when she came to the 4 Arrows before the fire. It's a small world this catering business Stefan, and you look in good shape too, so what have you been doing since the fire?'

Stefan had returned to Hungary to see his family and worked as a waiter until Hitler's advance through Europe had forced him to return to England, just in time. Eventually, he ended back in Cumbria at the Waterside Inn after several seasonal jobs at the coast. He was now the Head Waiter after the incumbent had retired three years earlier.

'Maybe fate has brought up together again Stefan because I'm looking for an experienced Head Waiter to develop the business where there's plenty of potential. Would you be interested in a move to the North East? I'll put you in the picture when you finish your shift?'

'About ten o'clock. I find you in the bar, yeah and we can talk about old times too, it would be good.'

After an enjoyable meal of poached salmon, crème caramel and a bottle of house white, they returned to the bar for coffee.

'Wouldn't it be marvellous if you could entice him to the Bay.' Mary said, thinking how much weight it would take off Don's shoulders. 'He's just the person to get things ship-shape.'

'We'll see how feels, but you're right Stefan would be an ideal appointment. I wonder what his deal is here.' Don was laying plans as Stefan appeared.

'Lovely meal Stefan, can I get you a drink?'

'Newcastle Brown Ale Don, thanks. Pleased you enjoy dinner, we hav a good chef here, yeah! So, tell me all about this new job of yours?'

A quick overview of the Bay's development, salary and conditions as the Head Waiter was an improvement on Stefen's current level. Initially they could also provide him with live-in accommodation, so Don suggested a visit to the Bay on his day off. He would also meet Tim and the other Leisure Consortium directors at the same time.

'That is good idea Don, I'll come on my day off and see for myself, yeah. Next Wednesday would be fine.' Don made a note to gave Stefan directions to Cullercoats from Newcastle Central, with lunch in the Bay restaurant to see the restaurant in operation.

CHAPTER 62

They had just taken their seats on the return journey from Haltwhistle when Mary gasped in pain holding her stomach. 'Oh Don, that's the second time I've had that over the past week, probably something I ate.' She explained unconvincingly.

'Well, we'll get you to see the doctor when we're back and put your mind at rest, can't be too careful.' Don's smile masked his concern because it wasn't the first time he'd noticed Mary grimacing and rubbing her stomach.

*

The doctor's tests proved inconclusive as he examined Mary and suggested further tests at Newcastle General's gynaecology department and made an appointment for Mary the next week and prescribed some medication to ease the pain. Don was naturally concerned when the doctor couldn't diagnose her problem and suggested Mary have a few days off work to rest until the tests were concluded. Mary refused saying she was better off at Dobson's and in any event they were short staffed and needed her in charge. Don knew better than to argue with his wife when her job was on the line.

The day before Mary's tests, Stefan duly arrived at the Bay Hotel, had an enjoyable lunch in the 'work in progress' restaurant and realised it's potential. He was in no doubt that under Don's expertise it would quickly take shape into a first-class operation. Stefan subsequently signed the employment contact and a start date set after his notice at the Waterside Hotel.

'Congratulations on your appointment Stefan, it's a good job we had that weekend break in Cumbria; it's the best decision I've made in a long time. I can't wait for you to get to grips with the Bay's development.' Don was looking forward to resuming his partnership with Stefan – they had been such great companions.

*

Newcastle General hospital has the finest gynaecological department in the country which made Don feel a little easier when he escorted Mary for her examination and tests. They were welcomed by Elspeth Gillespie the consultant surgeon and head of the department. After checking Mary's notes from her doctor, she explained that the series of tests that would take approximately two hours so Don was directed to the hospital's canteen where he ordered a tea and a fig roll while he waited, consumed with concern for Mary's condition and what might arise from the tests.

After what seemed an age, Don was summoned to the consultant's office where Mary appeared to be distraught, having been informed that urgent treatment was required as it was confirmed she had cancer of the cervix. This would require regular weekly injections of chemotherapy with follow-up examinations to ensure that the month-on-month treatment was working. Mary had been told that the side-effects of the therapy was hair and weight loss and feelings of nausea but her condition had been caught early which was a good indicator to effect a cure. She was provided with a treatment timetable commencing the following week and told to avoid stress and overwork during this period.

They were both were shell-shocked and decided to keep her illness under wraps from family and friends. Mary would continue to work at Dobsons until it was necessary to reduce her hours. Likewise, Don would continue with the Bay's development and work around Mary's weekly visits to the General. Having Stefan in place would provide Don with some breathing space by delegating the restaurant supervision to his newly appointed restaurant manager. Don's deep concerns made Montry tingle as **The Voice** intervened.

'You need to keep positive and upbeat for Mary's sake, because she's going to go through some rough periods. Your understanding and support will be vital for her to pull through.' Don looked around and nodded that he had to remain strong and positive for Mary's sake.

The surgeon's warning of the chemotherapy side effects appeared with the loss of Mary's fine reddish hair and a slow but perceptible loss of weight as her appetite waned and increasing tiredness set in. She was determined to carry on at Dobson's as this gave her some respite from the chemo sessions but as the weeks passed, Mary eventually had to curtail her hours to a minimum. By then she was bald and had taken to wearing a rather squish auburn wig which gave her morale a badly needed lift.

'Don, I don't know how long I can carry on, look at me, I'm a shadow, although the wig has given me a boost. I'm seeing the surgeon for an assessment next week and if I'm not making progress I'll stop the chemo and let nature take its course.' Mary's sombre feelings sent a shiver of despair through Don. It was as though a knife had been driven into him.

'Listen to me Mary, the chemo ends in two weeks and hopefully we'll have some good news so can you tough it out? Otherwise, you'll have gone through all the pain with no gain.' Unknown to them little Malcolm, now a sprouting eleven-year-old had been listening at the bedroom door.

'Yes Mam, please 'tough it out' please, I want you how you used to be so we can race each other on the beach at Tynemouth!' Her son's plea was accompanied by tears of hope.

'Of course I will Malcolm, and we'll have a good race on the sands and Daddy can be the referee.' As Mary embraced her son; unable to stop the tears. Don was similarly affected by his son's plea and joined in a group hug. For that moment all was well again.

*

Stefan made an immediate impact at the Bay, partly due to an emotional reunion with one of the senior waitresses whom he had worked with at Blackpool's Tower restaurant. Redecoration was now in full swing with the restaurant repainted, recarpeted, curtained in 30's art deco style mirroring the hotel's origins and complemented with scenes from the village's Victorian fishing heritage. At the same time Don had applied for a bar license and was due to support his application at the magistrates' court and was confident as Tim was a Rotary club friend of one of the magistrates.

Unfortunately, the Bay's chef had been unimpressed with Don's menu overhaul and handed in his notice. Stefan found out and spoke to Don just before the lunch service. 'I hear chef is leaving so I make some phone call and maybe I hav solution for you yeah? Stefan rolled his hands and smiled conspiratorially. 'Would you like to know my news Don?'

'At the moment Stefan any good news would be a bonus, so what's up your sleeve?' Don asked impatiently, more concerned with Mary's appointment with the surgeon.

'You remember chef at 4 Arrows, Gordon Strachan yeah? Well, I find he's not happy where he is so I told him about our chef vacancy and he says, yes he would be interested. So, what do you think Don?'

'Gordon eh? Where is he now?'

'He's very close, near Newcastle, a place call Wall, so thinking you'd be interested, I ask him to come tomorrow afternoon, is that good Don?'

'I'll say; well done Stefan, that could be a life saver.' Don exclaimed, buoyed up with some good news for a change.

*

Gordon's appointment was for 3.30 p.m. after the lunch service, so Don set off for home with a spring in Monty's step.

As Don opened the front door he heard sobbing in the front room and hurried in to find Mary, on the settee, head in hands with Malcolm by her side with his little arm barely reaching around her shoulder. 'Daddy, Daddy, Mam isn't well and she's crying.'

Don sat beside his distraught wife and held her close. 'We'll work it out Darling and get you back in shape. Just have faith you're going to pull through, whatever anyone says.'

'Oh Don, I wish I could believe you but I'm feeling worse now than at anytime during the treatment and I know I'm dying.' Mary shuddered with her admission and sobbed uncontrollably. How will you manage when I'm not here anymore? I can't bear to think about it.'

'Mary, *MARY, LISTON TO ME! YOU ARE NOT GOING ANYWHERE.*' Don implored, you're going to get better whatever it takes and whatever we have to do. We're seeing the surgeon tomorrow and I'll tell her the same thing.' Don knew he was flying in the face of reality but never, ever would he give up on Mary's survival, remembering that only a few years earlier when the Jeremiahs' had given him little chance of survival after his accident he had pulled through against the odds and with the same resolve and belief would do the same for Mary.

'OK Malcolm would you help Daddy make a nice cup of tea for your Mam because you know the right way to make it, don't you?'

'Alright Daddy, I know to warm the teapot and have the water very hot and let it stand a while and give it a good stir and put the milk in first.' Mary smiled at her sons recall and patted his hand, 'well done Malcolm.'

'We'll have a slap-up meal tonight as I've squandered our life savings on some prime fillet steak to show off my culinary expertise, with all the trimmings.' Don announced, taking Mary's hand as she looked up into his face with her sunken cheeks and tired eyes and smiled gratefully. 'I've checked with our 'live-in lodger' and she's volunteered to baby-sit – right Mam?'

CHAPTER 63

On the dot at 3.30 the next day a resurgent Gordon Strachan strode into Don's office at the Bay Hotel and announced his arrival in a broad Glaswegian accent you could cut with a knife.

'Aye, tis good to see aul the old crowd again, and my you've all weathered well except me.' He said fishing for compliments as he hugged Stefan and gripped Don's hand, vice like.

'I can't tell how pleased I am to see you again Gordon and may I say looking so bonny. You've been keeping yourself in trim obviously.' Don grinned at Gordon's querulous raised eyebrows in response. 'Many thanks for answering Stephan's call to arms so let me tell you what we can offer.' Gordon didn't take too much convincing in accepting the position as the Bay's chef de cuisine.

The 3 Musketeers waxed long on their experiences before, during and after the war and were surprised they had come through without so much as a scratch, especially in the case of Stefan who had reprised his role in the Polish AirForce, trained as a Hurricane pilot and narrowly becoming a fatality on more than one occasion. War service had also claimed Gordon with a recruitment in the Scottish Black Watch and a narrow escape from the Normandy beaches at Dunkirk. It was all good *Boy's Own* comic stuff and worth the retelling even if there was a whiff of incredulity in their accounts. Don's war experience was boring by comparison, so he glossed over his experiences except his exploits during the Hull blitz.

Once Gordon's contract had been drawn up and agreed he was put to work on an appraisal of the Bay's kitchen and service areas. An interim list of additions and necessary maintenance was agreed with Don for the kitchen upgrade. He would also interview the three-kitchen staff who had agreed to remain, one for his deputy. Gordon's review of the new menus added several dishes of a Scottish flavour including haggis and cullen skink (a smoke fish bisque) which gave a nod to the Scots invasion during the season. Another plus was that Gordon didn't need to give any notice which provided an earlier opportunity for him to put a personal stamp on the kitchen brigade. With Don's help he drafted advertisements for three more kitchen staff.

'That is really good news Don,' Tim said when told of the new appointment. 'Just shows how well the catering network works when you put your mind to it.' Then he added, 'I'll pop in tomorrow and introduce myself and tell them what a great company they've joined.' Modesty wasn't in Tim's modus operandi.

*

Holding hands with Mary in the surgeon's office the next day, Don realised only too quickly from Mrs Gillespie expression that her news would not be good. She opened Mary's file on her desk and after a slight pause revealed that the latest results showed that there had been a spread of the cancer to adjoining areas of Mary's uterus.

'We had great hopes for a full recovery as it had been diagnosed early but this cancer is aggressive, and the levels of chemotherapy required would be injurious. I'm sorry,' She paused to let her painful news sink in, although Mary had already steeled herself.

'So,' Don replied firmly, taking a grip on his emotions, 'in your view what else can we do? We're not giving up!' The ball was back in Surgeon Gillespie court as their first positive step.

'Well,' looking sympathetically at the desperate couple. 'There is radium treatment you could try which has had some success in the past, but it does replicate chemotherapy to a large extent and to that extent may not yield any better results.' She was just softening the blow which she felt was a lost cause.

'Isn't there any other new or revolutionary treatment available, we'll try anything.' Don responded, trying to disguise his desperation.

'Well, there is some research going on with various bodies. For example, Barminster University's Department of Medicine, in Birmingham has a very active clinical research department so you could speak to their chief scientist.' Elseth looked in her index, here it is. 'Professor Toby Maudling is the head of department,' she added, writing down the address and telephone number, 'please tell Toby I referred you, as we have worked together in the past. They thanked her for the referral but left under a cloud of despair at the finality of the verdict although Don still held onto a glimmer of hope that somewhere there was a cure for Mary.

On returning to the Bay Hotel, Don immediately contacted Barminster University and was put through to the clinical research department's secretary who said the professor was in a meeting so connected Don through to Preston Daly, one of the professor's researchers who was appraised of Mary's condition. Preston said he would have Toby return Don's call that afternoon.

As Don was discussing the next stage of the Bay's kitchen update with Gordon and a team from Sankeys' kitchen division, his secretary called to say she had a Toby Maudling from Barminster University on the line. 'Many thanks for returning my call, Mr Maudling,' Don answered, relieved they had shown an interest in Mary's condition.

'My pleasure and please call me Toby. I've read the notes that Preston made from your phone call and as you were referred by Elspeth at the General, I gave her a call to get some first-hand detail on Mary's condition. Now I understand her condition is not terminal, but speed is of the essence so would you be able to bring Mary to the University as soon as possible for some tests?' Toby wasn't going let the grass grown under his proactive feet.

'Would tomorrow or the next day be good?' Don asked, new hope surging through him at this chance encounter.

'We'll set up the tests tomorrow based on Elspeth's records of Mary and her treatment. We'll then have a better idea as to how to proceed. If you could bring Mary the day after tomorrow, that's Tuesday the 23rd; I'll give you the address and directions from New Street Station, it would be best to take a taxi which takes between 15 and 20 minutes.' Toby explained, sounding quite excited by the prospect of seeing a real-life research subject.

'Many thanks for your offer to help Toby; I'll confirm our arrival time once I've booked the train.'

'That's; fine Don I'll await your call. Just remember, these are exploratory tests and not cures or even treatments but let's see what we find out first and what can be done, OK?' Toby's warning was to dampen any unrealistic hopes, mindful that if he was in Mary's condition, he would be straw grasping.

'Yes Toby, I fully understand and look forward to meeting you and your associates, goodbye.' Don gave an involuntary thumbs up as he ended the call.

*

'Darling, pack your bags, we're off to the 2nd City tomorrow to see a man about your problem so things are on the move.' Don's upbeat tone gave Mary a boost too.

'How long are we staying Don because I'll have to let Dobsons know.' Mary was concerned at letting her employer down again.

'It will depend on what Toby finds out from your condition when we get there. I've booked one night to start with at the Station Hotel in New Street, with an option for another night if necessary.'

'I've a cousin on my mother's side who lives in a place called Edgbaston and we've kept in touch over the years, although I've never visited her. I'll give her a call from the Research Centre when we have more information as she might have a spare room.' Mary's positivity gave Don a boost.

'That could be a useful contact, Mary. I've booked the train from Newcastle Central and then we'll take a taxi to the university. We should arrive before 3 o'clock to see Toby and his team.' Mary's smile at this news was all he needed to feel better.

Don let Tim know the reasons for his Birmingham visit and that the Bay would be in the capable hands of Stefan and Chef Gordon in his absence.

CHAPTER 64

The LNER train Gods were in their favour with a comfortable journey, and a timely arrival. A black cab took them past the famous Edgbaston Cricket Ground and the leafy suburb of Edgbaston to the University which stood proudly in its own extensive grounds, overlooked by Old Joe, a clock tower close to the research facility.

'Welcome to Barminster University Mr and Mrs Sullivan, and especially to our medical research facility of which we are justly proud.' Professor Toby, the research head smiled a welcome. 'We have received a considerable donation, bequeathed by a distinguished old boy, which had given a considerable boost to our research programme, so you've come at an opportune time.'

'That is good news Toby and it's Don and Mary.' Don was warming more and more to Toby's informal manner.

'Before we start let me get you a drink, tea of coffee?' Noticing for the first time Don disability and Mary's gaunt appearance.

'Just water for me please, I'm quite thirsty after that journey.' Mary had a lovely smile Toby noticed and could see she would have been a very attractive lady before the cancer took its toll.

'Coffee for me please, milk, no sugar.' Don replied.

As they were waiting for the drinks Toby explained how they would proceed. Mary would have some blood samples taken and related tests to provide a profile of her physical condition. These results would provide the information on which various research options would be based. One particular cancer treatment programme had yielded encouraging results.

After they had their refreshments, Toby explained that their approach to cancer research was to look at the causes rather than the traditional remedies of chemotherapy and radium. 'Our approaches are non-invasive, that is to build up the body's immune system to fight the cancers from within. Does that make sense?' Mary and Don nodded, eager to learn more.

'In in other words our research is to concentrate on which of the body's cells are best to fight the cancer cells naturally and so far, test results prove we are on the right lines.' Mary and Don could not have been happier because, in a nutshell there was hope for Mary. 'I'll give you two research terms for the moment: Immune Memory Transmitter or IMT and Dentric Cell Therapy or DCT. In short IMT is the way the cells are managed to attack the cancers and DCT is basically the way we go about it, OK? It's important that you both believe in the eventual success of the project.'

Don was now more hopeful. 'You've given us something to cling onto for the first time since Mary's condition was diagnosed Toby. You'll have our wholehearted support however long it takes.' It took all of Don's discipline to resist giving Toby a hug of appreciation.

'Good, that's all I want to hear, now first things first, I'll introduce you to the research team and then we'll start Mary on stage one; that is finding out all we can about her present condition. The application of the DCT is not one size fits all, it's like being fitted for a haute couture dress, if you'll forgive the analogy.' Toby explained. 'So, Don, you can amuse yourself in the library while we check on Mary's condition, there's some information there on both DCT and IMT.

*

Three hours later Don was called from the library where he spent some time trying to make sense of the DCT and IMT articles that Toby had recommended and had to admit it was a bit out of his depth. He understood that IMT, was the elements of change that fought the cancers and DCT was the method identifying the process of processing the IMT, based on each person's profile. No two patients would have the same therapy, although there might be similar features within the programme.

Mary was seated in an easy chair and looked exhausted but not unhappy. 'Well, Don I've had a full MOT,' Mary grinned and looked at Toby for confirmation.

'That's right Don, part of the DCT is to find out as much as we can of Mary's profile because that way we can fine tune the IMT for the best results. Because of the chemotherapy treatment, Mary's body has basically had a battering and we need to return her to her normal, or an even better condition for the ICT to do its job effectively. The blood tests will tell us where Mary's body is under stress and where we need to build her up with an appropriate diet. It's the most important feature pre-ICT.

'What we are doing is groundbreaking in that it has never been applied so Mary you are in effect our guinea pig. To a degree, success is in the lap of the Gods, but we would not be embarking on this costly venture if we didn't think we had a good chance of success.'

'I'm no dietary expert but presumably that's not all that has to happen to get me in shape. I don't mind being a guinea pig if there's a chance of a cure - there's no alternative, is there?' Mary stated, looking a little disheartened with Toby's realism.

'I should have been clearer and followed up by saying that everything Mary does from now on will be clearly prescribed, both in terms of diet, supplementary vitamins, and lifestyle. All you must do is to follow our regime to the letter.' Toby paused to check her reaction. 'And it would be best to have Mary nearby during this preparatory period of between 4 to 6 weeks. Is that possible?'

'It will depend on whether I can manage to stay with my cousin in Birmingham. I'll let you know if it's viable but when does the treatment start Toby?'

'We're working against the clock so it's important we start the regime immediately. Could Mary come back tomorrow while you sort out her accommodation?' Toby was at pains for them to buy into the urgency of the treatment as the clock was ticking on her cancer.

'Of course, we'll return at the appointed time tomorrow with news of the accommodation.' Don promised, hoping for a start to Mary's recovery.

*

Mary's phone call to her cousin failed to obtain any offer of accommodation, as her only room had been allocated for a student. Don made a vow that even if it took him into bankruptcy, he would make sure that Mary had the treatment. On their return to the University, Toby was made aware of the problem and said he would explore another avenue to guarantee the continuity of Mary's treatment.

'Apologies for the interruption, but I've been talking to the bursar in charge of student accommodation and she can allocate a room for Mary over the treatment period. The charge won't be onerous, and Mary could use the University's facilities with a temporary student union card. You won't be out of place here Mary as we've several mature students on the campus. The positives from our point of view are that Mary would be onsite and close at hand for the ICT process so it's the best option for both of us.'

Don and Mary were lifted out of their trough of despair when Mary's accommodation was arranged. 'That is good news Toby and please convey our thanks to your bursar.' Mary could hardly believe their fortunes had changed within days.

CHAPTER 65

Toby was feeling chipper about the whole exercise and looking forward to organising a project that could have a dramatic impact on medical research, his unit and the University as a whole. He could see a new era opening for his own development so he must keep the University's vice chancellor in the loop with regards to the progress of the programme.

Susanne Thimblemill, the bursar was doughty lady in her late forties, wearing a light orange two-piece suit and a pleasant smile as she welcomed Mary and Don into her office. She gave Mary a University map and a student card and escorted them across the extensive campus and into the first floor of the Chamberlain Block. 'You'll find getting around a bit confusing at first but you'll soon get used to it.'

Susanne showed them a surprisingly large room which was compactly furnished with pleasing views across a lake busy with assorted waterfowl to a multi-purposed student facility. 'It's not a home from home but you'll have all the University's facilities at your disposal, so you'll never be bored. There are toilets and showers and a small kitchen on each floor with an oven if you need a hot snack. The Chamberlain block is all female but male visitors are allowed in the public areas.' Susanne explained with a smile.

'It looks very comfortable Susanne and I'm sure I'll fit in quickly and learn my way around the campus which is beautifully planned. I'm indebted to you for arranging the room, it really has been a Godsend and solved so many of our problems, so thank you so much,' Mary said with feeling.

'We try to help our sister departments when we can and, in this case, we had the accommodation available.' Susanne added, slightly embarrassed at Mary's fulsome praise but pleased by her gratitude.

*

'We must have someone up there looking after us with what's happened in the last few days Don,' Mary smiled and looked enlivened as she sat back in the Newcastle bound train squeezing Don's hand.

'Long may it continue,' Don replied, 'I just hope things are still on an even keel with the Bay Hotel operations. 'I'll come down with you to Birmingham and all being well I'll try to contact you every weekend?'

'Listen Don, I'll be in very good hands and don't forget, I'm a big girl now and you have your new venture to keep on track to prioritise. If I need to talk to you or Toby wants to check with you on the programme, you're only a telephone call away.' Mary pleaded with Don to take a back seat during her treatment. I don't want you to feel responsible for me when I'm at the research centre?'

'If that's what you want Mary I'll take a back seat but promise to contact me if you have any worries'.

*

Back home, Malcolm was jumping up and down excited at the return of his Mam. 'You know we really missed you, that is Dusty and me, and Granny of course. You're not going away again are you Mam, are you?'

Don intervened as Mary was rather emotional and on the brink of tears. 'Listen to me son, you know your Mam hasn't been well for some time and we went away to see a special doctor who thinks he can make her better. But, to do this your Mam has to stay for a while in a big city called Birmingham where she can get the treatment. You'll have to be brave, so she'll know you're not getting upset while she's away. Will you be brave for your Mam, because she's depending on you to look after Dusty and Granny?'

'Alright Daddy I'll try but it won't be easy because Dusty's always looking for her when she's not here.' Malcolm said close to tears.

'I know, and you'll have to make sure you feed Dusty and the kitten regularly and give them a good cuddle, right?'

Mary took over to give her son a long hug on the settee. 'I don't want to go away but it's necessary to get me well again. I'll be writing to you, so will you tell me how you're doing at school?'

'Oh yes, I like writing and I'll get Dusty to send you a message too.'

'He's been very good while you've been away,' said Gracie, 'doing his homework and writing letters to his friends. Each evening, we sit down before bedtime and he reads me some of his favourite stories from his Biggles and Just William books.' Gracie laughed at the memory, 'He laughs so much at William because he's always getting into trouble.'

'But he always finds a way out, so he's pretty clever really,' added Malcolm excitedly, 'would you like me to read some to you?'

'Yes, when it's your bedtime,' Mary says looking fondly at her son.

*

'I hav to tell you Don we hav some problems with suppliers and these workmen after you left yeah, but with Gordon's help we tell them. Hey, I say you need to provide the quality merchandise or we don't deal.' Stefan grinned, 'yes, we put them right Boss.'

Gordon chipped in with his version of their dealings. 'Och aye t'waas a storm in a teacup we just had to stand firm by changing some of suppliers who weren't up to the mark, they all try it on until they realise we're no a soft touch. They soon get the message.'

It sounded to Don as though they were making a meal of it to boost their status but that was fine if the developments were on schedule and the refurbishment of the restaurant was almost complete. 'So Stefen, Gordon, bring me up to date with progress on all fronts, including the new menus because I want to fix a date for our Grand Opening. We need to generate as much publicity as possible.

'We still not operating 100% yet Don because of refurbs but the restaurant looks good and all the new staff are trained, yeah? We still waiting for new curtains and wall lighting but we hav many new customers and sales in restaurant and bar have increase. Also, we gettin enquiries for parties and weddings too. Look!' Stefan pointed to a glossy brochure of the hotel's future accommodation now almost complete. 'Tis good, what you think?'

'Excellent, Tim had done a great job with the brochure. Well done Stefan I knew I could rely on you.' Don said clapping Stefan's shoulder, obviously delighted in his rejuvenated maître d'hôtel role.

Gordon told Don proudly, 'The new kitchen equipment has been delivered and is in situ and the air conditioning was sorted last week. I've trained up one of the old staff as my deputy and the rest are almost on song for a full team. A couple of young ladies from Tynemouth Catering College have come up trumps, one specialises in pattiserie although she's an allrounder and the other has some excellent skills with fish dishes. We're in vera guid shape staff wise.'

'That's great gentlemen. I've also been told that most of the rooms have been upgraded with only five more to be released. The head receptionist is rising to the challenge in her upgraded role.' Don concluded, delighted with his team's performance.

*

The night before Mary left for her treatment Don asked straight-faced, 'Have I told you before that I love you, and right from the first time I saw you?' Holding her tightly.

'Actually Don, you have many times, but I'll never get tired of hearing repeats.' Mary gave him a confirmatory kiss. 'And I hope you're going to show me that you mean it before I leave you tomorrow, so let's have an early night because good boys have to have proper rewards, don't they?'

'I'll say!' Don replied as they climbed the stairs.

Early the next morning the taxi delivered them to the Newcastle Central where they hugged and parted with Mary tearful as Don walked away engulfed in the train's steam.

*

Mary's first two weeks at the clinic were taken up with finding her feet by adjusting to the DCT regime which would build her fitness level up so the ICT could start to work on the cancer cells. Her mind was focused on the endgame and the belief in Toby's therapy that eventually she would be free to enjoy life. Gradually her hair started to grow back and her weight increased, although the cancer was still growing but at a much reduced rate.

'We can see distinct improvements in your overall health Mary so if you keep this up we'll be able to start the ICT in another couple of weeks and monitor its effects on the cancer.' Toby sounded a positive note.

'That's very good to hear Toby, thank you. I do feel much better now although I must admit to being drawn to the banned food on occasion and looking forward to starting the ICT treatment.' Mary replied, remembering the awful effects of the chemo.

'Hopefully if we've got our levels of the ICT right, you'll start to feel better within a few days with no side effects. At the same time, part of the DCT is to gradually improve your fitness because a healthy body gives a boost effect to the ICT. This is all part of a systems approach to the eventual cure; an all-body therapy.' Toby knew from other research studies that the psychological aspects of any treatment were a major contributor to success. Don was appraised of this during the weekly phone calls and was elated both with Mary's progress and curiously felt a little envious that he wasn't there to share the improvements with her.

CHAPER 66

'The Voice's appearance when Don was stressed after Mary's diagnosis required an explanation but that would have to wait until Mary was out of the woods and the Bay Hotel was well and truly established.' Don decided, his thoughts crowding in as he strolled for an afternoon breath of air around Cullercoats Bay just below the Oceanic research centre and lifeboat station. Many a time in his youth he would have 'dares' with his pals to dive off the bay's double pier as the tide turned to give just enough depth for their plunge. An impish urge made Don rattle his walking stick along the metal railings as the majestic sweep of Tynemouth sands and the open-air salt-water lido in the distance came into view. The sun had cast a sparkling, dancing reflection on the waves as they creamed softly onto the white sands of the tiny harbour, now devoid of the fishing boats that had brought income to the local economy and employment to fishwives outside their tiny cottages. Many years before, famous painters from around the world had converged on this part of England, Winslow Homer the American painter among them because of the unusual light that gave life and energy to their art. As he turned back, the Bay Hotel stood out proudly and brought out a feeling of personal satisfaction that his decision to reject Beck's offer had been the right one.

With only a week to go before the Grand Opening, Don wanted his previous colleagues at the Cliffe Hotel, to see that he had come full circle after his accident and that a lost leg was of little hindrance if you had the resolve and the support of your family and friends.

*

Malcolm had always been fascinated by Monty and would spend happy times with the limb when not attached, clipping and moving the three joints into their various positions. On more than one occasion he told a much-surprised Don, 'I've been talking to Monty and he tells me funny stories Daddy.'

Mmmm ..... Don thought, 'I wonder if there is any mileage in family thought transference.' Then turning to his son, 'well that's fine, you'll have to tell me one of these stories.'

'Alright Daddy I'll do that because Dusty likes to listen to them as well.' Malcolm continued, 'Monty told me that when I was little we lived in a big house at the end of a 'cul de sac' and you used to give me rides on a motorcycle, up and down. It was very exciting and I used to blow the horn as well.' Malcolm chatted on as Don felt his pulse race and a shiver down his spine. 'How could he know this, he was only a few months old, and I never talked about my accident or the motorbike?'

'All the things that Monty revealed to Malcolm happened *before Malcolm was born*, and yet Malcolm's stories were accurate.' Don was clearly unnerved but dared to ask if Malcolm had any more stories.

'Well Monty told me where you found Dusty where his mummy and kittens had died.' Malcolm explained and Don gasped, pulse racing knowing he never told Malcolm this.

'Stranger and stranger. Is **The Voice** having an influence in the animal kingdom,' maybe it was Don's overactive mind, counting 2 x 2 and getting 5, 'I'll have to keep a close eye on Malcolm and his stories; they're unnerving.' Don was at a loss to explain.

*

'We hav the problem with a party of five who have been complaining all through the service about the food and getting boisterous with too much to drink, yeah.' Stefan waved Don over. 'The other diners are being disturbed so is not good.' Stefan's efforts to quieten them had failed so Don had two more waiters to stand by and wait for his signal. 'Sod's law, the last thing I need before the Grand Opening,' Don thought as he approached the troublemakers.

'Good evening, I'm the Hotel Manager and hope you have had a pleasant evening?' Don said evenly looking directly at the loudmouth and leader of the disturbance.

'No, we haven't, the food was poor and service worse and we're not leaving until we get satisfaction – right?' The thirty-year-old look at his cronies, three young ladies and two younger men, all who nodded nervously.

'So, what satisfaction would you like?' Don smiled into the face of his tormentor. 'We pride ourselves at the Bay in having happy customers.'

'More drinks all-round would be a start – free of course.'

'Unfortunately, our licence ends at 10 p.m. but we could serve you outside.'

'We're not going anywhere Matey, until we get our drinks.'

'Well, that is unfortunate Sir, because that is the only way we can serve you.' At that point Don signalled to Stefan and his waiter who quickly removed the loudmouth's tableware and cloths, collapsing the table itself and removing it from the restaurant, leaving the 'nasty group' sitting on chairs with nothing in front of them. Don had also asked Stefan to alert the local constabulary in case of any disturbance and was told two constables would be on hand shortly.

'I think you've had your fun so it's time to be sensible and leave before you're escorted. You and your friends really don't want to have the law involved do you?' Don could see the indecision in the leader and without a table in support and his friends looking embarrassed, but he didn't want to lose face.

'C'mon Colin let's go before we get into trouble,' a sensible member of the group said moving toward the door, taking his arm which was shrugged off.

'OK. OK! We've had our fun and we'll be back,' the leader called out with more bravado than belief as the remaining diners gave them the slow handclap, hurrying them to the exit.

'Many apologies,' ladies and gentlemen for the interruption.' Don checked the remaining diners to find most were smiling. 'I hope it hasn't spoilt your evening but to compensate for the slight disruption please have a drink on the house.' His announcement triggered a round of applause which Don was relieved to hear and felt that the altercation had probably given the restaurant a boost, although he had had his fingers crossed.

'That's a new one on me Boss,' Stefan's cheeks blew out in relief that Don had been on hand. 'I never saw problem diners handled that way, but effective, yeah!'

'Neither have I, but a colleague once used it and I thought, let's try it out - there was little to lose and fortunately we did have a backup.'

CHAPTER 67

On the morning of the Bay's Grand Opening Don opened an envelope marked *Private*. Inside was a 'Good Luck' embossed greeting card with a message

Don Darling,

All the very best to you and your team for the greatest day in your life. I'm sure everything will go as planned as I know you've left nothing to chance. My only regret is I'm not there to celebrate with you, but I'll be with you in spirit. I'll call soon so you can give me a potted version of the highlights.

Your loving wife Mary.

Mary's letter brought tears and a lump in his throat, knowing she was fighting a battle many miles from those she loved. Just as soon as the Bay's festivities were concluded he would take a few days off, visit Mary and exchange their news first hand because he had been remise in writing to Mary in all the excitement. Don had a sleep interrupted night before the Grand Opening, constantly reviewing the programme for the day.

After a light breakfast he stepped out to check the special flower display on the hotel's front lawn which read. *'BAY HOTEL 1950'* above the Whitley Bay coat of arms.

*

'Good morning all – are we going to enjoy ourselves today?' Don asked and received a positive response from his managers. 'As we've all got plenty on our plates today, I'll make this meeting brief just to establish that all your sections are on track? Stefan?'

'So far, we're prepared for 45 guests, no exceptions yeah. So, all is good for a 1 p.m. start.' Stefan looked a cool as a cucumber.

'How's the kitchen Dougal?' The Chef gave the nod to Don.

'Oche aye, we've a full complement and all our suppliers have come up trumps with the special deliveries for the lunch and dinner service, do we're good.' His ruddy face glowing from his exertions. 'Aah'll be doing a tour of the restaurant towards the end of service as weel tae make sure aal the guests are happy.' Dougal added to reassure Stefan.

'The new American bar and the conference room are open and guests will be escorted through the new facilities,' the Head Receptionist Fiona

Cable confirmed. 'I'll be able to answer any queries and brochures will be available throughout the hotel.' Don thanked his team and ended the meeting wishing everyone good luck and an enjoyable day.

*

Don took a call from Gracie who sounded a bit flustered confusing Buttons A and B in the phone box which had already swallowed 5 pennies but she was determined to call her son knowing how important the day was. 'That's fine Mam don't worry, just let the receptionist know when you arrive and they'll find me. OK? Got to go, the Backworth Silver Band is just revving up, bye Mam.' Gracie sounded the happiest and proudest mam on Tyneside.

*

After changing into his best VIP meeting suit with crisp white shirt and black bow tie Don stood at the entrance taking in the sea air, pinching himself that most of his hopes for a new career had come to fruition. The final hurdle was Mary's cancer which, fingers crossed was responding to the Dentric Cell therapy.

'Why look at you Donald Sullivan,' Gracie stood back looking admiringly at her son dressed to the nines. 'Before you left home you looked like a rag and bone man, so give your Mam a hug.' Don couldn't help grinning as he was enveloped by Gracie and then in short order by his siblings Sadie and Sidney, both of whom looked well-scrubbed and sparkling in their best attire.

'Come on, let me show you my new empire,' as he escorted them around the redeveloped hotel.'We'll have a drink in the bar and then I'll leave you to enjoy yourselves. Just make sure you have your invitations otherwise you'll go hungry.' Don warned them.

Don and his fellow directors were on hand to greet the Mayor of Whitley Bay, resplendent in his Mayoral robe and chain of office, sparkling in the late morning sunshine. Then, right on cue to screams and whistles from his adoring football fans, an international icon, England and Newcastle United's centre forward Jackie Milburn, Wor Jackie, unfurled his 6'3' frame from the limousine, clad in his iconic number 9 shirt and beaming a wide smile at the public display of royal patronage – the King of the Gallowgate End had arrived and was led to the microphone to address his doting public! Don smiled inwardly at his coupe de grace.

'Aye well! Welcome everyone,' Jackie announced with shouts of 'Up the Magpies',' Ahm reet pleased to cut the taape for the Bay Hotel's grand reopening,' louder applause, 'aye and if ye give me time and a bita space ahl sign some autographs, but give the young'uns first chance,' louder applause. 'Thank you ahl for cumin.' Jackie turned, shook Don hand, signed Malcolm's autograph book, and was engulfed by the ecstatic crowds.

Tim had been given the opportunity to escort the Mayor through the hotel's refurbished areas and ingratiate himself by extolling the virtues of the Leisure Consortium which was bringing employment and tourism to Whitley Bay and the surrounding North East.

With one last call to his managers who gave him a thumbs up, Don took his seat for lunch between Wor Jackie and the Mayor who was given a round of applause after a short welcome to the guests. Throughout the meal, Don's intimate knowledge of football sparked Jackie to recall memorable incidents from his recent F.A. Cup win.

During the break before the dessert Don circulated to have a chat with his old boss Sinclair Beck and friends and ex-colleagues from the Cliffe Hotel who praised Don for his reconstruction of the Bay, hoping he wouldn't steal too many of their customers. Malcolm was in his seventh heaven with his Jackie Milburn autograph that would elevate him to the top spot with his school pals.

Don's menu for the lunch was one of Dougal's favourites with Brown Windsor Soup then Fillets of Sole Bonne Femme, a local Crusted Rack of Lamb with Pomme Parmentier, Spears of Asparagus, and Petit Pois Francais. Bombe Vesuvius was the spectacular flamed dessert, paraded through the restaurant just like the real Vesuvius. The Grand Opening was underlined by the mayor's thank you speech to the Bay's managing director, Don Sullivan and the Leisure Consortium's CAO, Toby Spalding for such splendid entertainment.

'The redeveloped Bay hotel will be a welcome addition to the area's tourist infrastructure and a major boost for the local restaurant scene.' The mayor concluded to all round applause.

If the mayor laid the Bay's benefits to the local economy and community on a bit thick, Don wasn't complaining as it would all be grist to their business development mill. Don estimated that the substantial outlay for the opening was a sum well spent, because the increased business would offset a healthy proportion of the costs.

It was a marketing triumph for Don and the Leisure Consortium with Tim and the directors jubilant at the outcome, especially from a publicity point of view – news photos and press articles covered Wor Jackie's visit.

Long before the end of that day Stefan confirmed restaurant bookings had doubled, booked rooms were almost at capacity and two wedding enquiries had been reserved. 'Our investment has paid off in spades and it's still early days.' Don believed that the seeds of his ideas had generated a harvest of goodwill.

CHAPTER 68

Monty's stump was giving Don a problem despite regular applications of white spirit because he had hardly been off his feet with preparation for the Bay's Grand Opening. He would switch to his crutches when visiting Mary at the University's Clinic, and hoped the progress report would be good news.

*

'Hi Don, long time no see,' Mary called out as Don paid off the taxi, 'let me take your bag. You look ready for a cup of tea, or something stronger.' Mary smiled and pecked him on the cheek as Don took a close look for signs of improvement.

'Never a truer word spoken Mary, and how are you?' Don replied looking at someone without a care in the world and in sparkling form. 'You're looking well and so much better now. Is that all down to the DCT treatment.'

'Yes, and my reformed diet and exercise regime is all part of it but come on in and let Toby give you the technical details. I feel so much better Don, I can hardly believe that only a few weeks ago I felt at death's door.

'Well let's hope that door is permanently shut and under lock and key,' Don said as they entered Toby's office to a warm welcome.

'It's good to see you again Don, how was the journey?' Toby stood and shook Don's in a firm grip, 'let me get you a drink before we go any further, coffee for you Don and a fruit tea for Mary, it's one of her favourites now.' Toby opened Mary's file onto the desk. 'Although we're only 4 weeks into the DCT programme we're all delighted with Mary's progress in preparing her for the next and most important stage. We have built up Mary's monocytes cells through the ITC which basically tells the Dendric Cells to isolate and destroy the cancer cells. The frequency and level of this depends on how quickly Mary's immune system responds to these signals. The treatment is formulated differently for each patient and that's why it is so different to the traditional treatments.' Toby hoped his simple explanation was clear enough.

'Yes Toby, I can see it's a whole-body approach using the body's own immune system to fight the cancer cells. How long will it take for the therapy to eliminate the cancers?' Don's grasp of the process was acknowledged by Toby's nod.

'That's the million-dollar question Don. If you recall, I said at the outside we are into clinical research, no one had done anything like this before with a living patient. The clinical trials we've now concluded have given us every confidence that DCT will work. We just don't know at this stage how long it will take or how effective it will be in the long run although we are set up for a nine-week trial period. If it takes longer, we'll apply for additional resources.' Toby paused to let the unspoken message sink in and hoped he hadn't pulled the DCT costs mat from under their collective feet, but he didn't want them thinking it was now plain sailing.

'The way I feel now is so much better Don, and I'm as confident as I can be that what Toby and his team are doing is going to work.' Mary gazed at Toby as though he was the deity while Don was almost overcome by Mary's positivity.

'There it is Don; I couldn't have explained Mary's situation better in making my point.' Toby returned Mary's gaze as a 'thank you'.

Mary noticed Don wincing with each step as they left Toby's office. 'You look uncomfortable Darling, what's the problem?' She asked, concerned that Don often suffered in silence.

'The stump is chaffing a bit with all the walking so if I can rest it for while it should be alright.' Don replied clearly in some distress.

'Let's get to my room so you can massage where its sore and rest up until supper time, although I could always bring some food from the canteen?' Mary asked knowing the stump played up if it wasn't rested.

'That's a good idea about supper but let's see the damage as it usually just needs a massage and rest.' Don was annoyed with himself for not taking the usual precautions.

An evening spent in Don's room was not wasted, and once the stump was massaged he felt much better. The next therapy stage for Mary would start in two days so they had a day spare for some leisure activity and decided to visit Birmingham's Victorian Botanical Gardens in Edgbaston.

The gardens covered a 15 acres site which comprised four sub-tropical glass houses containing, a huge aviary and a mini zoo. Scattered around the palatial grounds were 7,000 plants and horticultural specimens of all shapes and sizes, which included a Japanese and alpine garden. Inside one of the glasshouses was an enormous pool of Japanese koi, some over 18" long! One of the best things from Don's point of view was the availability of a self-propelled buggy – with Mary walking alongside for the exercise.

After a blissful hour later winding their way through the avenues of plants, bushes and trees, most of whom they had never heard of, they retired to the garden's café for refreshments. Additional entertainment was provided by the Erdington Silver Band playing a variety of popular melodies from inside the wrought iron bandstand. Below them an expanse of lawn allowed families to lounge and picnic, enjoying the music and singing along to some of the melodies as they watched their youngsters rolling down the grassy slope.

'What a marvellous feature for Birmingham residents, I'm sure they appreciate it,' Mary stretched out, admiring the idyllic scene, 'this was a good idea Don, and it's rested your leg, so tell me all about the Grand Opening and how you wowed Wor Jackie and the Mayor of Whitley Bay.' Mary said mimicking a yawn at the same time, accompanied with an impish grin,

For once Don didn't rise to the bait. 'It went better than I thought, mainly because everyone put 100% into making it work. I've brought some photos and cuttings you can read at your leisure.' Don handed Mary a folder.

'Thank you Don, that's very thoughtful, I'm a bit out of touch with North East news.' Don's reward was a fond embrace. 'Now what did you make of Toby's remark about the project funding that they'll apply for if necessary - if they don't get it that then?' Mary looked anxiously at Don for some answer to her concern.

'I'm sure Toby is on top of the situation and is thinking ahead. He's not going to risk any attempt to curtail the trial when the results so far have been on track. Try to keep positive Mary and let them do the worrying. Your job is to concentrate on sticking to the plan, mentally as well as physically.' Don kept any concerns to himself.

'Yes, you're right I must concentrate on my role above all because I'm excited about the next DCT stages and whether I'll actually feel physically different as the therapy takes effect.' Mary seemed to have regained her positive composure.

'Over the next few weeks they'll be monitoring the effects closely and will keep you informed of progress so just go with the flow.' Whatever happened, Don wouldn't embrace any negative thoughts.

*

After an emotional parting hug from Mary, Don was on his way back to Newcastle with his leg sitting a lot more comfortably. He was still thinking about the project funding and wondering how he might be able to help. He would write to Toby on his return to find out if project funding was really at risk. Better to know than wait for a potential Sword of Damocles to bring a premature end to the project.

Back in his office at the Bay, a full in-tray contained a host of congratulatory cards, business enquiries on the back of the Grand Opening and a letter from the Ministry of Transport that piqued his interest. He was reminded that some months ago he had applied for a car under the disabled mobility scheme and had promptly forgotten about it in all the excitement.

Dear Mr Sullivan

Thank you for your application of the (date received) for a vehicle under the government's mobility scheme. We are pleased to inform you that you qualify based on your war factory inspectorate record. If you would contact our vehicle provisioning section manager Mr Carter, he will provide you with a vehicle which can be adapted to your disability.

Yours sincerely

David Timberlake (regional disabled provisioning)

Don had been thinking long and hard about a car but the basic cost and the adaptation for his disability would be excessive. However, the mobility option might be worth exploring to make it a worthwhile means of transport.

That evening he discussed the government offer with some friends from the Cliffe who were pleased he would be independent of public transport. 'The offer is for a vehicle called an Invacar, which is powered by a motorcycle engine and has only space for the driver. Anyway, I'll see this Mr Carter and find out what the deal is, I've nothing to lose.' Don saw an opening and had the bit between his teeth again. Anything for a challenge, especially is it could result in his first personal transport since the accident.

*

Don showed Trevor Carter the disabled centre manager his letter from the ministry and was taken into a showroom to view a brand new Invacar and was given a demonstration of its controls which were handily placed near the steering wheel and meant the absence of a leg was no hindrance. Don asked the Invacar's cost which was in the region of £150 and enquired if that amount could be allocated to an adapted Morris Minor or a Ford Popular as he would be using it for his business.

'Well, I've never been asked that question before, but it might be possible if we made a case. Certainly, most popular cars would be easy to adapt, leave it with me and I'll make some enquiries. In the meantime, would you like to try out the Invacar on our test track?' Don agreed and was helped into the cramped space.

'Before the war I was more used to two wheels, but I'll be interested to see how it performs.' Don was quite excited at the prospect. 'What's its speed limit?'

'It has been test driven to 60 mph but 40 is the sensible speed for normal use.' Trevor advised, looking warily at Don.

The controls of brake, accelerator, clutch and gears, were handily placed and after a couple of stalls due to aggressive acceleration in first gear, Don got the hang of it. All he had to do was to relate the controls to those of a motorbike and change their position to each hand, left for the gears and brake, right for the accelerator. On the conclusion of his test drive Don decided to take advantage of the Invacar offer even if his pursuit of a family car wasn't feasible. He would wait to see if Trevor's enquiries bore any fruit but until then he would check out second hand car prices and costs of adjustment at Tynemouth Motors.

CHAPTER 69

'Let's do some research on family saloons,' Don decided as he checked the prices of a Ford Prefect at £240 (4 years old) and a Morris Minor £240 (5 years old) with mobility adaptation at £40. Don calculated that if either car were subsidised by the Invacar cost of £150 he could have a 4-seater for around £140 which might be affordable. If not, he might be able to convince Tim to provide him with a loan or an advance on his salary. Don wrote to Mary later that day to say he was mobile with a single seat mobility car and was also exploring a family car option. Malcolm did a cartwheel and asked if there would be room in the car for Dusty.

'I think we might be able to squeeze Dusty in somehow?' Don grinned, ruffling his son's hair.

'We couldn't leave out Dusty, could we, but as it would be his first car ride you would have to keep a tight hold on him.'

'Oh, I would have him on his lead to be sure. So will we have a car soon Daddy?' Tugging Don's arm for a response.

'I'm waiting to hear from a man who might be able to provide the money, so I'll let you know.'

'That alright Daddy I know you'll do your best. C'mon Dusty it's time for your walk.' Malcolm said magnanimously which made Don stifle a laugh as his son took the cat out the back door.

Don finished the letter for Trevor concerned with an Invacar trade and noticed in the Newcastle Journal a report of a disabled ex-RAF airman who was doing a sponsored wheelchair event in aid of an RAF servicemen's charity which involved a 24-hour run around the local Hill Heads sports stadium. Sponsor forms were available from the Journal's office and the local library with donations for each mile completed.

This got Don thinking about how he might be capable of raising funds for the University Research Clinic as it would be a popular cause. But how to get enough interest? It would have to be something eye-catching, dramatic and have public appeal. Later that week, Don had the answer at least in embryonic terms.

*

'Hello, is that Mr Sullivan?' Trevor Carter from the Invacar centre. I enquired further up the hierarchy about your request to offset a regular car cost against the nominal cost of an Invacar but I'm afraid it wasn't possible. It's the Invacar and that's it.' Trevor sounded genuinely apologetic which Don thought very considerate as his request had been a long shot.

'Many thanks for your efforts and I'll make do with the Invacar. When could I take delivery? Is a motor-cycle licence enough?'

'We do have a couple of the latest models in stock and ready to go so I'll organise the paperwork and you could pick one up at the weekend and your motorcycle license will suffice for the Invacar.' Trevor was a man after his own heart thought Don, *'put the customer first and no messing about.'*

'I'll be there at 10 a.m. next Saturday with my licence and many thanks Trevor?'

Don's next step was to contact Toby at the research centre and ask him if he had a linked charity to sponsor an appeal once he had worked out the details of his 'mission impossible'.

*

Don took possession of the Invacar after his licence was checked and a comprehensive policy organised through Prudential Insurance. Trevor checked that Don was still au fait with the control positions and pointed out the important features of the handbook, before handing him the keys.

'Don't forget it's a 197cc Villiers 4 stroke motorcycle engine with a maximum speed limit of 50 mph but I would advise keeping within the 40-mph range for safety, depending on the local speed limits.' Trevor suggested another 30-minute test around the track before venturing onto the open roads. 'I'll point out some 'do's and don'ts' on driving behaviour before you go, just remember it's transport for the disabled not a racing car.' Trevor warned, aware of Don's previous motorcycle ownership.

After a couple of circuits Trevor signalled Don to a stop. 'You're good to go Don, good luck,' as Travor waved goodbye. Don turned on to Turnbull Avenue that would take him onto the Whitley links road and towards St Mary's lighthouse for a spin before turning back to the Bay Hotel for a management meeting. After that he would head for home in time to meet Malcolm who would be cock-a-hoop when he saw the sparkling blue Invacar.

*

Due to the Grand Opening's publicity Don was delighted to see the restaurant almost full of afternoon tea clientele. 'We hav many enquiries since the big opening for meetings of local clubs on the back of the Rotary club President's supper. The Lions and Soroptimists have also enquired about monthly meetings so we're not resting on laurels.' Stefan announced proudly.

'Well done Stefan, best news today. Those afternoon tea pastries look very professional, did you get them at that upmarket French pattisierie in Town Gordon?' Don enquired thinking about the cost.

'Aye weel, that's down to the new pastry cook I poached from the Cliffe last month. With the permission of their head chef Dougal, tis always best to keep in with the local chef fraternity, you never know when you want a favour.' Gorden explained, pleased with Don's compliment.

'Fiona, how's the new housekeeper working out? Has she settled in now as she's been with us, what, six weeks? Don quizzed his upgraded head receptionist who was also responsible for the back-of-the-house operations.

'So far, she's getting on well with the three chambermaids. I've checked the rotas and the laundry schedules with her and apart from the odd room checks I'm happy to let her manage. She's compiled a room check list so the chambermaids have a routine and workload they can manage.' Fiona explained to Don's satisfaction.

'Well done Fiona. I'm pleased with how the housekeeping is working out. I see from the bookings that we're over 90% capacity for the next month?' Don asked, 'does that mean we're turning customers away?'

'Yes sometimes Mr Sullivan, but I try to rebook them on an alternate date if possible. I also remind them that early reservations would be a good idea because the demand is creeping up.'

'That's a good point. I'll be looking to add more rooms before long, but where can we put them? Maybe some adjacent properties might be encouraged to sell for the right price?' Don decided to leave that idea for another management meeting and alert Tim to do some local research.

'You may not have noticed but I'm now motorised, compliments of the Government's disability initiative. The small blue vehicle in the car park is an Invacar which is an ideal transport for two reasons. I don't have to rely on public transport or any more friendly lifts. It also costs about a third to run than even the cheapest motorcar at 60 mpg and to cap it all, I didn't need to pass a driving test - my motorcycle license was enough.' Don acknowledged the polite applause from his team. 'I'm still learning to get the best out of it and will give it a good runout once its bedded in.'

Don left the Bay in high spirits with the hotel's progress on track in every area and especially with Stefan's declaration that they were *'not restin on their laurels.'* That was the attitude he had been at pains to instil in the staff because in the hospitality business if you didn't look forward, you stagnated.

*

'Ooh Daddy what a lovely car, can I have a ride please, my friends will be so jealous.' Malcolm could not contain himself with whoops of delight as he ran around the Invacar, as Gracie attempted unsuccessfully to calm him.

'Well, and there's a fine vehicle Donald, is it yours or just on loan.' She asked admiring the sparkling three-wheel motor.

'It's mine alright Mam, compliments of the government and a nod to the disabled. I knew that losing a leg would eventually have its compensations.' Don's attempt at black humour nose-dived.

'That's as may be Donald so can you leave your new toy and come in for your supper, it's one of your favourites, steak pie and baked potatoes. And that's you as well Malcolm.' Gracie called to her grandson who was gazing at the Invacar, lost in admiration.

'That was a grand meal Mam, you haven't lost your touch,' Don kiss on her cheek made Gracie tut with embarrassment. 'I'll write to Mary with the news of the car, and you can add a post-script if you like son.'

'What's a poscrip Daddy?' Malcolm's brow wrinkled in puzzlement.

'It's what you add at the end of a letter Malcolm, often something you forget to say earlier so write something in your best handwriting and then I'll add it to my letter.' Don handed his son some spare paper and pencil.

*

Don intended to drive to Birmingham in the next couple of weeks once he was confident with the Invacar and stay a day or two and hoped the DCT injections were starting to make a difference. Malcolm added a 'poscrip' with a little help.

Deer Mam, hope you ar(e) wel(l) and getin(g) bet(te)ar. Dusty and me re(a)ely miss y(o)u

and hope y(o)u ar(e) ba(ck) soon. From yo(u)r su(o)n Malcolm xxxx

Malcolm licked the 1st Class stamp, stuck it to the envelope and dashed off to the post-box at the end of the street.

*

Mary was now in the fifth week of he DCT treatment and her immune system had been boosted by a selected programme of diet, exercise, antigens and supplements and she was now prepared for the injection of the Dentric cells which, through the addition of the IMT (immune memory transmitter) that would programme her cells with the anti-cancer vaccine. Over the next four weeks, injections would be applied at regular intervals and the results monitored for their effects on the cancers. During this time Mary's immune system would be enhanced and supplemented for the anti-cancer fight. For six to nine months the Dentric cells would search out and eliminate the cancer cells.

'So far Mary the mix of cells and vaccine are doing their job in isolating and inhibiting the cancer cells, so you can tell Don that the DCT is working as we hoped.' Toby confirmed on their daily progress session.

'I'll be able to tell him face to face as he's coming in just over a week. He hopes to stay a couple of days as the Bay has a good management team in place.' Mary did look in good shape and had filled out almost to her pre-cancer weight.

'You mentioned last time Don was here that additional funding might be necessary to continue with the DCT research programme so is that still a concern for you?' Mary always thought it best to know as it was her way of preparing for bad news.

'Not at all,' Toby emphasised, 'research studies are always at a risk of having funding dry up and especially with clinical studies. We're now moving from research into the application phase, as in your case but we're a long way from any financial constraints and we have a great many sponsors who are confident of a breakthrough.' The last thing Toby wanted was to upset the delicate balance of her treatment. 'We're all OK Mary, so remember just concentrate on keeping positive and try not to be diverted. The DCT must be your only focus as we want to give you the best chance of success so we're relying on you to play your part.' Involving Mary as part of the team ethic would help her remain in the zone. Toby would have a quiet word with Don to have him reassure Mary that all was well with the project funding.

'You're right Toby, I've got to concentrate on staying positive. Maybe I'll go to that comedy show the students are putting on at the Barber gallery this evening.'

'Good idea Mary, you can get tickets from the library in the Chamberlain building. It should be well attended so I'd get over there asap.' Toby thought it would help if she went with someone. 'Marjorie in the office was talking about going, so why don't you ask her?'

Mary often had lunch with Marjorie and when asked about the show readily agreed to team up for the evening with a meal before the show. Mary was enjoying herself for the first time since starting the therapy and realised that once away from the clinic she hadn't made any proper friends, frequently feeling homesick for Don, Malcolm and even Dusty who was often her knitting companion. Mary mentally shook herself and resolved to get out a bit more, she would ask Don to bring her knitting and find out what was on in Birmingham's cinemas. Marjorie had confided that she didn't get out much as her husband's was a traveller so trying to book anything was a gamble.

'Do you fancy seeing The King and I with Yul Brynner Marjorie, it's on at the Odeon in Birmingham next week.' Mary asked as they were having coffee.

'Oh yes I've heard the show has been a sell out on Broadway and Deborah Kerr is one of my favourite stars, so I'd love to see it.' Marjorie was delighted to be asked out again because she really liked Mary and her Geordie accent.

CHAPTER 70

While Mary was cosseted in a newfound friendship Don was working out how or even why he was embarked on a questionable journey of 400 miles in a motor designed for journeys around the block. He had always considered himself a pioneer whose role was to challenge the status quo and wouldn't Mary be surprised and delighted that he's pushed the car's boundaries above and beyond just to see her?

Monty's catches started jingling as **The Voice** *queried*, **'Don, isn't it about time you considered your family? Aren't they a tad more important, than this escapade with the Invacar?'** The voice had been quiet recently but perhaps it was apropos to reminded Don of his primary obligation.

'I suppose you're right as usual, but how am I going to test out the Invacar for a long charity run if I don't test it on a run?' There was no response to Don's justification for such an arduous undertaking. It was left to his conscience as to what were in his family's and his career's best interests. He was now older and should be wiser to be even thinking of such a journey without really having done any research into whether the Invacar was capable of such a continuous journey. 'Maybe a few circuits around the area would provide some indication, a hundred miles and back to Berwick shouldn't be a problem.' Don concluded. 'Maybe a more sensible option to would be to contact Trevor Carter at the disabled vehicle centre for his opinion on a 400 miles round trip.'

'You want to do what?' Trevor could hardly belief his ears, 'do a return journey of 400 miles plus in the Invacar on open roads – tell me you're having a laugh at my expense?' Trevor raised a tight grin that this was somehow a knowledge test of disabled reliability. Surely, he couldn't have been set up by the Ministry so see if he would approve a *'test to destruction'* of an Invacar? No, that was a too fanciful an idea.'

'No Trevor, I'm seriously considering this journey to see if the motor will stand up to a real test because if it can then I was planning to attempt the ultimate charity run; John O'Groats to Lands' End.' Don explained with a straight face much to Trevor's bemusement.

'Oh, this gets better and better,' Trevor thought, 'I have a serious fruitcake on my hands.' But he decided to take it on face value just to see how far this ludicrous idea would go. 'So, a marathon from one end of

Britain to the other and tell me Don why would you want to do this, especially in your disabled state which can't be something on the plus side.?' Trevor was beginning to enjoy the conversation - it would make a great story when retold to his pals in the Frog and Nightgown. Don realised Trevor was not taking him seriously, and why would he but decided to find out a bit more of the Invacar's long range potential.

'I want to raise a significant amount of funds for a cancer research clinic because my wife is being treated with an alternative therapy. Until they accepted her as a patient this treatment was still at the research stage. So, the more bizarre the challenge the more it could attract in sponsorship, especially if the press were involved. So, could you give me some performance information on the Invacar, for example; what's its range on a non-stop journey before it needs a rest?' Don explained.

'It sounds as though you're serious, so first things first.' Suggested Trevor, 'The Invacar is not designed for long journeys but having said that, the Villiers 197 cc engine is very reliable and hard-working. The tank holds 3 gallons and has an approximate range of 150 miles dependant on an average speed of 37 mph. Its top speed is around 50 mph but being a three-wheeler, I wouldn't want to exceed 40 mph. In addition it's made of fibre glass and being light for its size is at risk in cross winds. It has been known to blow over, so checking the weather forecast is a wise precaution.'

Don made some notes as Trevor spoke. 'Thanks for the information Trevor and have you any Invacar drivers that I could talk to?'

'I'm not allowed to divulge confidential information about our customers, but I'll contact a few and see if they're willing to talk to you.'

Two days later two drivers who lived locally contacted Don, one of whom, Bill Stanley a 45-year-old had driven his Invacar for five years with no problem and had travelled around the region as far as Berwick-on-Tweed. His only breakdown was when he forgot to top up the oil and the engine seized. His longest single journey was just under 100 miles into Yorkshire to visit a cousin in Sheffield and on a couple of occasions he had exceeded 50 mph but wouldn't advise it. Bill confirmed the Invacar was seriously averse to cross winds in anything over 30 mph when the Invacar became unstable.

'This is good stuff,' Don realised and spoke to 60-year-old David Chalmers who had owned his Invacar for 7 years and was now due an updated model. There were plans to add a fourth wheel to improve stability, but nothing had materialised so far. David told a similar story to Bill as he had the embarrassment of being blown over on the Coast Road. 'I really shouldn't have gone out as it was very draughty, but I had to visit a sick relative. Fortunately, a motorist with three large passengers on board managed to get it upright with a couple of scrapes and took it easy until I got home.' David smiled at the memory, adding a warning, 'as long as you look after its maintenance and drive carefully it will serve you well, just don't push its boundaries.'

With all the evidence Don could muster by those in the know coupled with personal accounts in the Disabled Drivers magazine, it was evident that the journey Don envisaged would be foolhardy, at the risk doing damage to the car as well to himself. He would do some longer local test runs and see for himself what the Invacar could handle but for now a train ride was the sensible option to visit Mary. 'Better get a ticket and review the Bay's progress with his team before I leave.' Don thought as he pondered whether his quest was really *'pie in the sky'*.

CHAPTER 71

Mary looked radiant when she met him at New Street Station and was looking forward to the last period of the DCT, even though the weeks and months after that would require regular monitoring to ensure that the cancer was on the retreat.

'I've made a new friendship at the Uni. and it's made such a difference because I think being on my own had an adverse effect on my progress.' Mary was clearly more upbeat than Don had ever seen her which gave him a surge of confidence for their future. 'Oh Don, I'm so pleased all your efforts have paid off in the end. Incidentally, you did get my letter wishing you all the best?' Mary asked, hopefully. 'On that day I was so miserable because I wasn't there to support you but that's the price I had to pay.

'Yes, I did get your letter – I forgot to mention it last time, and if it's any consolation you were in my thoughts the whole time Mary, so I felt you were there in spirit.'

'OK Don enough of this mutual congratulation, lets decide what to do over the next two days to make the most of it. I've booked us in to a local comedy at the University theatre and tomorrow I thought we could visit Coughton Court, a National Trust property where the gunpowder plotters met. It's not far and there's a good bus service with a stop close by, so what do you say Mr Sullivan, is that something that appeals?' Mary asked, giving him a playful dig.

Don was so puffed up with Mary's progress and positive demeanour as he travelled back to the North East after his two days with Mary and discussions with Toby about his plan to generate sponsorship for the research department in some way. It was the least he could do to acknowledge their efforts. In fact, Don still hadn't given up on the possibility of an ultra-marathon in the Invacar but more research was needed before Don would decide whether to *'eat the elephant'*.

*

Mary had now completed her DCT treatment and the result had been encouraging with the cancer in remission but she was not out of the woods yet and would need to return every three months for a scan and a top up boost of Dentric cells.

Don's dream of completing a marathon run for charity had hardened into a 'possible' rather than a 'maybe' after a long run to see some old friends in Carlisle, a return distance of almost 200 miles. Apart from some hairy moments crossing the top of the Cheviots at Hartfell Pass when he was almost blown off the road.

*

Shortly after his return to the Bay, Don received a call from his brother Sidney that Gracie was receiving treatment at the Grosvenor Hospital in South Shields after another fall at home. He gave his excuses to his Bay managers and checked his Invacar before the 20-mile trip to Shields.

Grosvenor hospital was a late Victorian building near the centre of town with an austere high windowed outlook that was in urgent need of an overhaul with grounds that had once blossomed with flower beds, a fountain and shrub lined pathways with benches for patients and visitors as Don remembered. Now, it was overgrown with a cracked fountain and broken benches, it was a sorry sight and inside the smell of disinfectant was almost overpowering as Don was directed along the green tiled undecorated corridors to where he found Gracie in a ward with five others elderly ladies. They were similarly incapacitated, in beds that were functional but in need of updating. Gracie smiled painfully as she saw Don and attempted to sit up to give him a mother's welcome.

'Hello Mam how are you feeling?' he asked giving Gracie a long hug, presenting her with a mixed bunch of flowers and a bunch of grapes from his shoulder bag.

'Not so bad Donald, they're looking after me. I just tripped, fell heavily and banged my head.' Gracie replied, her face was badly bruised as were her arms, but she seemed lively enough and in good spirits. 'Sidney's coming at the weekend and the doctor thinks I can be released once they've checked *'my vital signs'*, that's the phrase they use when they're not sure.' Don was relieved that his Mam had not lost her sense of humour and hoped she could be released from this depressing place.

'I'll ask Sidney if he could bring you over to Sycamore to convalesce. Would you like that Mam?' Gracie was visibly cheered by Don's offer and agreed straight away. 'I'll get a wheelchair if you're not fully recovered by then.' Don suggested as the ward sister called the end to visiting time. Don squeezed his Mam's hands and kissed a damp cheek. Don was appalled the hospital's general state of repair and vowed that in future he would find somewhere in better trim and nearer to Whitley for his mother.

*

Tim was excited when he called Don from his office at the Leisure Consortium two weeks later. 'Have a look at this brochure Don and let me know whether it's worth a visit as it could be another feather in your corporate cap.' Tim certainly didn't let any grass to grow, which was all very well but the Bay Hotel was still in its transitionary phase and Don didn't need any distractions. Tim met him just after he had parked with the news that the hotel in question, the Angler was in the Northumbrian countryside not far from Hexham.

Mary's condition was another issue that took a toll on Don's time and he wouldn't prioritise Tim's new venture, plus and he had concerns over Gracie. Sidney had brought her to convalesce from Shields the week before. 'Certainly Tim, give me a couple of days and if it's worth a look I'll take the Invacar for a run out.'

CHAPTER 72

Early the next morning Mary rushed down the stairs calling for Don. 'I can't wake Gracie Don, she's not responding, come QUICKLY,' Mary called out desperately. Don bent over the still form of Gracie and gently felt the main artery on her neck where his finger sensed an almost non-existent pulse.

'Mary, ring 999 for an ambulance from the phone-box, there's not much of a pulse but I'll move her into a better position, until they get here.' Don relied on his wartime experience of bombed out casualties. 'It could be a stroke or possibly a heart attack,' but time was of the essence if Gracie had a chance of pulling through. Within minutes of Mary's call an ambulance screeched to a halt, disgorging two medics, a stretcher and a holdall containing emergency life support equipment. Gracie's faint pulse was holding as they strapped on an oxygen mask which immediately boosted her pulse.

The gurney rushed into the critical trauma theatre where the team connected various lines to monitor Gracie's vital functions. Don kept his fingers crossed as they were directed to a bleak waiting area to fret and worry. An interim report from a medic would have been some solace, but none was forthcoming. Don brought Mary a tea from the volunteer stand and went in search of a phone to contact Sidney, leaving messages to contact him at the hospital.

Another hour elapsed before a medic informed them that his mam had had a bleed on the brain which had led to a massive stroke. In normal circumstances this would have been fatal but their quick action and the ambulance staff had enabled the surgeons to stabilise her condition and arrest the worse effects of the stroke. Whether the trauma team could stabilise Gracie's condition would be revealed in the next 24 hours. Don and Mary could only hope and pray that she would recover from the induced coma. They were allowed into the monitoring unit to sit by Gracie whose pale face was encircled by wires and pipes linking her to a range of servers, which were checked every 30 minutes.

'She couldn't be taken care of any better than this?' Mary whispered as she gently stroked Gracie's hand as Don nodded in agreement, too concerned to speak. Sidney and Sadie arrived an hour later, visibly traumatised and were given an update on Gracie's condition, their grief and shock all too clear to see. Don eventually arranged a taxi to return them to Sycamore

Avenue where they talked in subdued tones to wait a long night. They all returned to the hospital at 11 a.m. the next morning, fearing the worst but hoping against hope for an improvement in Gracie's condition. They were met by the same medic as they sat nervously sipping their drinks, hoping for some good news.

'I'm very sorry to tell you that despite all our best efforts Mrs Sullivan's condition deteriorated throughout the night as a result of the initial stroke and she passed away peacefully at 5 a.m.. We had hoped for a better outcome.' His expression clearly showed how low he felt having to give this sad news. 'Would you like to see her?' He asked looking at each in turn.

Don nodded a thank you and led the way to see Gracie who looked peaceful as they all stood respectfully, heads bowed, broken in grief, holding onto each other and desperate for some comfort in their inconsolable loss of a woman who had been their rock and example all their lives.

*

Don took charge of the arrangements for Gracie's funeral which was held at St Patricks of the Blessed Virgin and then she was buried close to her mother and father in the adjacent cemetery. As befits a Catholic service the church was standing room only because Gracie had been a popular and long-term resident of the area. The pastor provided a moving and personal eulogy of Gracie which included amusing memories of a strong willed but loving mother who had raised a successful family without the personal support of her husband. Afterwards the packed local church hall provided a fitting reminder of how highly regarded Gracie had been and how sorely she would be missed by all her friends.

For two weeks after the funeral Don emersed himself in developing new projects for the Bay as a means of filling the void left by his mother, but no matter where he was her presence was always on his mind. Things she said, things she did, advice she gave, help and support she provided – it was a constant reminder of how much they had lost.

Monty tingled during his grief. **'Don't beat yourself up Don,'** *the Voice said,* **'don't even attempt to work yourself out of the grieving, it's a natural process so embrace it and gradually all the things you remember about her will become a pleasant memory, as her spirit lives on in your own behaviour.'*

*

As part of 'keeping busy' Don browsed the brochure of the Angler Hotel that Tim had asked him to appraise as possible acquisition for the group so he gave the Invacar a 50-mile round trip workout as part of his research. The hotel was just South of Hexham and a stone's throw from the A1 with tourist access. Although its main business was the restaurant it did have ten rooms, with 50% ensuite. Its position in a third of an acre was ripe for development as most of the land was taken up by a small wood and an orchard of apple and plum trees. The hotel was not as yet on the market but the owners were nearing retirement having apparently owned the hotel for 25 years. Don scouted the nearby village and estate agent to gauge what a realistic price might be and then booked a room with dinner for some onsite research.

*

Don's assessment of The Angler's suggested a worthwhile acquisition for the Leisure Consortium. 'It's not in bad shape overall Tim but the rooms and restaurant need updating and some sales promotion locally could increase take up for both rooms and restaurant. The menu is attractive, and the chef is experienced with many years of service.' Don did not want to sound too enthusiastic but the potential was there. 'I suppose the next stage would be to trawl the business estate agents in Hexham to get a realistic guide price, without arousing any alerts. Why not take a run up there yourself and see whether you agree with my appraisal?' Don hoped this would get Tim off his back for a while so he could fine tune the Bay's projects that he had originally planned. Mary's return had provided some badly needed family stability after his mother's death.

Mary was looking fit and well, much to Don delight, knowing she was not yet out of the woods and would return to the research centre to check on the cancer remission. She was even able to help at the Bay when the housekeeper was absent and being the professional with her Rubicon training had kept the operation shipshape, introducing some of the Rubicon's systems as the need arose. Having Mary around for a coffee or lunch had been a comfortable way to keep in touch and have some stress-free family time, before she returned to the clinic that week for her periodic check.

CHAPTER 73

Don had been celebrating with Tim on the completion of the renovations with his favourite, Bells 12-year-old scotch and had rather over imbibed. Tim was also enthused by Don's assessment that the Angler hotel could be a possible addition to the Leisure Consortium's hotels portfolio. 'It's a going concern and if the couple were offered in the region of £10,000, they would snatch my hand off.' Tim thought. 'Anyway, I've left it in the capable hands of the Hexham estate agent to see if they'll bite.'

'Don't get too excited Tim, there's a long way to go. We don't even know if they want to sell.' Don cautioned Tim about thinking too far ahead but knew he might as well save his breath - Tim had already extended the restaurant and added 20 rooms.

'You're right Don, slowly, slowly catchee monkey, but it's nice to dream.' Tim said, buoyed up at the prospect of another acquisition for the Consortium.

'Well, I must be off to finalise plans for the speciality evenings. Our 'Stars and Stripes', the last one was well received, and the Latin American evening was a hoot teaching guests the samba. I've never laughed so much at the *'trainees'* having a go. You'll have to come to the next one.' Don suggested to keep Tim abreast of the Bay developments and make him realise that the Bay was Don's priority.

*

Don walked carefully to the car park knowing he was really in no fit state to drive. 'I'll take it steady,' Don said to himself as he eased himself into the car. The Coast Road home took him into Whitley and along an ill-lit road adjacent to the golf course. He had successfully negotiated the round-about at Monkseaton when a badger ran across the road. In his befuddled state he swerved out of the way and ended in a wayside ditch from which there was no escape.

'Damn and blast my sister's cat's bottom! That's blown it,' Don's swore loudly, realising he was well and truly stuck but fortunate to have escaped injury.

It wasn't long before a local resident had seen the disabled vehicle disappear off the road and alerted the police who had been cruising the local night scene. 'Tap, tap, tap,' on the Invacar's side window as the constable peered through the misted glass. 'Tap, tap, tap' again, 'Are you alright sir, can we help you? Are you injured?' The constable asked, who didn't look old enough to have left school.

'Thank you constable, I don't appear to be injured, but if you could help me out, I seem to be at the wrong angle for an easy exit.' Don gave a nervous laugh, breathing through his nose to minimise the alcohol fumes leaking out.

'That's no problem sir, we'll have you out of there in a jiffy if you're sure you're not injured?' He checked to err on the side of caution after noticing Don's disablement and the recognisable fumes.

'No constable, I'm as right as rain, just shaken up a bit trying to avoid running down that damn badger. As soon as you get me out of here, I would appreciate a taxi as I don't live far away.' Don explained, still breathing through his nose, now with some difficulty as the two policemen gradually eased him out, like the pip from an orange.

'There you go that wasn't too difficult now, was it? We'll have you home in no time now what's your address sir?' The constable took a closer look, 'why it's Mr Sullivan from the Bay Hotel isn't it? We were on duty when you had your Grand Opening and Wor Jackie opened the proceedings. That was a grand day, wasn't it Sir?' Now Don had been recognised he hoped this might help overlook his mild intoxication.

'It certainly was a grand day for all concerned. Are you sure you can take me home? I don't want to take up valuable police time.' Don thought his concern might speed things up.

'It's no problem at all Mr Sullivan, we were going that way anyway.' The constable was obviously impressed by Don's links to VIP's such as Jackie Milburn. Don was duly returned to Sycamore with a promise that the Invacar would be towed from the ditch to the nearest garage and have its roadworthiness checked.

Don thanked both constables for their prompt action, taking their names and number and invited them to come for lunch or dinner at the Bay, 'just contact Stefan, the restaurant manager and he'll take care of you.' Don's farewell was followed by a sigh of relief at his close shave.

'That was a small price to pay,' thought Don, 'let that be a warning - I must be more careful in future,' he remonstrated with himself as he sank into the armchair, with a loud purr and a plaintive meow from Dusty as a welcome. 'You'll have to do with me until Mary returns,' he said stroking Dusty's ears as it settled onto his real leg, drifting off into a Bell's haze, dreaming of happy times picnicking with Mary and Malcolm on Seaton's dunes.

A week later the receptionist called to tell him the local garage would be delivering his Invacar, now restored from its brush with the badger and ditch, (*sounded like a good name for a pub, Don thought*) as he inspected a gleaming car and gave it a spin round the block to check he was back in business.

*

Early the next morning Don confirmed with Stefan that all the speciality evenings were now fully booked that, despite the continuing hard times on Tyneside, there was more than enough customers to want some relief from the economic straight jacket of the 1950's.

'Excuse me Boss, I thought you'd like to know we had the two constables in for dinner last night and were well impressed. So, if we have any problem in future there are two officers we can rely on, yeah?' Stefan said grinning, as Don knew his 'accident' had been discussed at length by the Bay staff.

'Good, well-done Stefan, it always pays to keep in with the law.' Don stated evenly, giving Stefan a warning look.

*

As a result of Tim's sleight-of-hand with the Hexham estate agent, the Leisure Consortium had been able to acquire the Angler hotel, including all the fixtures and fittings for a sum that Don considered a smash & grab for £8,000. It was now up to Don to conduct a full survey of the restaurant and hotel and plan an upgrade. So far, the takeover had been problem free mainly due to the cooperation of the owners who had been considering retirement so the Consortium's offer had been a blessing in disguise.

CHAPTER 74

Mary arrived at the clinic to be met with a smiling Toby for her DCT bi-monthly check. 'Well so far, the cancer is still in remission so all we can do is keep to the regime. Another few months and we should be out of the woods. I know it's been hard at times but you've stuck to the therapy conditions and it's paying off. Toby sounded much more upbeat than he felt because there appeared to some disquieting changes in the cancers, but it wouldn't do to raise any alarms now when all seemed to be on track. Mary's second check at the University clinic two weeks later with Toby showed that the cancer remission had stopped, a worrying sign but to be expected with newly applied research. It was decided to increase the Dentric Cell count which would boost Mary's immune system and kick start the remission.

'Don't worry Mary, this minor blip is to be expected with new treatments so we'll take some blood tests now and if you could return in two weeks, we can monitor the changes.' Toby smiled encouragingly.

Mary left the clinic depressed by Toby's news and dreaded having to give Don the results of the test, but she had to stay positive for everyone's sake. She could hardly believe that only two weeks ago she had been the happiest person in the world. Homeward bound, Mary's mental state fluctuated from negative to positive and back again reminding herself of the dark days when the chemotherapy had failed. Then the soaring hope when the DCT was making inroads into the cancer and feeling she was getting her life back. Now it appeared that all the weeks and months of the therapy might be in vain. She knew Toby was doing his best to stay positive, hoping the additional infusion of the Dentric Cells would shrink the cancer into a final remission. His body language seemed to Mary that he was just being brave for her. She had to keep fighting for Don's sake as she dozed through the last miles.

'*Newcastle Central, Newcastle Central, all change,*' called the platform guard, jerking Mary into the present. Don agreed to meet her at Whitley Bay station and was buoyed by Mary's voice. From a bright and sunny day the weather turned to match Mary's mood. Gloomy, overcast and now incessant rain as she scampered towards Don in the waiting taxi.

'Wow, summer and winter in one afternoon,' exclaimed Don ruefully as he gave Mary a welcome hug. 'And how are you Mrs Sullivan, you certainly look very good to me, as usual.' Don looked closely at Mary who smiled at the compliment.

'I'm fine Darling and much the better for seeing you.' Mary squeezed Don's hand, happy to be with the only one she loved.

'Home sweet home Darling. You must be exhausted after that journey. Make yourself comfy, I'll put the kettle on and you can tell me all about your review with Toby. Malcolm's out playing football with his pals.'

As Don poured the tea Mary bit the bullet. 'Don it's not good news I'm afraid, although Toby is still positive about the cancer remission. They've increased the D cell dose and hope to boost my immune system but if that doesn't work, I don't know Don.' Mary explained tearfully, her voice reduced almost to a whisper. 'I have to return in a couple of weeks for the results of the blood test and hope the increased DC therapy had worked.

'We've just got to stay positive to help the D cells do their work. If Toby is still upbeat then we have to be as well.' Don's mind was in a turmoil after Mary's news, but he had to remain confident and supportive, whatever the outcome.

Rather than stay in and listen to the radio with Edmundo Ross and his Orchestra, they decided to eat out at their favourite Italian restaurant and keep their minds off Mary's condition to enjoy the camaraderie of a busy restaurant. Not having eaten much during the day worrying, her appetite returned exponentially due to the mouthwatering Italian aromas and duly demolished starters of fried squid, a dish of pasta carbonara and a mixed gelati (vanilla and pistachio ice cream).

'After that I won't eat for a month,' Mary grinned, wiping away the ice-cream residue with the linen napkin. 'And you just about matched me,' Mary grinned as Don patted his waistline.

'Got to watch the calories to keep in shape, overwise Monty will be complaining.' Don deferred, thinking the voice hadn't been in evidence for a while. The meal guaranteed them a deep dreamless sleep wrapped contentedly in each other's arms and all their cares forgotten.

'Oh Don, I'm really worried about the consultation with Toby, and can't help thinking about it even though I try to be positive.' Mary's face etched with concern as she feared the worst.

'I know it's tough Darling, but you must stay positive whatever the result of the sample. You have everyone behind you and we'll support you all the way, you know that.'

With Don's thoughts in her mind Mary decided to be strong for the family, even if the cancer returned.

*

Her consultation with Toby confirmed her fears; not only had the D cell treatment failed, but the cancer had also returned, and with a speed that had taken Toby completely by surprise when he saw the results of the scan. His course of action was to increase the D cell count to a level that previously he was reluctant to do because of the side effects. An ashen faced Mary took the news that the cancer had returned with a calmness that Toby considered remarkable in the circumstances.

'What we must do now, and it's our last throw of the dice, is to increase the D cell count and hope it works in your favour. I'm sorry to give you this news Mary after all you've gone through. I was very confident after the initial DCT we were on the right track and I still believe it's the best approach, but in your case it wasn't enough. Stay positive and the team will analyse the results again and see if there is anything else we can try.' Toby had to be realistic but it was no good sugar coating the pill. He was a clinical researcher and stranger things had happened when all seemed lost. Miracles of a kind did happen, so he had to convince Mary of that possibility.

'Thank you, Toby and your team for all your efforts. I know you've gone much further than you expected in searching for a cure and as you say, DCT is the way forward because I'd never felt better after the therapy.' Mary gave Toby a hug as she left the clinic with dry eyes and a clear resolve to keep her head held high, whatever happened.'

*

Don was struggling to keep his feelings in check after Mary had summarised Toby's news and could barely believe there had been such as major turnaround in Mary's condition. From hope and excitement to grinding despair. Was there any chance of a remission of the cancer? Toby had held out the slim possibility that the additional D Cells could still effect a cure because his team were re-examining the test results for positives.

Mary bravely summed up her situation. 'We have to be realistic Don and plan for the end which could be months or even years away, no one knows at this stage but my progress will be monitored by Toby. I'm resolved to live as though the cancer never happened until I physically can't, and I want you and the family to carry on in the same way because it's the only way. None of us know how long we've got to live and so we've got to apply the old expression. *'Plan as if you'll live forever but live today as if it were your last!'* I don't want anyone else aware of my condition, as pity has no place in how we conduct ourselves Don, we carry on as normal, right?

Don choked up, and tears flowed as he listened to Mary's nerveless analysis of her condition, as though it was someone else. He couldn't help admiring her courage in being able to accept what now seemed to be inevitable. He took her into his arms and sobbed uncontrollably. 'Oh Mary, Darling I'm so sorry I wasn't there when you were told.' His feeling of devastation subsiding. 'You're right, our way forward for us is to carry on as normal.' His tear-stained face was wiped gently by Mary as she smiled sympathetically, knowing how difficult it must have been for Don to be told.

'I think it's about time for a cup of tea Darling, don't you, and you can bring me up to date on what's been happening at the Bay while I've been away enjoying myself?' Typical of Mary to keep her sense of humour. Don pulled himself together and organised a pot of Lipman's and some fig rolls as Dusty wound himself around his ankles, hoping for a snack.

Mary looked wistfully around the room and wondered just how many more times she would enjoy these enjoyable family days and evenings. She would saviour each one as though they were the last. Little did she realise at that moment there wouldn't be many more. Would they break the news to Malcolm when he returned from college or save him the pain until Mary's condition was obvious? For now they decided the status quo would remain.

CHAPTER 75

Within two weeks the cancer had spread with lightning speed, taking Toby and the team completely by surprise. Chemotherapy had been ruled out at the earlier consultation. The tests by the clinical team recognised only too clearly that this cancer was particularly aggressive, giving Mary only a short window to say goodbye.

Mary's decline tore the heart out of Don as he saw his beloved wife of fifteen years disappearing visibly before his eyes. Within days Mary had gone from a lively working family member to one barely able to walk a few yards unaided, with the increasing pain a constant reminder of the cancer's rapid progress. Her doctor had prescribed sufficient painkillers to ease her condition and to be able to communicate with some fluency.

'I'm sorry Don, I was hoping to have more time with you and the family but hey, no one said life was fair.' Mary managed a crooked grin, and simultaneously gave a shudder as Don held her hand tightly as she grimaced in pain.

The morphine drip attached to Mary's arm could be adjusted to increase or decrease based on Mary's pain tolerance. 'Do you want me to increase the dose?' Don asked, his eyes pleading for her suffering to ease.

'No, I can manage that, because anymore and I'll be a zombie. It's powerful stuff Don - could you hand me the water; it makes me thirsty.' Don was constantly amazed at Mary's resilience and reluctance to be sorry for herself. It was a quality he had always admired and soon it would all be a memory. He helped her to drink with the aid of a straw and saw her face tense again as the pain returned.

'I'll just increase the dose a little and maybe I'll rest Don, it's so good to see you. Will you be here when I wake?' Mary's voice now a whisper.

'Don't worry I'll be here and Malcolm will be here to cheer you up.' Mary smiled a thank you as her eyelids slowly closed as the morphine dose increased.

Don just sat there a figure of despair, holding onto Mary's hand, his tears dripping onto her arm, now thin and mottled. 'If there is a God why take the life of someone so full of goodness and in her prime - Mary was barely 53 years old? Weren't there more less deserving of life than Mary?' Don agonised as his throat constricted.

The Voice returned, 'Don, soon Mary will be gone and then all you'll have are the good, happy, meaningful memories of your time together so treasure these when you feel down and resentful that life is not fair.'

Don couldn't help himself and always looked around to see if anyone else had heard. He knew they never would as Monty's catches twitched.

A subliminal nerve jerked Mary awake as her son entered the bedroom and she gave them a watery smile of welcome. Don had dozed during Mary's brief sleep, holding her hand to ensure she didn't slip away while he slept. Although Mary had visibly deteriorated both in weight and demeanour over the past week, she had tried to engage with her family. This spoke volumes of her indomitable spirit to live her life to the last as her body and mind faded away.

The next evening as Don gripped her hand and chatted about his day at the Bay, Mary smiled weakly at his amusing anecdotes and said in a whisper, 'Goodbye Don, I love you' as her eyes close and he felt her pulse gradually slowed.

'I love you too Darling and always will,' Don cried, as Mary's life ebbed away to the end. He kissed her for the last time, breaking into racking sobs of anguish that his life partner had gone forever. Don had steeled himself for this moment but when it came, it seemed his whole body dissolved into a state of shock that the unthinkable had happened. Don felt his life had gone where Mary had gone. He could feel nothing, just a numbness as he held her lifeless hand in his.

Malcolm had returned to visit his Mam and heard his father sobbing as he opened the door to see his mother. 'Oh no, no Mam, oh Mam, what's happened Dad?' he cried sobbing, holding tightly to his father. 'Oh Mam, Mam I really loved you, and you've left me. What will I do now? Dad what will be all do?' Clinging to his father for support and tortured with a grief that to him was inconceivable.

Gradually their collective grief subsided, and Don realised he had to assume the responsibility as head of the family to take charge, however difficult that would be. Don contacted the colliery office to inform Sidney, who was shocked by the news because he had been unaware of Mary's deteriorating condition.

*

Don had contacted Turnbulls the local funeral director to make the necessary arrangements when he knew the end was close and steeled himself not to break down when they arrived to take Mary away. He could barely function through the next few days as Sidney and Sadie took time off to help with the chores and housework and take his mind off the tragedy, if only briefly. Malcolm and Dusty supported Don as they grieved together, the tears falling at each mention of Mary's brave, but futile fight. A notice in the Newcastle Journal and the local Whitley Bay Gazette generated a flood of cards and condolences from friends, family, business and even patrons of the Bay Hotel. This outpouring of sympathy helped to support Don through the grim two weeks before Mary was buried in St Peter's graveyard in the family plot, attended by family, friends and colleagues from Rubicon.

*

Life eventually returned to some normality at the Bay Hotel, and to a lesser extent for Malcolm but not for Don - he was inconsolable. Every day he would spend hours at Mary's graveside, rain or shine and on more than one occasion Malcolm had to take him home for a rest and a meal. It was as though half his life had been ripped out. He couldn't bring himself to concentrate on the Bay's developments he had initiated. His responsibilities for the Angler hotel took a backseat which meant that Tim had to take over. He was not at all happy with Don's lapse, even though he had every sympathy for his friend's condition.

Similarly, his managers at the Bay held the fort magnificently during the funeral period but without Don's firm control, presence and interest their motivation slackened and things began to slide slowly but to a noticeable degree. Tim was in a quandary when this became evident and called Don to the Consortium's HQ for a make-or-break meeting.

'Good morning Don, how are you and the family?' Tim smiled and saw a shadow of the normally well-turned-out Don Sullivan, as he shook hands.

'As well as can be expected,' Don replied noncommittally, anxious for the meeting to be over so he could return to the graveside.

'It's now over five weeks since your loss and I appreciate that it has taken a heavy toll on you. Can we review the development plans both for the Bay and the Angler. Tell me Don are you ready to resume? The Bay needs your commitment and leadership because no one else has the ability and experience.' Tim had said his piece in making Don realise he had to get back into harness full time, otherwise he was little use to the Consortium in his present state.

'Sorry Tim, I'm still not straight in my mind. I can't concentrate on anything but this gaping hole in my life. I did think after a few weeks' things would settle down but it's almost as bad as on the day Mary died. My family have been helpful to a fault and my managers at the Bay have stepped up to fill the gap but there comes a time when grieving must take a back seat in the interests of others and the business. I understand that and have tried to come to terms with my loss but it's no good. I can't rationalise the way I feel or the way my mind is working now.' Don felt he owed Tim this explanation which didn't really do anything to help Tim or the Consortium.

'I've tried to put myself in your shoes Don but I can't, although I really do sympathise with how you feel. So, what do you want to do now Don? I'm sure you've given some thought to the void in your responsibilities.' Tim was desperate to discover if Don's condition was just a short-term blip, but his behaviour was so alien to the norm he feared it wasn't.

'I haven't come up with anything that would make sense to you and I'm not really sure myself, so the best thing is for me to resign as the CEO with immediate effect because I'm no good to the business in my present state.'

'That's an extreme decision Don. Why don't you just take an extended leave of absence, say two months until you feel ready to return?' The last thing Tim wanted was to get embroiled in an unnecessary search for a replacement which would be a major headache.

'Thanks for that option Tim and I know you've always had my best interests at heart but I just think I have to sever all my ties to the past. Hopefully this might help me reset my mental state. I'm truly sorry to put you in this position Tim, especially as you provided me a lifeline into hotel management.

'OK Don if that is really what you want, I'll put in place arrangements for your resignation and work out a severance package which will include some shares that were part of your contract. I won't do anything for a few days on the possibility you might reconsider your decision, and I'll inform the other directors as to what we've agreed.' Tim still held out some forlorn hope, that he would reconsider but knew in his heart that Don was resolute. Don's next task was to inform his managers at the Bay of his decision because his mind was made up. After that he would work out what would be his next move into a future that was gaping hole. He didn't know what he wanted but maybe time away from work would provide the answer.

'You need the break.' The Voice interrupted his thoughts as he drove home in his Invacar. 'Some time ago you talked about a major charity appeal with the research centre in mind that would help the research clinic.'

'Lands' End to John O'Groats in an Invacar, would be some publicity generator with the press to drum up interest and sponsors.' Don mused as Monty's catches tinkled and **The Voice** faded.

Don felt an enormous weight of responsibility lifted having made the decision to do something else but not yet. He had to get away from home and area and the constant reminders of Mary. It had been Mary's death to make him realise that since his accident he had been 'running' to keep up with everyone and everything and he had paid the price. Life with Mary had made all this frenetic pace justifiable but now his support, confidant and partner had gone. Don would have to find an alternative raison d'etre,

CHAPTER 76

After his resignation from Leisure Consortium Don said goodbye to his friends at the Bay hoping they would continue with his reforms and rented out his Sycamore home. Malcolm was happy to be boarded out to a recommended school until Don was able to bury his grief away from places and people that served to remind him of what he had lost. After wandering aimlessly around Cumbria for many months in several odd jobs he ended up in Westmorland and was appointed a bursar (caterer) at a residential boy's school, St. Wasps. He had accommodation on site and provided popular and filling meals for the 60 odd pupils aged 8 – 18 years who were always hungry.

After two years immersed in this isolated area developing his culinary skills and walking in the countryside to help with his grieving. Don resigned amicably and moved away from the coast. Two weeks later in a chance encounter in a village pub the Crown & Sceptre, Don was hired as the chef where the incumbent had been sacked for fiddling the takings. Don established a popular menu which soon obtained a local reputation for quality and price. In a subsequent deal with the owner based on sales and profitability Don boosted his earnings substantially with gratis accommodation as part of the deal.

After an enjoyable two years Don moved on to find lodgings in Workington where he made friends with a Rotary club member, Bernard Tearse, head of the local college. Aware of Don's hotel background and training Bernard asked him if could take his students through a City & Guilds Catering programme. Relishing another challenge, Don was duly hired and after a steep learning curve in the vagaries of teaching regulations and City & Guilds systems, Don directed his trainees seamlessly through their City & Guilds modules and examinations. Don had rarely touched his savings during his self-imposed exile and added additional sums as a popular speaker on a range of subjects which included his life in hotel & catering and as a war factory inspector.

Financially, Don was thriving and although Mary's memory was still a daily constant, Don's aching void had been replaced by a more positive way to preserve her memory. These experiences did not give him "closure," whatever that was, even if it was possible to find such a thing, but it did mean that the memory did weigh less heavily on him than before. And as a result he was no longer certain whether he wanted, or needed to address the pain of her memory.

After four his years in the 'wilderness' coming to terms with the death of Mary, Don was now homesick to return to his beloved North East, ready to reconsider his charity quest in her memory. During his absence Don had kept in touch with Malcolm whom he had initially sent to a boarding school and had occasionally met to check on his progress. He had reluctantly conceded that Malcolm's career interests were clearly directed towards journalism and sponsored him a year at Pitman's Commercial College and subsequently as a junior reporter on the Newcastle Journal. In Don's absence Malcolm had met Barbara Macdonald at Pitman's and were already engaged, much to Don's surprise. At the time Don was unaware that Barbara was 'obliged' to get married with a rushed Registry Office wedding during a time when Don was unavailable. When Don was informed it seemed only five minutes ago that Malcolm and Dusty were an inseparable duo.

CHAPTER 77

The more Don thought about his marathon 'mission' from John O'Groats, the more he realised how much planning would be required. He didn't even know the exact distance or what route would be best, how long it would take or realistically how many daily miles was feasible for the Invacar. It was a daunting project the more he thought about it – 'foolhardy,' 'reckless,' 'madcap' were the more printable adjectives offered when he first aired the project. As Don compiled a list of 'to-do's', he started to relish the put downs as challenges rather than reasons to chuck the idea into the nearest basket and do something less fanciful.

Would the Invacar's reliability be up to the journey was the first question. Trevor Carter the Disability Centre manager agreed that the Villiers engine and mechanics were reliable enough to travel nine hundred odd miles but not on a continuous journey. Despite Trevor's efforts to dissuade Don from his mission by comparing his quest to someone entering a marathon of 26.2 mile having only ran 400 yards but his mind was set! He took all this information on board in good heart and Trevor had to admire Don's determination despite his misgivings, crazy as it was. Nevertheless, Don was supplied with a list of equipment he would require and disability centre garages that could provide breakdown assistance on route. The RAC supplied a road map, avoiding busy carriageways and trunk roads enclosing a membership application form. O'Groats to Lands' End was the direction Don decided as the weather would likely improve as he travelled South, ending in the county of Cornwall.

*

Mary, he felt was by his side as he planned this 'impossible' quest and hoped it would lessen his heartache. Don would honour her memory by raising funds for the research clinic that would help cancer sufferers in the future. The pre-requisite to get the ball rolling was publicity and what better contact than his son for advice.

'Dad, you've got to be joking!' Was Malcolm's reaction.

'I know it sounds mad but until I get over the loss of Mary this is my outlet, and for it to succeed I needed your help to raise awareness for the cancer research clinic. This clinic spearheaded the alternative non-invasive cancer treatment that almost succeeded in curing your Mam. Wouldn't it make good copy for the Journal?' Don pleaded, 'they could track my daily progress in maintaining reader interest and I could contact you every couple of days with news and progress to engage your readers as to 'will he, won't he' make it?' Also, there are thousands of disabled drivers and Invacar owners who would have a personal interest and possible involvement in the 'mission impossible' scenario.' Don hoped his son would see the potential benefit for his career and to honour his Mam's memory. Come what may, he was going to finish or fail spectacularly and, in the process, bring closure to his bereavement.

'Ok Dad, I'll have a word with my editor and see what he thinks but first let's get some detail down as to the key features of your marathon. Where are you starting and when – Scotland or Cornwall? The charity's name and reason for the run. Also, I want some quotes from the disability people – i.e. 'He's mad to try this,' 'Invacar's not designed for this distance', 'would the Guinness book be interested as a new record?' 'How will his disablement affect the attempt?' 'How much will be raised? Etc, etc.'

Malcolm had the feeling that Don was resolved to go through with it whatever the obstacles. 'Dad hadn't survived his accident and his war time escapades being a shrinking violet or lacking the necessary guts.' Malcolm thought. 'OK Dad, I'll do an introductory piece as the opener but there needs to have some dynamic elements to boost interest e.g. 'marathon in wife's cancer memory' 'fund raising for cancer charity,' 'is a 1,000 mile Guinness record marathon attempt in an Invacar possible?' Malcolm felt the personal and emotional tag could help generate more interest. 'What about seed funding? How much will you need as a start-up for supplies, transport, accommodation etc.' Don still had reserves from his 5 year 'walkabout', but Malcolm's article could also initiate some funds as it was for cancer research.

'My biggest expense will be getting to the start so if a garage could sponsor a lift that would be a big plus. Accommodation and meals on the way is a major outlay but as an ex-hotelier I might attract some offers in exchange for the publicity, once each stop-over is agreed.' Don was getting more enthused as the project took shape.

'Yes, that could work. Also, stopping points and dates would let the public to know where you are on any day. Our photographer will take some pictures with the Invacar but what about a name for the car, the more dynamic the better? Something eye catching. What about disabled driver's clubs networking where you are to help with publicity and even sponsorship? Maybe local papers would provide readers with bulletins on your progress, if they had your location?' Malcolm knew you could never get too much coverage and if his dad's crazy venture touched a nerve because he was putting himself on the line in memory of his wife, then the public could be attracted and the cancer research clinic would be the beneficiary.

*

'You'll need a team behind you before and during the event. Who has spare time or at a loose end? If you draw up a list of activities I could include them in the start-up piece to attract volunteers?' Malcolm realised a 'one-man-band' operation would limit its effect and sponsorship, so the way forward was to drum up a team to spread the word and organise jobs. 'Incidentally Dad, did you come up with a dynamic name for the Invacar?'

'Right, the car's name. It's a bit silly but being blue, how about the Blue Bullet?' Don raised a questioning eyebrow.

'Great just the over-the-top name we need.' Malcolm agreed grinning. 'Yes, it has a ring to it Dad.'

'Now first things first Mal. I'll list some job titles for the team and plan out as many activities to delegate so let's meet again in a couple of days, if that fits your work schedule?' Don could see his son was now committed to help preserve his mother's memory.

*

Malcolm's subsequent article in the Journal sparked interest from disabled drivers clubs, the DDA (Disabled Drivers Association) and cancer charities such as the Imperial Cancer Research Fund (ICRF) who agreed to publicise the quest in their monthly magazine. Another of Don's 'to-dos' was to join the DDA and he sent Malcolm's article to the President with a covering letter with his proposed route. After a hesitate start Don's quest was on the move and from almost every DDA branch Don received a positive response and offers of help.

One major spinoff from the article was an offer from the Minories Group in Newcastle, to transport the Invacar to John O'Groats and a return to Tyneside from Lands' End. Malcolm's article also included a sponsorship form with Don's address and this attracted varying amounts in cheques and postal orders, made out to the 'Fund for Clinical Research into Cancer', the name of Don's charity. Several residents volunteered their support so Malcolm and Barbara, his wife, compiled a list of volunteers and arranged a meeting to allocate duties and responsibilities in Hill Heads' village hall.

*

A flurry of Invacar drivers had also written to provide valuable information on the various anomalies and useful features associated with the vehicle. In many cases they had also pledged sponsorship and attached 'good luck' cards. Malcolm's article was picked up by the national dailies including the Daily Mail and Daily Mirror, with readership in the millions. This press publicity piqued the interest of BBC TV and ITV channels who sent their reporters to verify details of the charity marathon.

'I can't believe your article has generated such a national media storm; your editor must be ecstatic Mal, so well done you.' Don's eyes glistened with pride.

Don and Malcolm set to and planned the marathon schedule, identifying the daily stages for the marathon and for each stage a list of overnight accommodation was drawn up asking for a night's sponsored bed and board. In view of the uncertainty of the Blue Bullet's optimum daily range Don had erred on the side of caution. Between 50 and 70 daily miles seemed to be a realistic average with an overall journey period of between 14 and 15 days, allowing for breakdowns and bad weather. The route was circulated to all interested parties including the DDA clubs and media.

CHAPTER 78

Don and the volunteer team put on their thinking caps to identify which organisations, groups and individuals could be approached for sponsorship. The brainstorming was flooded with ideas as to who to approach, including Invacar manufacturers, local businesses, clubs and social groups in the North East. Don's Blue Bullet logo could be displayed as the basis for their adverts and promotions linked to cancer research.

*

As the day for his transport to JOG (John O'Groats) drew near the extra phone lines Malcolm had installed were red-hot either with offers of sponsorship and requests for information on the route. The DD clubs on the route had already provided emergency contact details for Don in the event of an accident or breakdown. Local press on route also offered to publicise Don's progress. Both BBC and ITV said they would do a piece before the start and at Lands' End (hopefully). The Guinness Book had also approved the record attempt and would supply an official recorder at the start and finish but warned Don to ensure a verified log was maintained of times, dates and places. 'I'm not sure I'll have the time for all that.' Don thought, 'they'll just have to take whatever information I can record and hope that's enough.'

Trevor at the local Disability Centre had offered to give the Villiers, engine an overhaul to ensure the Blue Bullet was in the best condition. Goodwill messages from all sides flooded into the quest's H.Q. to the amazement of Malcolm and the team.

'What have I started?' Don thought, as a frightening and chilling realisation overwhelmed him. 'I can't pull out now, can I?' as he tried to dismiss the negative thoughts. 'but have I finally embarked on a project too far – it's too late for second thoughts.' Don realised that 'shit or bust' would have to be his mantra from now on.

Funds had been rolling in since Don's marathon attempt had been broadcast on national TV and local papers had picked up the TV broadcast and agreed to include sponsorship forms. The flow of funds into the charity account was growing at a pace and had already exceeded £2,000, a sum well beyond the team's expectations, and Don's marathon hadn't even started!

*

The 'Blue Bullet' logo on each side panel had been waterproofed in reflective midnight blue capitals by a local artist. 'This is it! There's no Plan B Mary so look after me please!' Don said to himself, raising his eyes heavenward.

Resplendent in their black and gold uniforms and brightly polished buttons, the local Backworth Colliery Brass Band gave Don and the Blue Bullet a rapturous send off from the Bay Hotel by Don's family, a boisterous crowd and his former employees waving Union Jacks. The Bullet now had an additional slogan 'Land's End or bust' on the bonnet as it was hoisted carefully onto the low loader, strapped and locked in place. Malcolm and Barbara hugged Don as cheers and cries of 'good luck' and 'God's speed Don' erupted from crowds of flag waving supporters. The Bullet was now festooned with bunting for the record attempt as the lorry eased away on its 400-mile, 10-hour journey to the start of Don's epic marathon at John O'Groats. Don's tears were in full flood as he waved and acknowledged the lined streets and onto the A1 North.

*

They were making good time until a puncture in a rear tyre brought them to a full stop fifty miles North of Edinburgh. A village phone call alerted a nearby AA patrolman who helped change the tyre with the spare. The puncture was then repaired after a brief comfort stop in Perth. After seven hours they were through the Cairngorms and into Inverness with 100 miles to go, when a multiple accident on the main road put a brake on their progress for over an hour. After that hiatus, traffic free roads enabled driver Bert to increase his speed and with a clear run over the Dornock Firth and onto the A9 they eventually arrived in John O'Groats (JOG), to a flag waving, noisy reception and only an hour behind schedule.

'Well done Bert, that was 10/10 driving,' Don said clapping him on the back, 'I didn't think we'd make it before nightfall'.

A couple of Invacars tooted a noisy welcome along with a cheering group of locals. Angus Robinson the manager of the Seaview Hotel made himself known as the generous hotelier who had sponsored their accommodation. 'I suppose a wee bevvy weid be in orrrder?' Angus asked in a thick accent.

Don readily agreed and shook hands with all the DD's (disabled drivers), the local dignitaries and media who had been alerted by Malcolm's publicity team - thanking them for their support and posing for the obligatory photos and interviews. Don breathed a sigh of relief that the start of his charity run had been negotiated with minimal delays and trauma. A sharp flurry of biting rain soon dissipated the crowds as Don and Bert made their way to the hotel for a late meal and a well-earned rest. Earlier, Don had contacted a relieved Malcolm that all was well and would be ready to start at 10 a.m. the next morning. Butterflies were already having a field day as Don contemplated the next 1,000 miles with frequent visits to the facilities. 'I must be nuts, getting myself involved in this venture but it's too late now Mary, you'll just have to help me out!' Shaking his head in disbelief at what he had initiated.

*

After a disturbed night tossing and turning, a hearty breakfast of local porridge oats, bacon and eggs steadied Don's nerves. Despite the blustery, cold wind a hardy group of well-wishers, assorted media and Invacar owners turned out to cheer Don with much hootenanny. As flags waved the Blue Bullet away into the unknown Don choked back the tears as he read a banner by an elderly lady, **GO WITH GOD DON – MARY IS WITH YOU!** A pair of Invacars and motorbikes provided an emotional send-off for his charity run with villagers lining the street and young children waving bon voyage flags as they briefly ran alongside. Don was now on his own.

CHAPTER 79

CANCER MARATHON - STAGE ONE

Don's plan was to ease into the first leg to ensure the Bullet was functioning as expected. His first overnight stop at Brora was 60 miles into the journey where a local guest house had sponsored his accommodation.

The A9 took him alongside the magnificent coastline at a steady 40 mph towards Helmsdale where he stopped to chat to the villagers before continuing towards Brora. 'So far, so good,' Don thought, breathing more easily. The Bullet was running well within its range and arrived mid-afternoon into a deserted market square apart from four teenagers having a kick-about. 'Our publicity machine must have failed with this lack of any interest but it's early days.' Don concluded, noting down his milage and time for the Guinness Book.

A short horn blast caught the youth's attention, one of whom wandered over. 'Sorry to interrupt your game but do you know where the 'Lochview' guest house is in Braikie Street?' Don enquired hoping his pronunciation was understood.

'Och aye, tis chust around the corner ower theer, a Mrs Macintosh is in,' the youth replied in an accent so thick, it was barely comprehensible, but his pointed finger was enough.

'Many thanks young man,' Don said, smiling at the 'Just William' look-a-like in scruffy attire and hang-dog socks.

The Lochview guest house opened to reveal Mrs Macintosh, a well-built lady in a pinny. 'Ah and a grraaand welcome to you Mr Sullivan, we didnae expect you this early but in you come and al tak your case. The welcome committee will be heerr about 5 pm but ah'll expect you'd like a cuppa?'

'Thank you, I've made much better time than I thought,' Don replied asking if he could make a phone call.

'Aye, tis in the hall, chust leave a sixpence in the pot unless it's long distance and Maisey at the exchange will know the cost.'

Barbara took the call and was relieved to hear that the first stage into Brora had been problem free and was expected to be on schedule for the next overnight at Inverness.

'I'll be averaging between 50 and 60 miles and the Bullet is on song so far. The local support on route has been amazing.'

'I'm so relieved to hear. The local radio is keeping a check on your progress with Malcolm's Journal readers receiving daily bulletins.' Barbara confirmed as Don said his welcome committee had arrived.

'Give my love and thanks to everyone – onwards and upwards.' Don grinned as he turned to greet his supporters.

Considering Brora was a small village, the mob clustered around the Bullet suggested the whole community had turned out to view this nationally publicised phenomenon. The council chairman gave a short welcome and escorted Don to the village hall like a modern 'Pied Piper' with the Hamelin style crowd, buzzing with excitement at the local press's involvement.

'If this level of interest is any indication,' Don thought as he was seated on the stage, 'our sponsorship expectations are going to be exceeded by miles.' He thanked everyone for their welcome, apologising for his early arrival and said every penny raised for the cancer research charity would be spent on finding a cancer cure as every member of the team were volunteers. After a filling meal of steak pie, neeps and tatties (swedes & potatoes) Don mingled with the villagers and an Invacar owner who was revelling in the press attention.

*

After a filling breakfast of porridge, black pudding, toast, Scottish marmalade and strong tea that would keep him well away from starvation - he would have to watch his weight - Don was waved away by the villagers with his speedometer on 61 miles and only 850 to go! 'Downhill all the way!' Don shouted to himself in good humour as the Blue Bullet meandered through the tiny villages of Dornoch, Dingwall and Mur of Ord. Hadn't his Mam mentioned an auntie who lived at Dingwall many years ago, as part of his Scottish heritage?

Inverness, affectionately referred to as the capital of the Highlands and situated at the tip of Loch Ness, famous for its mysteriously elusive monster 'Nessy'. The thriving town had been a medieval Pictish settlement dominated by King Brude's castle in the 6th century and a target for the warring Clans until the infamous (to the English) Robert the Bruce attacked and destroyed the castle in the 16th century. Oliver Cromwell aware of its strategic importance built a citadel there in the 17th century only for it to be destroyed five years later. Inverness's battles, bloodshed and strife over the centuries were long gone as Don arrived to a grand Scottish welcome by a kilt clad bagpiper playing 'Bonny Scotland' and ably supported by the mayor, townsfolk and owner of the Loch Lomond Hotel, Don's sponsored overnight. After the photos, speeches, press interviews and dinner Don graciously declined second helping of haggis having already been initiated in the delights of Cullan Skink, an extremely filling starter and later slept like a log.

At 11 am on the dot Don bid farewell to his hosts and thanked the local garage for a sponsored tankful, cheered to the echo by the Saltire waving Invernessians. Stage 2 had been safely negotiated with 111 miles on the Bullet's speedo. Fifty odd miles down Loch Lomond was Stage 3 and another strategic Scottish centre, Fort William, named after William of Orange. The town traversed the banks of Loch Eil on one side and the commanding presence of Britain's highest mountain, Ben Nevis on the other.

A few miles South Loch Lomond was a major tourist spot and given the national publicity the Bullet had received, was surrounded by well-wishers and tourists snapping photos of this mini phenomenon, offering donations of every denomination to the charity's coffers. It was here that spawned the famous Scottish ballad which told the tale of the ill-fated Jacobite rebellion and a Bonny Prince Charlie supporter who was captured by the English and incarcerated in prison lamenting *'Oh, me and my true love will never meet again on the bonny, bonny banks of Loch Lomond.'* It's probable that this kilt wearing revolutionary came to a sticky end.

Don's reception outside the Highland Hotel was thronged with kilt wearing locals and children who danced an energised reel accompanied by two youthful bagpipers before an enthusiastic group of supporters and tourists who applauded Don's short speech and 'thank you' for his welcome which initiated a flood of donations into the collection boxes offered by his supporters who then escorted him to the official reception with the town mayor Hamish McDonald, a red bearded giant who squeezed the breath from Don with his embrace, congratulating him for his cancer quest as they were served a traditional Scottish of haggis and all the trimmings after which Don decamped to a cosy first floor room and slept fitfully, happy to be well on his cancer marathon way the next morning, escorted briefly by an Invacar.

The Loch monster was nowhere in evidence as Don negotiated the lakeside road in driving rain and hoped that he was away from the downpour before his next overnight stop at Tarbet, a small village at the head of Loch Lomond and the Trossachs National Park.

After a comfort stop through the tiny village of Tyndram continued to a reception at Tarbet and his Stage 4 overnight. An enthusiastic crowd of villagers, headed by the mayor, applauded Don's welcome speech in the tiny hall and then tucked into a traditional stew he assumed had a beef origin but was too polite to ask. His residence was a beautifully restored bothy on the lake shore with Don's window providing magnificent views of the Beinn Min, a Monroe towering some 3,000 ft.

Don was now close to the divide between Scotland's lowlands and highlands in Dunbartonshire. The Bullet's performance so far had been exemplary but would his luck last? Don was ever mindful of his flight into the unknown for an Invacar and kept well within the Bullet's comfort range for speed and distance. So far Don's daily stretching regime for hands, arms, neck and leg had kept cramp and tiredness at bay.

Sponsorship in notes and change was piling up in the Bullet and would need to be banked in the next town of Dumbarton. After a tiring 55 miles Don duly banked £210.13.6 and collected a receipt after the cashier had added a further ten-shilling note and a blessing for his cancer charity. 'An indication that the public were buying into Don marathon.' Don realised. Twenty miles further on the A82 Don was buzzed by six Invacars who ceremonially escorted hm into Glasgow's centre - Sauchiehall Street opposite the Theatre Royal. The President of the local DDA greeted Don like visiting royalty along with Glasgow's Mayor and a famous international Scottish goalkeeper Fred Martin who had played in the World Cup. His presence helped to boost Don's donations in cash, notes and cheques.

Despite his exercises Don was starting to ache from the effects of his incarceration in Bullet's cramped space and needed a well-earned rest for himself, Monty and a service for the Bullet. As a result, a later start at noon was agreed with the DDA President which allowed Don some precious hours of rest and a massage for his aching stump. At the next stage maybe he could organise a proper massage of arms and shoulders?

CHAPTER 80

The evening reception in Glasgow was another surprise for Don. It had been arranged at the Theatre by the local DD club and attended by club members, local sponsors and City dignitaries. BBC TV and news photographers had also been alerted by Don's team. During the reception Don's heartfelt thanks for their support was applauded as he emphasized how important it was and that every penny would go to the research clinic to spearhead alternative non-invasive cancer cures. After Don's speech donations flowed into the collection boxes and his later call to Malcolm revealed that the fund's sponsorship had risen to £8,000 due mainly to the TV coverage.

Kelvingrove Hotel's disabled owner had close links to the DDA and provided an attractive room for Don on the ground floor. This allowed him some relief from Monty as his daily incarceration in the Bullet that was becoming increasingly uncomfortable and had caused a rash to develop around his vulnerable stump. For a while he would use the underarm crutches for mobility then see a chemist about the rash. He couldn't let this minor problem get any worse and threaten the project. At the later start time of noon, Don thanked his host the DDA president for arranging a very relaxing massage. His next stop would take him to the village of Moffat, noted as a regional wool trade centre and spa, fifty-five miles down the A73. A rainbow passed over the Bullet's speedo and across Don's smiling face as it dawned that he had driven over a third of the way towards his epiphany.

Don was worried. Would the Bullet find the going too tough as he climbed through the rolling hills and stunning views of South Lanarkshire. The daily respite for the Villiers meant that the rejuvenated Bullet crested each incline with some ease in the late morning sunshine. His sunny disposition was soon to be rudely interrupted. As a section of the A73 morphed briefly onto a dual carriageway Don eased into the nearside lane and a jangling ringing alerted him to an approaching police car which motioned him to pull over just North of Abington. 'I knew things were going too well,' thought Don as he wound down to window to be told by a burly red headed Scotsman that his vehicle was not allowed on dual carriageways.

'I beg to differ officer; I have a letter from the Ministry of Transport giving this vehicle permission to use dual carriageways. Would you like to see it?' Replied Don, evenly but groaning inside.

'Aye ah weid Sarrh,' asked the officer in the thickest accent so far, as Don opened his satchel and retrieved the letter.

The officer scrutinised the letter and announced triumphantly, 'aye this disnae apply in Scotland, sarrh,' emphasising the last word.

'Doesn't the Ministry of Transport cover Great Britain, which includes Scotland?' Enquired Don, trying to keep calm.

'Aye but no on these roads, yourr slow speed maeks you a danger te yousel so weel ha to escort you onto another minor road, so please folo me Sarrh,' brooking no arguments as he strode to his police car.

'That's done it, I've now got to find another road South,' Don cursed, consulting his road map. He would have to take a 'B' road and then rejoin the 'A' road North of Moffat and inevitably lose valuable time. Half an hour later the police vehicle pulled into Abington, whereupon the officer approach the Bullet and wished Don a pleasant journey, grinning from ear to ear as he swaggered away. 'And have a nice day too, you over-officious, jobsworth, numpty!' Don called after him, soto voce.

Fortunately, the B719 branched off at the end of the high street heading South, and Don hoped that if the road was reasonable, he might be able to increase his speed and make up time. It was and he did with barely a half hour lost and entered Moffat stopping at the village green to get his bearings. He eased himself out and approached the only shop he could see to ask for the Craigburn Guest House, his overnight accommodation. 'Och, you'll be Donald Sullivan, wont ye be?' The shop assistant chirruped warmly. 'We didnae expec you til tomorrah, but ahl mak a caal to the guest house, an put the worrd oot you've arrived.'

'Why thank you kindly, that would be very helpful,' Don replied, concerned that his schedule had briefly gone off track but relieved that there might be a formal greeting by the local DD's. A group of youngsters and locals followed in Bullet's wake chattering amongst themselves, pointing and smiling at the car's logo as he drove slowly to the guest house. Don felt a tap on his shoulder and turned to see a smartly dress lady in McDonald tweeds in her 50's announce she was Angie McPherson chairman of the local council.

'Welcome to Moffat Mr Sullivan, it seemed our dates were out of synch but you're here now and aye that's aall that matters.' She stated in a lilting, but understandable Scottish accent.

'Thank you, Miss McPherson and many apologies for the mix up with my arrival and hope it hasn't inconvenienced you too much.' Don replied, in a suitably self-admonishing manner.

'Oh no, tis no problem and my that's a bonny logo, Blue Bullet, did you name it?' Angie asked Don.

'It was a team decision, and please call me Don. I'm so pleased to see you all as I had a brush with the law and thought I might be delayed but made good time after that, though a day early.'

'Thats noo problem. I've put the word out and I'll show you where we'll meet later then you can settle into your accommodation, and please call me Angie.' Don's apology to Mrs Turnbull, the guest house owner for his early arrival wasn't a problem and she welcomed him with tea and cakes and showed Don to his room. He removed Monty with a sigh of relief and massaged the sore stump with a moisturising cream. Later she escorted Don to the village hall to meet the reception committee. After Don's misgivings that Moffat might be a damp squib, the reception and buffet, an appetising spread of local delicacies was one of the best especially as it had been drummed up a day early. Another surprise was the number of generous donations that was collected from such a small community.

Despite a sombre morning accompanied by light rain, it seemed the whole village had turned out to wave Don away, leaving the Eskdale Forest and Galloway behind with fond memories of his lengthy traverse of Scotland. Don was now on crutches and feeling much more comfortable having obtained some antiseptic cream from the Moffat chemist for his stump. The rain had eased as he headed to the tiny watering hole of Gretna Green, made famous for eloping couples to marry in defiance of their parents. A stunning view of the glittering Solway Firth to the West greeted Don as he attracted a curious group of sightseers. Near the village green where a wedding was in progress provided Don with a eureka moment and despite the alternative attraction, he generated more sponsorship and enjoyed a deserved coffee break. After the comfort stop he was enthusiastically waved away towards the City of Carlisle and his 7th Stage, feeling euphoric, now 375 miles into his cancer quest and approaching the half-way mark with the Bullet running like a dream.

*

Don approached Carlisle's centre square, as a banner fluttered in the breeze on the Town Hall; '**Carlisle *Welcomes Don and the Blue Bullet.*'** His publicity team had done a first-class job. After 400 miles completed, he was now in England and with no concerns for the Bullet, testament to the Villier's reliability. Don was in high spirits but wouldn't allow himself the luxury of being complacent and was always tuned in to the Bullet's rattle, hiccough and sigh as each might signal a future problem until its source was uncovered. Don's problem antenna was fine-tuned for preventative maintenance as he entered 'Fortress' Carlisle.

As part of his welcomed by the Mayor and DDA President, Don was given a short history lesson of this important border city. Carlisle had been a key Roman fortress on Hadrian's wall and bulwark against the marauding Scots. Mary Queen of Scots had been for many years imprisoned in Carlisle castle until her incarceration in the Tower of London until her decapitation on the orders of her cousin, Elizabeth 1. 'In addition to fund raising I'm getting a history lesson at each stage,' Don thought as he existed the Bullet on his crutches to the delight of his reception committee.

*

Don's 'thank you' was roundly applauded in the packed City Hall with the press having a field day. His interviews with local press and national news outlets expressed his gratitude for his welcome and charity sponsorship. 'I will never, ever be able to thank you enough for your support in helping to defeat this terrible disease that affects so many thousands. The University's cancer research clinic is working towards a cure every single day.' Don ended his speech emotionally, feeling that Mary was with him, as the applause for his cause rang out.

The amount of interest generated for his charity quest never ceased to amaze Don. Was it the link to cancer research? Or the 'impossibility' of his quest? Maybe it was just a 'good news' story for these straightened times in post-war Britain? Or maybe it was his quest as a disabled former war factory inspector? Or in memory of his wife as a cancer victim? Whatever the reason, Don and his team had picked the right time for sponsorship and Carlisle was no exception. One DD told Don, 'We are so pleased you've embarked on this marathon because the publicity for the disabled community has provided the recognition and awareness we've never had – it's just spectacular!' This one single comment was all the justification Don needed to underline his 'foolhardy' mission.

CHAPTER 81

After Don left the reception for his accommodation, he updated his diary for The Guinness Book and had it authenticated by the DD president, with dates, and places. Stage 8 would take him through the mountains of the Lake District National Park, and finally to an overnight stop at Lancaster, adjacent to Morecambe Bay. The Cumbrian hills provided another good workout for the Bullet and proved that the Villiers could handle the gradients with ease, provided sufficient breaks were built in for rests. The bustling market town of Penrith gave Don a comfort break and then after lunch at Kendal, capital of the Southern Lakes, a DDA whip-round provided another boost to his sponsorship total. South of the Town and on the lookout for Bullet busting transport police, he comfortably negotiated a 6-mile stretch of dual carriageway without interference but all too soon Don had something more threatening to worry about.

Back on the A6, the heavens opened, and visibility was down to zero and with the wipers unable to cope the Bullet came to a full stop in a dip and his lights on full. The downpour continued for over an hour until Don realised that his part of the road was rapidly filling with flood water with the low-lying Bullet threatened with partial submersion. He hoped a Samaritan motorist would stop but they were too concerned to get out of the deluge themselves. Don's concerns went up a notch as the water started to seep into the cabin and he knew that if the downpour continued he might be floating, but to where?

*The Voice resonated through Monty's catches. **'Don't worry Don, help in on the way,'** The tone was soothing but firm, **'stay focused for Mary.'***

Another quarter hour passed as the storm continued, accentuated with cross winds blasting across the open fells that added another level to Don's concern for the Bullet. Minutes later a lorry pulled up ahead of him flashing emergency lights, and a tall figure dressed for the conditions asked Don how he could help.

'Many thanks for your timely arrival just get me out of here if you can. I'm Don Sullivan on a mission and need to get to Lancaster for my reception committee.'

'Yes, I know who you are and I'm going that way myself. It's only 15 miles to Lancaster so happy I can help Don Sullivan on his marathon quest.' The man smiled and in a broad Geordie accent gave his name as Duncan

Jacobs, with an aura about him which Don found mystifying yet comforting at the same time.

'That's very kind of you Duncan, I'm much in your debt as will the Lancaster disabled drivers.' Don shook a damp hand through the window and hoped his reception committee at Lancaster would understand the reason for his tardy non-arrival.

'OK Don, here's what'll happen, I'll fix a tow and when I blink my lights put your gear in neutral and take off the brake. I'll pull away slowly and if I have to brake just ease on your brake and you'll be fine.' Receiving a confirmatory nod Duncan attached the towrope and the van moved slowly away with Don holding the steering wheel a little too tightly until they were moving still buffeted by the relentless elements. After half an hour swaying through the downpour with Don's eyes narrowed to see through the rain lashed windscreen they came to a stop in Lancaster's Cathedral square. Despite the chilling temperature Don was bathed in sweat and slumped forward onto the controls with relief, his nightmare over. Duncan untied the towrope and after a handshake and a heartfelt 'thank you' Duncan wished him the best with his quest and disappeared South into the gloom.

'What a life saver' thought Don, 'I'll give him a heartfelt *'mention in dispatches'* for his timely intervention. So, what now? I'm in a rain-soaked City with a non-functioning motor and hours later than expected so how do I find my accommodation?' Don wriggled into his waterproofs, unfurled his umbrella and headed for the nearest shop through the rain-soaked pavements.

'I'm looking for the Riverside guest house on Lisle Street, is it far?' Don enquired of a small middle-aged lady in a green overall with a kind face, blue eyes and her hair in a bun.

'Oh no, tis maybe five minutes' walk around the far corner of the square.' Marjorie Clements you'll need, I'll give her a ring,' she shook her head at Don's proffered phone number and dialled.

'Hello Marj. it's Bessy from the shop, I've Donald Sullivan here who says he's staying with you, yes, the disabled car man. Hmm, hmm, yes, yes, alright I'll tell him thank you, bye Marj.' Bessy said Marjorie would be waiting for him. Don thanked Bessy and offered to pay for the call, which was politely refused. Marjorie waved a welcome to Don as she saw him approaching.

CHAPTER 82

'Come, come in Donald, it's a dreadful day right enough, so take off your coat and leave those wet shoes at the door. Have a seat and I'll make a cup of tea, I suppose you're gasping? Where's your car, I understand it has broken down?' She had hardly drawn breath as Don sat down thankfully in a voluminous sprung armchair, looking around a room substituting as a lounge, with an open coal fire, a paisley designed carpet, prints of mountain scenes and a small round polished table with family photos, obviously taken over the years. All in all, it had a comforting feel. Don was nodding off as he was stirred by the rattle of cups on a tray with slices of homemade cherry cake as Marjorie continue her discourse.

'I've contacted the DD's president Jason Smith to tell him you've arrived and he's going to come around in about half an hour or so. I gave him your apology and said you'd been delayed by the storm, it's been dreadful, the worst we've had in years you know. Now, how do you like your tea and there's some cherry cake if you like,' as she drew breath Don asked for milk no sugar and thanked her for the help with the president. 'Do you have a number for a local garage?' Don asked.

'Oh, you must have been terrified, in all that awful rain and wind and little hope of rescue until that Good Samaritan turned up, it must have been God's will; what a blessing you were not far from Lancaster when it happened;' pouring the tea as she chattered on. 'I'm sure Jason will organise a garage,' Marjorie said reassuringly.

The arrival of DD President Jason gave Don the opportunity to explain the reason for his delay and recounted his rescue and Bullet's condition, 'It's certainly waterlogged so the electrics must have shorted out and the engine will need a good check. The next stop is Warrington for stage 9 so can any garage help?' Don had his fingers crossed that some speedy repairs could get him back on the road without delay.

'I'm sorry to hear about your problems. It couldn't have been much worse, but I think we can get you mobile again as we have a local garage that specialises in disabled transport and what they don't know about Invacars isn't worth knowing.' That was good news for Don. 'If you give me your keys, I'll drop them round to the garage and they'll take the Blue Bullet in for an inspection. I'll tell them the repairs are an emergency, as they'll know you're on a mission. We've got to get you back into your marathon as we're all depending on you.' Don was cheered by Jason's enthusiasm and a joy to hear that so many people were actively supporting his project. 'Our branch is cock-a-hoop that you stopped at Lancaster.'

'That's good news Jason and I can't thank you enough. When I was marooned in that downpour, I feared the worst until that Samaritan showed up. Will it be possible to meet the DDs tomorrow because I'd like to thank them for their support. We're now at stage 8 (440 miles), and halfway to Lands' End and so far, donations have far exceeded our expectations; it's just unbelievable,' Don said proudly.

'I'll organise a get together tomorrow, after all we all want to meet the TV star and Blue Bullet after what we've seen on TV and in the papers. I'll leave you to rest up and call about nine-thirty to take you to the reception.' Jason shook Don's hand firmly and bid him good night.

*

He had to get more surgical spirit to massage the stump with only one bottle in reserve and realised his marathon had almost come to premature end, if not for the Samaritan's intervention. In retrospect Don thought his rescue puzzling as it was only a few minutes after **The Voice's** call to Duncan's arrival; maybe it was just a coincidence? But when he shook Don's hand before leaving, Monty's catches rattled as though **The Voice** was there. He had meant to thank Duncan afterwards for saving his marathon by taking his van's registration, but the plate was missing – maybe it had fallen off in the storm? As Don pondered these curiosities, another voice called from below. 'Supper's ready Donald.'

Marjorie had prepared a mouth-watering supper of pork sausages, mash and cabbage followed by steamed jam sponge and custard. It was all Don could do to stay awake after the meal, and within minutes he was sound asleep and dreaming of swimming in a river followed closely by the Bullet until a firm triple tap on the bedroom door heralded Majorie with a cup of tea at 8 a.m.. Don had slept like a log for 9 hours.

Jason was as good as his word in having the Bullet repaired and had organised the reception for 11 a.m.. A slight seizure in the electrics, was sorted by the garage's knowledgeable mechanics in double quick time and the Bullet was deposited outside the venue. 'A*près le deluge'* a group of DDA members and locals were determined not to miss Don the TV star and photos of the Blue Bullet. 'I'm indebted to you all, firstly for your generous donation to the charity and especially for Jason's prompt repair of the Bullet. My overnight in Lancaster has saved the cancer charity marathon from a premature end, so thank you all.' Don clapped the assembled supporters as they applauded his thanks and cancer mission, now back on track.

Preston 25 miles South was Don's next lunch stop where he contacted Malcolm to summarise the previous days drama. The press report of his submersion had reaped donations for the charity and it seemed that each of Don's hiccoughs seem to heighten the national apprehension as to whether he would make it to the finish.

CHAPTER 83

'The charity fund could top £10k' Malcolm said, 'and the nearer you get to Lands' End, the more interest is being generated.' Malcolm's excitement was infectious as Don marvelled at the surge in donations.

Stage 9 would bring Don to Warrington, Lancashire by 4 p.m. with a lunch stop at Preston. As the weather warmed, the crowds came out and Don's Bullet was surrounded by a few, blue Invacars; there was no other colour! Tom Finney the renowned footballer who played for Preston North End and England was cheered by the crowd of locals who were hoping to be seen with him on the monitors. At the reception Tom shook Don's hand to congratulate him on his marathon efforts and signed Malcolm's autograph book. 'It's a pity you don't play for Newcastle (United) and team up with Wor Jackie (Milburn), we 'ed win everything'. Don said smiling. Although past his prime at thirty Tom was still scoring goals in the First Division.

Don's route took him through a dreary industrial cluster of belching factories and abandoned mines, sandwiched between glimpses of verdant countryside that would all be gone in the pursuit of industrial development struggling to survive in the 1950's. A couple of miles outside the industrial blight the countryside opened to rolling hills and pastures of Lancashire and Don's mood brightened as the sun peeped through the cloud cover. Wigan drew ever closure with the Bullet cruising along at a comfortable 40 mph with Don keenly alert to the slightest rattle that would made him sweat and edgy, and well he might.

Wigan is famous for two things; Wigan Pier, though many miles from the sea, and the inspiration for George Orwell's 1937 novel *'The Road to Wigan Pier'*, a socialist treatise. Wigan's rugby league team is equally famous having been at the zenith of the game for many years winning top league and cup honours. The market square was tense with anticipation at Don's arrival and gave him a vibrant cheer by the local DD group as the Bullet entered the square to be engulfed by well-wishers. They all wanted photos of Don with the Blue Bullet, a publicity magnet.

Don was starting to believe Lands' End was more than a pipedream with Warrington in his sights, at stage 9 and 500 miles into the marathon. A dour but friendly Lancastrian town, Warrington held fond memories for Don as an eight-year-old when Granny Tearse, Mary's mother, was visiting relatives. Thereafter he had always supported Warrington RFC which rarely won any national honours, despite his nightly prayers. Situated on the River Mersey it was a major conduit to the Irish Sea and only fifteen miles from Liverpool, Britain's biggest East coast port. Much to Don's surprise was a presentation granting him the **Freedom of the City of Warrington** for his charity efforts and shear bloody-mindedness in tackling his 1,000-mile marathon. It was apparently an ingrained Lancastrian trait.

*

Don was indebted for his Warrington accommodation to Darren Baker, owner of the Patten Arms Hotel, who gave him a warm welcome along with the DD's president Henry Wainwright and twenty club colleagues. 'Don, we're honoured that you chose Warrington for one of your stages because the publicity has rejuvenated our membership.' Well-wishers surrounded the Bullet while the local press were on hand to garner the Bullet's exploits.

'Many thanks' for your welcome Henry.' Don replied, delighted but always surprised that his charity marathon was a 'must see' event. Don was not religious but was ready to believe that Mary's spirit had something to do with it.

Don passed the *'Thank you for visiting Warrington'* sign as he left Lancashire, and had his fingers crossed that the fine weather would continue to Stoke-on-Trent, the centre of the Potteries about 30 miles away. As he neared the town's centre, he had to keep his wits about him with the spaghetti style road network that became more tangled with traffic coming at him from all directions. His pedestrian pace slowed to read the plethora of signs only served to frustrate other motorists, blasting their horns in annoyance. 'Don't they realise the Bullet is on a marathon mission?' Don seethed at their insensitivity.

Just when he had given up finding the meeting point, a frantic wave from a diminutive middle-aged lady, gestured Don to a parking spot next to the Town Hall.

'Hello Don, I'm your reception committee or rather the secretary of it, you can leave your car there as it's only a short walk to the meeting, I'm Kyla Leadbetter by the way so welcome to Stoke.' As she beamed a lovely smile she led Don to the venue, where a group of about 30 assorted locals gave a rendition of *'Don's a jolly fine fellow, and so say all of us,'* much to his embarrassment, his previous traffic woes forgotten.

'We've already had a whip-round and collected about £50, in addition to the cancer charity tins, so the total could top £100.' The president announced proudly.

'Thank you for your generosity, every penny goes towards cancer research,' Don confirmed, relieved to be out of the traffic's maelstrom for a while. An hour later and the sponsorship boosted by over £100, Don was on his way toward Stafford on the faster A34 on route to Birmingham, his next overnight at stage 10. 'Brum' as it was popularly referred to was known as the City of 1,000 trades and the beating heart of the Black Country. He was helped from the Bullet by a smiling Brummie adjacent to Victoria's statue next to the Council House to meet his flag waving supporters.

William Tefrn Bowen the Lord Mayor, a dyed in the wood Welshman embraced him in a congratulatory hug followed by the DDA President. A guard of honour of sparkling Invacars, put his mud-spattered Bullet to shame which nevertheless added to its attraction for the cameras. A loudspeaker had been set up which enabled Don to thank the crowd for their sponsorship and raised his crutch next to the Bullet in thanks. The official reception included a gourmet meal for a 'starving' Don as a stomach bug had denied him sustenance for twelve hours. Don's aching arms and hands were a result of the longest daily total of 70 miles, and he gratefully accepted a massage from a DD who happened to be a physio. Don thought a crystal ball might have helped him to know what lay ahead – with another 400 miles still to negotiate as he steeled himself for more challenges. His years as a boy scout reminded him to of their leitmotiv *'be prepared!'*

*

Once at his accommodation, the Hagley Hall Hotel, one of Birmingham oldest he was able to update Malcolm on his picturesque journey through Derbyshire and the Peak National Park the first to be created in the UK. Malcolm was bursting to inform Don that charity sponsorship had surged to over £14,000 which took some believing but put Don in good humour. He was much happier that his stump had responded to the antiseptic cream so Monty was back in favour.

Before setting off the next morning Don turned to the DDA President, 'Many thanks for arranging Bullet's service and could you pass on my thanks to the garage proprietor and tell him he has probably made the difference between success and failure of the marathon.'

'He'll be delighted to hear that and good luck with the remainder of your cancer marathon, we'll all be watching you roll into Land's End before long, I'm sure.' The President shook Don's hand warmly as he prepared to leave. Washed and polished, the Bullet stood out proudly in Victoria Square at 10 a.m. for the official send-off where a phalanx of Invacars, toot, toot, tooted his departure as 'God speed Don' calls echoed around the square. Britain's

2nd City was in his view the 1st for its welcome and generosity. The Bristol Road was lined with well-wishers as he headed from leafy Warwickshire into Worcestershire and on to Alcester village. It was not to be the plain sailing as disaster struck on the A46.

After Evesham the road climbed steeply, and Don failed to notice in the half-light a rain damaged pothole in the middle of the road. The single front wheel, one of the weaknesses of the Invacar's construction disappeared into the water filled hole with an enormous crack. The Bullet lurched to one side almost turning over as Don wrestled to control the car's sideways motion and came to rest on the brink of a ditch. Don crashed into the right-side window, his shoulder taking the brunt of the impact. After pausing to assess his injuries and get his breath back, Don gingerly extricated himself from the stricken vehicle hoping it wasn't an inglorious end to his marathon. A quick inspection in the gloom revealed a punctured tyre and a cracked supporting axle which meant Don realised in despair that he wouldn't be going anywhere soon. 'I knew things were going too well.' Don thought, agonising over his bad luck.

CHAPTER 84

The Ribbon development around Evesham had placed a row of semi-detached houses on the car's offside, one of which had lights on and curtains open. Don approached as quickly as Monty would allow with his shoulder starting to ache. A doorbell resounded though the house and shortly after a young mother with a toddler by her side opened the door and looked at Don nervously.

'Yes, can I help you?' Her hand ready to close the door quickly.

'I certainly hope so Mam,' replied Don in as cultured an accent as he could muster and explained his predicament and urgent need to make a phone call. After a wait while she assessed that Don was a low risk being disabled, she opened the door and pointed to a white telephone on the hall table. Don dialled the Invacar emergency number to report the problem giving his location from the mother and phone number. The emergency service said they would relay the problem to the nearest garage that dealt with DD's vehicles and ring back with an approximate call-out time.

'Many thanks for your help Mrs …..? I'm Don, Don Sullivan on my way to Cheltenham as part of a charity marathon, I hit a pothole and broke a wheel. The emergency service will ring back once they have a rescue vehicle, so is it alright if I wait for their response? It would be a big help.' He pleaded, leaning on his walking stick for effect.

'My name's Debra, Debra Forrister. Oh yes, of course, I've heard of you from the papers about your cancer charity marathon, you must be very brave in that little car. Would you like a cup of tea and maybe a sandwich while you wait?' She asked smiling, her manner and attitude doing a 180 degree turn from suspicion to cosy familiarity.

'Yes, many thanks, if it's no trouble.' Don replied taking a proffered seat.

Tea and sympathy were in wholesome amounts for Don by the young housewife and three cups and a snack later a phone call confirmed that the cavalry would arrive in an hour. So it proved in the shape of a low loader. The rescue would shorten his marathon by 15 miles and deposit the Blue Bullet in Cheltenham where hopefully repairs could sort the damage and get him back on track with no threat to his quest of his Guinness record attempt. Don promised to mention Debra in his next interview as he was assisted into the low-loader's cab and waved goodbye heaving a sigh of relief that his quest might be still on track.

*

The local DD had been alerted and organised a healthy turnout of its members in Cheltenham despite the unscheduled overnight stop. It was a bonus attraction for the locals who turned out in good voice. The amended schedule would add an extra day with Bath at Stage 11 but it was a small price to keep Don going. Malcolm rearranged the Bath stopover and later that evening he rang the hotel with good news that had Don turning somersaults, figuratively.

'Hi Dad, the Bath organisers heard about your accident and have rearranged the reception for your arrival tomorrow? I take it the Bullet will be up and running with the repairs?'

'Great news, well done. Yes, the garage will have the car repaired before lunch so I should make Bath by mid-afternoon.' Don's fingers were crossed as he ended the call.

Unaccustomed to this level of luxury Don made the most of it after the reception and a 4-star meal where he was fawned over by the star struck personnel who were overwhelmed to be serving a national personality, 'I could easily get used to this treatment,' Don thought, as the head waiter deftly served the crepe suzette and the wine waiter topped up his glass from the chateau bottled wine. 'Sitting all day in the Bullet is not conducive either to fitness or weight control, I must have put on half a stone since John O'Groats.' Don rued as he immersed himself in a hot bath to ease his aches. 'I'll have to limit the sandwiches and cake from now on although healthy food isn't a realistic option.' Don made a mental note to resume a sensible diet, but not yet.

Repairs to Bullet took the best part of the following morning and necessitated the reorganisation of the stages and overnight accommodation, but at least his marathon was still live. The Queen's Hotel in Cheltenham was happy to donate the room, especially as the publicity featured Don at the hotel's entrance with interviews conducted by a hastily arranged press team.

Just after midday Don was called to the hotel reception to take possession of the Bullet, which on inspection looked 100% with a new wheel, tire and bracket. 'We were lucky to have the parts in stock as it's not something we get much call for,' the mechanic explained as Don thanked him for his quick repair and pressed a £1 note into his saviour's pocket with grin. The Spa Town bid him farewell towards his next stop at Bath, another noted Spa Town with Roman connections. Don was ever closer to his objective in Penzance with Mary forever in his thoughts.

Don felt completely rested after his luxury hotel night at the Queens and his VIP treatment. 'I'll have to remember that hotel for a future treat.' Don deliberated as he eased onto the A46 towards Bath and wound the Bullet up through Stroud, Nailsworth and Old Sodbury then across the county line into Wiltshire. He was making good progress keeping within his self-imposed speed limit with the Bullet purring like a contented Dusty.

*

Bath was a beautiful City with its Nash and Georgian terraces, Roman heritage and mineral baths open to the public and proud of its links to world famous artists and novelists, such as Jane Austen. It had cultural offerings to suite every taste and persuasion. Don's accommodation, the Avonmouth Lodge was convenient to Don's reception where the attendance of the Lord Mayor made it a win/win situation for attendees and especially for cancer donations, flowing in from a £5 a head charity dinner with 100 supporters. As each stage was completed it seemed the public interest rose, fuelled rocket like, by the press hype to levels which to Don was a completely unexpected reaction to what he had envisaged as a modest fund-raising exercise. His accidents and delays had only heightened the public's whirlwind of affection for his resilience and spirit and hoped that Mary understood the 'carnival' was to honour her memory and bring Don some closure.

*

'You have been our beacon in boosting the importance of the DD community and have our sincerest thanks.' The Bath DD president enthused as Don was moved by his praise.

Now back in his room, tired and still aching from the Bullet's pothole incident, Don set to compiling evidence with times, dates and places for the Guinness Book requirements, which after an hour gave him a headache.

After the charity dinner the president had offered to give the Bullet a checkup which Don gratefully accepted. Next morning the Bullet was delivered to Don's hotel with the mechanic providing a glowing endorsement of the previous garage's wheel repairs and overhaul. Tire inflation had been slightly increased to provide an improved miles per gallon and the carburettor had been adjusted as the mixture had been a little rich. In addition, the controls had been lubricated after Don said the brake and clutch had become a little stiff after his 700+ miles wrestling match with the controls. His Blue Bullet was back in rude health for the last lap, and it needed to be for what lay ahead.

Don left Bath just before noon on a fine Autumn morning, with a spring in Monty's step after a good night's sleep and a lively send off by locals and tourists. Soon he would be passing the famous Glastonbury Tor then onto Taunton and the 12th Stage. Don felt he was driving a new Bullet into Somerset and cider country where he stopped for a pub lunch and a glass of *Scrumpy* at the Glastonbury Arms. Don was immediately encircled by tourists and a DD in his Invacar who had become Don's unofficial escort and provided him a rare opportunity to exchange Invacar horror stories.

South of Glastonbury Don briefly lost his concentration on the A39 and realised he was travelling in the wrong direction. His compass clearly showed his direction as West and not South so after consulting his map Don realised his error and made a U turn. Fortunately, the 5-mile error wasn't a serious diversion and by 3.30 p.m. he was on the outskirts of Taunton, a small market town with a rich heritage. It was otherwise known as the Silver City because of its links to decorative silverware as well as a magnet for the equine community with its long-established racecourse. An additional attraction for tourists and visitors was the Somerset cider factory. The Invacar lookout soon spotted Don and with flashing lights escorted him via the War Memorial into the Town square where a welcoming crowd had assembled in the late afternoon sun, slanting over the Georgian buildings and thatched roofed cottages.

CHAPTER 85

Suddenly, at a hidden signal a group of strange men ran threateningly from the side of the town hall brandishing sticks and dressed in garish tops, braided hats and breeches tied with ribbon and held up by multi-coloured braces. An assortment of bells hung from every dress point and each carried a fearsome painted club tied with ribbons. It was a curious site that the watching crowd viewed with amusement rather than concern. Bringing up the rear was a young man similarly dressed, playing a quick, catchy folk tune on a penny whistle in 2/4 time. His eight colleagues lined up in two groups and danced to the music with a hopping motion, the bells tinkling in rhythm. On a signal each dancer threatened their partner with the stick, clicking them together and twirling about as they danced, their polished shoes glinting in the sunshine. Don's reception group quickly encircled the dancers and kept time clapping their hands and tapping their feet to the infectious rhythm as the dancer's changed formation at the end of each reel.

The group were obviously well versed in their routine and carried on with a short break. At the end of each interval the growing crowd showed its appreciation with loud applause, whistles and donations into the penny whistler's hat. The entertainment for adults and an assortment of youngsters who joined in the dancing was in festive mood. Don followed the crowd's example with a donation and made his way to join the reception, leaving the Bullet surrounded by the crowd who laughed as they pointed at the Bullet's sign "John O'Groats to Lands' End or bust! As the DD president described the entertainment as a traditional Morris dance hundreds of years old, Don cast his mind back and remembered a similar gathering many years ago on a day trip to Rothbury, a village in Northumberland close to the Kielder Forest.

'The Morris dancers travel from village to village in the season and the contributions help to pay for their costumes, equipment and travelling,' the DD president explained as they tucked into tasty meal of beef casserole and local vegetables. In thanking the reception committee Don provided an amusing summary of his journey's trials, which were applauded.

After bidding good night to his hosts Don wrote in his marathon log that Stage 12 had been completed with 794 miles on the Bullet's speedometer. Now with less than 200 to go he felt an increasing glow of self-satisfaction that his mad-cap scheme was nearing completion and with it an enormous boost to Mary's cancer research.

*

A gloomy overcast sky, threatening rain, greeted Don the next morning as a resolute group braved the elements to cheer him away from Taunton. Don's choice of route to stage 13 to Plymouth via Exeter was either on main roads or the B3212, across Devon's Dartmoor National Park, which in Winter, was a desolate and dangerous 25-mile route to be avoided, but not now. He would decide which route to take when he reached Exeter about 90 minutes away and by then he hoped the weather would have cleared.

The weather had improved by the time he arrived in the quaint market town of Cullompton, situated in Devon's Culm valley, its wealth built on textiles and paper sufficient to build one of England's most magnificent churches. The Bullet's signage had been a masterstroke, attracting curious interest wherever it stopped, thanks to the press coverage. As Don enjoyed a mid-morning snack, he was button-holed by an Invacar owner who asked Don to sign his logbook to remind him he'd met the famous Don Sullivan and Blue Bullet. 'This must be what fame is like', Don imagined.

Exeter, Don's next stop was one of Devon major coastal cities and boasted a magnificent cathedral, close to the river Exe. A Roman garrison town in the early centuries and an important centre of religion in the Middle Ages, its fortunes had been built almost entirely on the wool trade. A watery sun filtered through a hazy canopy as Don drove into Cathedral square to a noisy reception whose grapevine had monitored Don's departure from Taunton. As so often happened on his journey, Don would become depressed thinking how much he missed Mary and worrying about how many were depending on him to finish. Even questioning the fund raising as a means to banish his depression over the loss of Mary or perhaps a self-serving ego boost. It was at these low points that he would hear ***The Voice,*** reminding him of the importance of his mission in helping to develop cancer therapies that would save many lives. At each stop, he would be buoyed by the enthusiasm of his welcome, giving a lift to his spirits and to finish the job for the cancer clinic. The Exeter contingent brought out all the stops with the local brass band striking up shortly before Don's arrival. The crowd's size resembled one of the city's major events such was the fervour and good humour of the onlookers. Whatever their reason for being there the locals were going to have a jolly good time with Don's charity the beneficiary. Rounding things up after the official welcome, reception, and speeches relayed to the appreciative audience, Don was overwhelmed by another City accolade so went with the flow with a well-rehearsed thank you speech.

*

By mid-afternoon he was on his way towards Plymouth, the 13th Stage and 38 miles nearer his epiphany with no drama in-between. Being a fine day Don decided to take the route across Dartmoor, to avoid the busier A38. Through a jumble of city roads, he eventually found his way onto the cross Moor 'B' road and for ten miles it was plain sailing with beautiful views across undulating vistas of uncluttered moorland, dotted with meandering sheep. Then, seemingly out of nowhere the wind picked up, clouds misted over the sun and the temperature plummeted. He was climbing up onto higher ground with the cross wind increasing in strength, buffeting the lightweight vehicle and making steering an effort to keep the Bullet on the narrow road. At either side were dips and indentations best kept at a distance. Rain was added to the wind, slight at first but increasing with gusting ferocity, rocking the flimsy car perilously on its three inadequate wheels. Don was becoming increasingly concerned for his safety as the risk of being overturned increased and rescue miles away. 'I must find shelter quickly or I'll be blown over any minute - the next big gust will be my last.' Don realised, trying to be calm while wrestling with the controls to keep the Bullet upright.

The Voice intervened in his panic. **'Don, Listen to me! Just up ahead and to the right there's a dip in the road and a narrow path just wide enough to take the Bullet. You'll be safe there until the weather eases.'**

Don cranked the accelerator slight to boost his speed and saw the dip ahead just as a fearsome blast lifted the car off its front wheel at a 40-degree angle. Don leaned with all his weight to his right and forward, fighting to maintain control as the Bullet, surfed on two wheels surging down the incline, and into the dip. Now thankfully out of the wind, and onto the narrow path **The Voice** had indicated Don braked to a halt, breathing heavily. Although the temperature had cooled significantly Don was bathed in sweat from his efforts and nervous energy he had generated. He sank down in his seat, head bowed in defeat and exhaustion. Moments later a fatigued Don fell into a deep sleep thankfully out of danger.

CHAPTER 86

The Plymouth welcoming reception had been waiting expectantly and had been informed Don had left Exeter hours ago and should have arrived mid-afternoon. Concern grew as minutes turned into hours and still no Don, so the BBC TV and press reported his absence and packed up their equipment and left. The DD network requested to report any sightings of the Blue Bullet and supplied an emergency phone number. Malcolm had heard about his father's disappearance on the DD grapevine and was told that Don had not decided which route to take when he left Exeter. It was now dark so any search and rescue would have to wait until first light, when a helicopter would be scrambled to resume the search. TV and the press featured Don's vanishing act on the late news bulletin and announced in the next morning's newspaper headlines.

CHARITY CANCER MARATHONER VANISHES ON DARTMOOR - A SEARCH FOR THE 'BLUE BULLET' IS MOUNTED BETWEEN EXETER AND PLYMOUTH.

Don Sullivan, the famous 53-year-old disabled man and his Invacar the 'Blue Bullet', disappeared yesterday when crossing Dartmoor as part of his John O'Groats to Lands' End cancer charity marathon. He was due to arrive in Plymouth for a big city welcome mid-afternoon, and the alarm was raised after he failed to show by 6 p.m. Don had already covered almost 900 miles of his 1,000-mile record busting Guinness Book record attempt.

Fears were growing for his safety when it was reported by the Fire Services that the weather on Dartmoor yesterday afternoon was atrocious and worsening with rain and high winds; certainly no place for a lightweight, 3-wheel vehicle. It was hoped that he had found some shelter to await rescue.

Emergency services had been alerted with their search covering many square miles of the Moor by helicopter, a Dartmoor rescue team and local DD's but no trace has been found. The public have been asked to keep a lookout and phone an emergency number with any information (number attached). 'Dartmoor can be a dangerous place off-road with many gullies and old mine workings,' said the Chief of Dartmoor Rescue.

*

Don had kept himself well wrapped up and switched the engine and lights off to save fuel and battery power. He was deeply asleep when startled awake by a prolonged, urgent tapping on his windscreen and sat bolt upright so see a large crow pecking and tearing at his wiper blades. 'What the hell is that?' Don shouted loud enough to startle the crow into flight, squawking at being denied its breakfast. On closer inspection, a small, very dead gorse bunting that had been storm trapped in the wipers for the crow's next meal. Don checked his watch and realised he had been asleep for over 12 hours and concerned that his welcoming committee and family must be desperately worried by his absence.

'A search and rescue mission must have been mounted.' Don thought but being off-road wouldn't have help so he and pulled out of his hide-away and onto the road. 'Maybe this is time for my emergency aids,' as he ferreted around his boot-box and eventually found a distress flare. He read the instructions twice then opened the housing to reveal a small red barrel on a handle and a cord hanging from one side. Don read the instructions twice then gingerly held the stick aloft and pulled down sharply. After a two second delay, an ear-splitting whoooosh catapulted an orange projectile 300 ft. into the morning air, bursting into a multi-coloured firework that would be seen miles away. 'Do I wait for the cavalry or just continue on my way to Plymouth and hope they catch up?' Don wondered, refreshed from his self-imposed slumbers as he nibbled on a Mars bar.

After a few minutes above the noise of the Villiers engine he heard the unmistakeable flap, flap, flap of helicopter rotors immediately above and stopped to get a better view. A RAF helicopter with British roundels landed about 50 yards away on a flat area of moorland and as the rotors gradually slowed and drooped, sad to be at rest, two men jumped out clad in regulation mufti carrying an all-purpose first aid satchel and delighted to have found him.

Don slid back the Bullet's door as the navy personnel, grinning from ear to ear with the satisfaction that they would be the ones to initiate the headline; *'RAF recue Don Sullivan and his Blue Bullet.'* Assured by Don that he was in good shape and able drive the 20 miles to Plymouth, they radioed their HQ that all was well and took their leave leaving Don a small bottle of 'pick-me-up' brandy to help him on his way. 'Much appreciated,' said Don as the Sea King soared skyward and banked towards Plymouth.

*

Forty minutes later, on the outskirts of Plymouth, Don was met by a hooting, tooting, honking mass of vehicles of all sizes, including local residents who were out in force, having seen and heard the rescue helicopter. Don opened the window and proceeded to wave to the cheering lines as he slowed to a snail pace behind his escort. Just before noon Don ended up in the town centre opposite the cathedral and slowly exited the Bullet, smiling but looking a trifle dishevelled to be eagerly embraced by the mayor, the DD president, and the CAO of Plymouth's cancer charity. Those who had the temerity to break through the official circle, were welcomed to shake hands and a give Don a congratulatory pat on the back and a handshake.

'We're so relieved you made it, we were really worried Don,' was the response from all the hand-shakers so Don waved a thank-you to the rest of the crowd. This out-pouring of relief that he had survived a night on the Moor, moved Don to tears as he made his way among the crowd towards the press who wanted every detail of his disappearance and survival.

'How did you evade all the rescue services who had been searching over the Moor the previous evening and from the crack of dawn?' An interviewer asked.

Don didn't think it a good idea to credit the **The Voice** for his survival. 'Luckily, just as I was about to be blown over, I chanced on a small defile down a track, out of the wind and under a sheltered area and fell asleep until a crow tapped me awake on my windscreen.' Don explained, 'I'm very sorry to have worried all my supporters and family but I must give thanks to all the rescue services and the DDs. I didn't know how variable the conditions could be on the moor which took me completely by surprise.' Said a contrite Don. 'I was hidden from the air so I'll try not to do it again!' Don joked as the crowd laughed in relief that he was still on course for Lands' End.

*

'How are you Dad and has the Bullet recovered from its mauling? We were worried when you went missing.' Malcolm said, pleased that all was well.

'Yes, we're both fine now but at the time, I was panicking in the conditions but as luck would have it I found a haven of sorts to ride out the storm.'

'We are so relieved you're in one piece Don, we really feared the worst', Barbara added tearfully.

'You're nearly there Dad so we'll see you at Penzance shortly – please take the last stages easy and no short cuts!' Malcolm insisted grinning to himself, the weight lifted.

'Understood. I'll have the Bullet checked over tomorrow in Plymouth for the run in and sorry for putting you all through the mill by going missing.' Don said honestly.

'Since your disappearance and recue the sponsorship on the helpline has gone haywire with donations pouring in due to the press and TV coverage. The latest total we have now is over £30k and doesn't include the donations you've accrued on the road. It's beyond amazing Dad.

'That's an unbelievable amount Mal, so well done to you and the team. Look, I'm being called for another interview so love to Barbara and see you soon. Bye! Bye!' Don had difficulty getting his head around the burgeoning cancer sponsorship total and send a silent prayer to Mary; she was after all responsible.

*

During an interview the host gave the cancer charity a plug providing the helpline number for donations, after Don had described his life-threatening plight and subsequent rescue. 'The Bullet has taken a beating,' Don explained, 'but I'll have it checked before the 14th Stage to Truro, and fingers crossed for the final legs to Penzance and Lands' End. There's about 900 miles on the clock so we've already exceeded the official distance.' Don confirmed as the reporter shook his hand with some feeling.

Don ended the interview thanking everyone for their support. 'You kept me going in my darkest moments. But for the various rescue services on the way I wouldn't be standing here,' Don smiled for the crowd's acknowledgement and pledged that every penny would be donated to the research effort. After the Bullet's battering the previous day Don was indebted to the local DD's who had it serviced at a local garage with more air in the tyres and with an oil top-up it was pronounced good to go. Don's supporters had turned out in force to cheer him on his way to Truro, despite the chill wind over Plymouth Hoe, where Drake first sighted and subsequently vanquished the Spanish Armada.

Don was still exhausted after his battering and was escorted to his up-market, accommodation at the City Gate hotel. 'Oooh, Ahhhrd, Owwwh, Urrrrh, God that aches!,' Don exclaimed loudly as he painfully eased himself from the Bullet. Being tossed about in the car during the storm had bruised his arm and shoulder which he reckoned a hot bath and menthalatum rub would ease. 'Hopefully, I'll get a massage at Penzance but will make do with a couple of aspirins every 4 hours in the mean time.' Don promised himself. Monty had not been spared and the previous evening he had added new holes to the limb straps and oiled the knee and hip catches to Monty's satisfaction.

Don's escort peeled off at the City's edge to direct the Bullet onto the A38 and on to Truro, and the penultimate stage 14 at Penzance. 'I'm 50 miles from my epiphany, so thank you Mary.' Don shouted and laughed out long and loud as he slapped his steering wheel. 'Yes! Yes! Yehhhhhs! I've made it. Against the odds I've made it Monty! I've made Mary!'

CHAPTER 87

Don listened intensely to the Bullet's vital signs, satisfied at its recovery from the previous day's Dartmoor beating and negotiated the bridge over the river Tor and through Saltash (strange name) in relatively balmy conditions – no rain, little wind, sun peeping through the cumulus. Along the roadside, sycamore and ash were starting to turn Autumn shades of yellow and brown. Don reckoned at his current speed of 40 mph he would be in Truro by 2 p,m. with a short break at Liskeard then pick up the A30. The nearby Bodmin Moor was a desolate place and perfect for the British army exercises but not for the Bullet after his 'moors' mauling.

Liskeard town square was awash with locals and tourists who formed a funnel for the Bullet. A tall white haired male sporting a colourful tricorn hat and a mayoral chain of office glittering off the afternoon sunshine approached the Bullet with his entourage wearing a wide smile of welcome. He was soon engulfed by those on the bush telegraph as Don squeezed out of the Bullet to be offered refreshment in a temporary gazebo on the square which Don thankfully accepted. A Cornish scone, strawberry jam and clotted cream was offered as he sat, aching whenever he moved. The proffered bullhorn by the mayor enabled Don to express his thanks to the crowd for their welcome and their generous donations to the cancer charity. Even the smallest of places would turn out and donate generous sums for the right causes. 'The British are truly a benevolent Nation,' Don realised.

*

A lone Invacar guided him back onto the A38 with a wave as Don checked his mileometer which tripped over onto 880 miles. Don eased back and reflected on the charity bounty of such inconceivable amounts that would provide for research for many years to come. Mary's face suddenly appeared in his mind's eye and hoped she would see his quest as a confirmation that her early death would be the birth to save countless lives. Momentarily, his attention wandered and the Bullet almost collided with a large errant sheep, braking just in time as it wandered casually over the road from its pasture. Taking on a fully grown sheep Don knew it would have been Sheep 1 - Bullet 0, so he leant on his horn in frustration as the sheep bolted away, barr, barrring in protest.

*

His thoughts returned to his fortunate escapes due mainly to the timely interventions of **The Voice.** Where was its origine and why did its presence consider him worthy of help or guidance? Was it a feature of his alter-ego, only surfacing when practical, common-sense answers were of little use. Monty always seemed to vibrate as though there was some ethereal connection from who knows where. Extra sensory perception was said to illuminate these inexplicable events, so why not for **The Voice?** Would a psychologist or even a medium provide an explanation? It was a secret he would keep to himself – for now.

Don dismissed these reflections for another time to concentrate on getting to Truro in regulation time. The forecasted rain did nothing to dampen the reception which was literally on song with a buoyant group from the local choir singing popular Cornish melodies; the Cornish Floral Dance among them. An umbrella and handshake appeared from nowhere as he was embraced enthusiastically by a well-developed Lady Mayor and a popular film star, Jean Symons who was on tour to promote her latest comedy '*Guys & Dolls*'. She was one of Don's favourites and had attracted a growing number of locals to snap memorable photos of the famous film star, the Blue Bullet and Don Sullivan, everyone's hero. Three for the price of one no less!

'Can I congratulate you Don on such an amazing and worthwhile venture in generating so much for cancer research and raising public awareness for this largely secretive disease. An immense effort and God's speed to you and the er… Blue Bullet?' Jean beamed. My mother died of cancer well before her time so I know that any effort to find a cure is to be applauded.' Jane said, tearful at her mother's memory and kissed Don on both cheeks and held both his hands in gratitude, Don blushed to his roots at the totally unexpected praise from someone who he'd previously only seen on the silver screen, mumbling his tearful thanks for her kind words. Later he was told that Miss Symons had made a significant contribution to the charity funds. The next morning papers quoted Jane's tribute to Don in full, next to his photo alongside the Bullet. Gasps of astonishment from the Truro crowds greeted Don's announcement that the sponsorship total had almost reached £40,000, a barely believable amount. This bombshell announcement set off a cacophony of cheers, whistles and backslapping, much to Don's satisfaction.

*

The simplest route to Penzance the 15th stage was to drop down on the A39 with a lunch stop at Helston switching to the A394 about 20 miles South. Maybe the Bullet could sense that the end was almost in sight as the Invacar was about to break all kinds of records for a motor that had been designed purely as a local run-around for the disabled. To Don it had become a living breathing friend and confidant over the 1,000 miles of close harmony; complaining to the Bullet with his frustrations, railing against the weather, cursing when held up and talking to Mary about their precious memories and occasionally a dialogue with Monty. Don and the Blue Bullet had become a single entity, battling the elements together. They were two peas in the same pod.

*

The DDA would be thrilled to know that given regular maintenance and careful handling, the Villiers engine could handle much longer distances in its stride than previously envisaged. Of course, major improvements were required to improve stability – a fourth wheel would help. Otherwise, as Don had discovered, long distances travel in an Invacar was a risky business.

A fluttering sign brought a lump to Don's throat as he acknowledged with a wave. *'God bless Don for Mary's cancer appeal – you're nearly there!'* He was so buoyed up by the immense support that tears flowed as he approached Helston and into the village centre. The Lobster Pot café wouldn't hear of any payment for his lunch of local lobster salad and chips when he stopped for a short break. Finally, along the scintillating Cornish coast to Marazion in 70f temperatures, Don slid open both windows as he cruised past St Michael's Mount, replicated by France's Mont St. Michael and entered the town, his last overnight in Penzance, best known for two things, the Minack Theatre, hewn out of the Cornish cliffs and home to iconic Shakespearean plays where audiences could always watch dolphins gambolling offshore if the performance bored. Penzance is also famous for its smuggling heritage where ships were lured to their doom by lanterns masquerading as lighthouses. It's said the tradition still exists today although it's a rare occurrence - apparently.

*

Malcolm had booked two rooms in Penzance at the Queens Hotel, well in advance of any mass incursion by the press. Expectations were high that Don would establish a Guinness record and also break the longest continuous Invacar journey. As Don approached the town's centre the press coverage of his epic journey had touched the nerve of the nation, resulting in an unprecedented turnout in the town's square, where a whole 'flotilla' of Invacars were assembled in a horseshoe shape, to surround Don as he came to a stop and marvel at the size of his reception.

'Hi Dad, how are you? You're looking good?' Malcolm gave him a hug then Barbara kissed him on both cheeks.

'All the better for seeing you all.' Don said enthusiastically. The brief family reunion was interrupted by press interviews as microphones and TV cameras were thrust in his face, so he shrugged resignedly to Barbara, shouting above the melee, 'see you all later in the hotel and get me a cold beer, will you?'

Don was happy to provide headline gems from his 1,000-mile trek to the BBC and ITV, and newspapers (local and national). After all, they had been the conduit by which the cancer sponsorship had been raised. Finally, the big question was 'how much have you raised for cancer research, and will it all go to the University Research Clinic?'

Don announced the good news, 'So far, sponsorship has almost reached £40,000. The original plan was that everything we raised would be for the University Cancer Research Clinic but because the donations have exceeded our wildest expectations our intention now is to split the amount raised between the University clinic and Cancer Research UK. This is to spread the funding for the widest possible cancer research effort.' Don paused for cheers, 'and we have already been in touch with both charities to organise the distribution. You are all to be congratulated for this magnificent effort.' Don's closing words were drowned out by the crowd's exuberance.

CHAPTER 88

'How will you celebrate when you reach Land End tomorrow, Don?' A local reporter asked.

'I'll raise a glass of bubbly to all the DDs groups across Britain who have kept the Blue Bullet on the road with their incredible network of emergency aid. I'll raise another big thank you to the British public because throughout my 1,000-mile marathon they have come out in rain and shine, from early in the morning to late at night to wave me onwards and kept my spirits up, which were pretty low at times. Mary was with me too.' Cheers drowned Don out. 'My journey would have been impossible without their support.' Don had to stop to wipe a tear away and compose himself. 'Without the Government initiative to develop disabled transport, the Blue Bullet would not exist, so no Invacar - no fundraise; so, cheers for the Invacar!' Don raised his glass.

'It would also be remiss of me not to thank all those who provided accommodation and sustenance for me at each of the 15 stages, arriving early or sometimes, very late. Finally, this marathon has only been a success because of all the volunteers who have provided their time, ideas and efforts to oil the wheels, organise the funding and generate publicity across the country. If I have missed out anyone or any group who has helped me on my way I most humbly apologise.'

'Before embarking on this 'madcap' adventure I talked to my wife Mary about this venture while she was undergoing the DCT cancer therapy. The fundraise has now come to fruition after she died so I had to preserve her memory in some way and help the revolutionary cancer research that came so close to saving her life. It was those two things that were my motivation to raise the maximum amount for cancer research. I'm still pinching myself at how much has been donated – it's truly incredible! Thank you.' As the applause subsided, Don looked particularly drawn and was escorted to rest and be ready for the procession of 10 miles to Lands' End the next day. To thwart any souvenir hunters, the famous Blue Bullet was securely garaged overnight at the hotel.

*

'Would you consider another fund raise, Don?' A reporter asked the next morning.

'First things first, we've the little matter of getting to Lands' End tomorrow and I must collate all the data for the Guinness Book. A Guinness official will hopefully record that the Blue Bullet reached Lands' End to approve the record.' Don's fingers were firmly crossed.

With a klaxon hoot from the DD's president Don set off for the coast 9.5 miles away in fine weather with light winds and a temperature of 55f. A perfect September end to Don's marathon quest but would another wrinkle be added to Don's brow?

*

Don's 'caravan' included Invacars from many parts of the South West, honking their support along with a mixed assortment of other vehicles and even elite runners keeping up at the Bullet's pedestrian pace. Before Lands' End the village of Sennon was packed with supporters, some standing on lampposts to witness Don's completion of his 956-mile marathon in a little over two weeks. Shortly after the Bullet broke through the official tape at the sign, *'John O'Groats 874 miles'* a cacophony of cheers and horn blasts erupted from the assembled crowds. Don had exceeded the official distance by 82 miles knowing that he had honoured Mary's memory in full. Don's feelings were on an adrenaline high relieved that he had made it but sad that his quest had ended.'

Still in some discomfort from his aches and bruising Don raised his arms in a victory salute. Flash bulbs erupted like November 5th as the crowd cheered Don and his achievement to the echo. A loudspeaker was handed to Don. 'Thank you, my friends and supporters, for all your help and donations which in Mary's memory will help the research to beat cancer. The battle starts from today!' Don cried out.

Bathed in the crowd's euphoria, Don was again with his family. The CAO of the DDA UK, a Guinness Book official, Toby from the University's Clinic and the president of Cancer Research UK were also present to celebrate a breakthrough in cancer research funding. Naturally, the press had a field day with interviews, photos from every angle of the Blue Bullet with Don getting writer's cramp signing autographs and posing for photos. A washed-out Don accompanied by Malcolm, Barbara returned to their hotel in Penzance and allowed some well-earned R & R and a chilled beer. Next morning, a refreshed Don met the press for a final debrief on his epic marathon and to reveal the charity marathon had exceeded £40,000 and bid the waiting supporters a fond farewell. A few more surprises were waiting for Don.

CHAPTER 89

In discussions with government officials from the DFD (department for the disabled), Don agreed to publicise the Invacar provided that the design faults that he had discovered on his marathon were addressed. His exposure by the British press had made Don a very valuable marketing commodity for a range of products and services who wanted him to promote. Don created Don Sullivan Promotions (DSP) and established Malcolm as the Managing Directorship. The DDA asked Don to join their board of directors and help to publicise the concerns of disabled drivers and he readily agreed. Don had difficulty keeping up with this whirlwind of offers but was buoyed up by these marathon spinoffs and more was to come.

*

During Don's two-day 500-mile return to the North East the Bullet was a social magnet whenever they stopped. With the precious cargo of the Bullet on board, Nigel kept his speed down to 50 mph for the most part and they finally arrived home two days later to be greeted by a crowd of Don's family and neighbours as well as the local press. Malcolm had completed a feature article for the Journal on Don's marathon, supported with photographs and quotes from the supporters. It was a stella piece of journalism and clearly showed that Malcolm had made a mark in his chosen profession.

'All my friends and workmates were cheering you on, and you know Don I was the most popular person in the office.' Sadie said proudly giving her older brother a hug.

'It was the same at the pithead,' added Sidney smiling, 'they all wanted to know how far you'd got as they finished their shift. They wouldn't let me go until they had the whole story. You are truly an amazing brother. Mam and Mary would have been over the moon, especially with all the sponsorship you've raised, and they probably are.' Sidney's shed tears of emotion as he hugged his younger brother, unwillingly to let go.

'Thanks Sid. There were times when I'd bitten off more than I could chew – on Dartmoor particularly. It was only my stupid resolve and Mary at my side that kept me going.' Don wasn't going to reveal ***The Voice's*** involvement.

*

The final amount of sponsorship was confirmed by Malcolm, as the chairman of the Cancer Sponsorship committee. 'It's well beyond what we expected and has reached a whopping £52,000 to date so each charity will receive a cheque for £26,000.' Malcolm shook his Dad's hand as his thoughts of his Mam stopped him dead for a few moments; his family aware how difficult it was for him. 'Dad knows that her legacy will live on with the research effort now on two fronts. These funds will in future save many lives who would otherwise succumb to a lingering death, if not for Mary's legacy.' Applause rang out from all the volunteer members present as Malcolm wiped a tear away.

Barbara's mother, Janet McDonald, provided a tearful tribute and was applauded as her husband Fergus, gripped her hand in support. 'I'm thankful that Don has preserved Mary's memory in this way because in the too short time we knew her we were impressed with her stoic approach to her illness. Even when her expected hopes of a cure were cruelly dashed, she remained calm and strong, an example of how to approach the inevitable.'

'I know Mary would have been moved by your heartfelt tributes,' Don wiped away tears with the back of his hand, 'and to know you are an important part of our family.' He smiled, and hugged Janet warmly then turning to shake Angus's hand.

Malcolm held his hand for silence. 'I've one, or rather two little surprises for Dad which had to remain a secret until his marathon was over. Barbara! Show time!' A large pram was wheeled into the room in which two quite small bundles were fast asleep. 'Dad, meet your first granddaughters, Fern and Rowena!' Malcolm announced to Don's total bewilderment.

'I'm sorry father-in-law, we couldn't tell you earlier and upset your focus during your marathon, so we decided when all was done and dusted it was time.' Barbara apologised as she hugged her father-in-law. Not surprisingly Don was lost for words and could only stare in wonderment at two very different twins, barely four weeks old, one with black hair and one fair.

It later transpired that Malcolm and Barbara, sweethearts from Pitman's Commercial College were obliged to get married in a hurry while Don was on his travels and decided not to divulge their secret to their respective families until they had to. The twin's middle names were Tearse and Mary, in recognition of both family's grandparents.

*

'It looks like the party's started so let's have a toast to Don's new and unexpected arrivals – to the twins Fern Tearse and Rowena Mary,' announced Sidney as applause rang out.

Don winced as he gazed in wonderment at the twins and Sidney noticed. 'I'm truly amazed Monty lasted the whole journey, how is he?'

'Fine, although we had some help at times when the stump became sore, usually after each stage, then I'd use the crutches and store Monty in the Bullet.' Don explained, leaving out any link to **The Voice,** as he locked Monty into the hip position. 'My next visit at the Longbenton Clinic is to see if they know about a new lightweight material being developed called aluminastic, a mixture of aluminium and plastic that I discovered during my war factory inspectorate. It's durable and half Monty's weight but I haven't told him yet!' Don grinned as he tapped Monty and the catches rattled in response.

CHAPTER 90

ENDINGS

Don embraced Stefan and Douglas who had assembled a 5-star buffet at the Bay reception with a celebratory cake, topped with a Blue Bullet in royal icing.

'You look in good shape Boss, maybe a little thinner. I watch your progress and pray for you, so it paid off, yeah! Stefan grinned and bear hugged Don.

'Your prayers helped me through my worst moments Stefan because I felt someone up there was looking after me, as well as Mary.' Don looked thankfully at his managers knowing he had hired the best.

'You don't look as though you've wrestled with the Blue Bullet for a thousand miles Boss.' Chef Douglas beamed and gave Don some good news. We've attracted some more groups, the Soroptimists for one – a great bunch of ladies.'

'Thanks for all your efforts in keeping the Bay on track and for tonight's efforts Gordon – a magnificent job all round.

Don circled the room meeting Toby from the University clinic and the CEO of Cancer Research UK's who were overwhelmed by the size of the donation. He was prised away by various sections of the press whom he thanked for their coverage. The DD UK President offered his congratulations and thanks for joining the board. Sidney called the meeting to order and asked the Guinness official to make an announcement regarding a World Record attempt for an Invacar.

'The fastest John O'Groats to Lands' End record by an Invacar.' Don Sullivan in the Blue Bullet on 1st September 1954. 956 miles in 15 days 4 hours and 31 minutes. 'In due course Don will receive a signed certificate to that effect.'

'Thank you, Guinness Book, my cup truly runneth over.' Don said smiling from ear to ear as he shook the official's hand as the group erupted.

'And now the primary outcome of Don's 'mad escapade,' paused for laughs, 'Don will present cheques to the University's Cancer Research Unit and to Cancer Research UK for £26,000 each.' Gasps of astonishment were followed by sustained applause.

Don stepped up to the mike, 'On behalf of Mary Sullivan I am truly delighted and somewhat stunned to present these cheques to two worthwhile charities.' Don handed them over Toby Maudling (Clinical Research Unit) and Jim Davison (CAO Cancer Research UK). 'I know I've already expressed by thanks and gratitude to many individuals, groups, volunteers and organisations who have made my journey possible but now we know the total donated by the generosity of the British public the length and breadth of Britain, it doesn't hurt to give thanks to them all, ONE-MORE-TIME!' Don cried out.

'Finally, ladies and gentlemen I haven't given a public thank you to my son Malcolm, his wife Barbara, my brother Sidney, my sister Sadie and Barbara's parents Angus and Janet McDonald. They have all been in my thoughts throughout the journey and along with my memories of Mary have kept me going on the many occasions when I felt about to give up, but *'all's well that ends well'* some noted playwright once wrote.' Don's emotional tribute generated a tearful response by many in the group.

'Ladies and Gentlemen,' Sidney called for order, 'we have one more presentation to make and I believe it is an important one. Don, it gives me enormous pleasure to present you with this engraved plaque in recognition of your cancer charity marathon.'

'The Mary Sullivan Cancer Charity Marathon Run, 956 miles.' Presented to Don Sullivan and his Invacar, the Blue Bullet. John O'Groats to Lands' End. 1st September 1954.' Don was speechless as the applause rang from the rafters as he gazed in awe at the plaque.

*

If this presentation hadn't been a surprise, Don was flabbergasted two days later when a knock on the door revealed a representative from the Austin Car Company who handed Don the keys to a shiny, brand new 12 hp Austin A50 Cambridge four door saloon (on loan in perpetuity), complete with leather seats and a handbook on the modifications. Don would be required to pass a road test for four wheeled vehicles but was given a temporary dispensation as it was a car for the disabled.

*

A few days after the dust had settled, Don received a phone call from Tim Spaulding, to find out if he would reconsider his position as CAO with the Leisure Consortium. Don thanked him and promised to consider his offer.

Trevor Carter the disability centre manager was delighted to meet the famous Don Sullivan when he returned the Blue Bullet. He had followed Don's progress throughout the marathon. 'You put us all to shame with your awesome performance Don. We had a 'book' on how far you'd get but only one of us bet on you finishing.' Trevor admitted, 'it wasn't me sadly, but we were all rooting for you as the miles built up.'

'Thank you, Trevor, now here's a thought. What if the Blue Bullet was donated to the Transport Museum in Leamington? Wouldn't it be a great advertisement for the Government's Mobility scheme and a permanent reminder of the Blue Bullet's place in motoring history?'

'Yes, it's a great idea Don and I'll to refer it to the Regional Head, David Timberlake with my recommendation.'

Two weeks later Don's suggestion was approved, and the Leamington Motor Museum would take delivery of the Blue Bullet and publicise it as their latest entry. Don was invited to the unveiling and was like a dog with two tails, delighted that the Bullet would be preserved and admired in future, it was the least it deserved.

*

Don agonised over Tim's offer to return to the Leisure Consortium as their CEO and eventually agreed as it was something he enjoyed as the CEO. As for Don Sullivan Promotions, Malcolm would continue to oversee its operation and development.

*

It was now over four years since Mary's death; his self-imposed walk-about and the marathon charity run. All of this had drawn the sting out of his grieving with the knowledge that he had honoured Mary's memory. Over this time he had thought about a headstone for her grave and the following inscription was inscribed in Scottish granite.

MARY TEARSE SULLIVAN. Beloved wife of Don, son Malcolm, Barbara, Gracie, Sidney & Sadie. 20.5.1900 – 23.5.1953 Age 53. 'Gone before her time and loved by all'.

Family and friends gathered one afternoon on a bright October day for the memorial stone to be installed surrounded by chrysanthemums, Mary's favourite flower. The vicar from Mary's church St Peter's gave a short prayer and blessing with Mary's favourite song '*As Time Goes By*' accompanied on the acoustic guitar. Not surprisingly, the tune prompted tears and muffled sobs, but Don had done all his crying and stood stone-faced, his eyes riveted on the inscription, then excused himself for a while to honour her memory in silence. Don now had a new life, the support of a growing family and memories of Mary that would last until he joined her.

*

Don's cup was full to overflowing, yet a final surprise was in store. A special delivery embossed with Buckingham Palace included the following citation:

Donald Robinson Sullivan has satisfied the Honours Committee that he fulfils the following criteria for the award of MBE (Member of the British Empire). 'An achievement or service to the community which has delivered a sustained impact, and which stands out as an example to others.'

'**Donald Robinson Sullivan – For services to charity and national morale – the award by Her Majesty Queen Elizabeth 2nd of the MBE (Member of the British Empire) medal.**'

THE END

www.ingramcontent.com/pod-product-compliance
Ingram Content Group UK Ltd.
Pitfield, Milton Keynes, MK11 3LW, UK
UKHW020704030125
452938UK00017B/82